BOOST!
50 Legs Up to Become a Better Business Leader

BOOST!

50 Legs Up to Become a
Better Business Leader

THOMAS E. HENNING

Copyright © 2023 by Thomas E. Henning

All rights reserved. No part of this book may be reproduced, scanned, or distributed in any printed or electronic form without direct permission from the author or publisher.

First Edition: April 2023
Printed in the United States of America

ISBN: 979-8-9880733-0-7 (paperback)
        979-8-9880733-1-4 (eBook)

Printed by

Kramer PRESS

Redbrush

Dedicated to

my life partner and wife, Candy,
our daughters, Cassandra and Madeline,
our four grandchildren,
and
the talented associates I've had the privilege
to have as colleagues at Assurity Life.

Contents

Preface 1
Introduction 3

Chapter 1: Right People, Right Seat 5
Chapter 2: Servant Leadership 13
Chapter 3: Communication 20
Chapter 4: Trust 28
Chapter 5: Recognition 34
Chapter 6: Ethics 41
Chapter 7: Conflict Avoidance 50
Chapter 8: Change 54
Chapter 9: Making Good Decisions 60
Chapter 10: Delegation 66
Chapter 11: Leaders Are Readers 70
Chapter 12: Clear Writing Produces Clear Thinking 75
Chapter 13: Managing Information 80
Chapter 14: No 83
Chapter 15: Time 87
Chapter 16: Becoming a Humble Narcissist 94
Chapter 17: Majoring in the Minors 98
Chapter 18: Lies, Damned Lies, and Statistics 103
Chapter 19: Relationships 109
Chapter 20: Persistence and Resiliency 115
Chapter 21: Behavioral Biases in Management 121
Chapter 22: Bureaucracy / Corporate Politics 132
Chapter 23: Accountability 139

Chapter 24: The Virtuous Cycle 143
Chapter 25: Creating a Great Place to Work............................. 147
Chapter 26: Initiative and Hard Work...................................... 154
Chapter 27: Innovation 160
Chapter 28: Meetings... 167
Chapter 29: Benign Neglect 173
Chapter 30: Narratives 176
Chapter 31: Strategic Planning... 180
Chapter 32: Strategic Opportunism 186
Chapter 33: Luck 191
Chapter 34: Paradox... 195
Chapter 35: Achieving a Competitive Advantage..................... 199
Chapter 36: Expense Management 205
Chapter 37: Embrace Uncertainty.. 211
Chapter 38: Risk 218
Chapter 39: Measurement and Metrics.................................... 224
Chapter 40: Too Hard.. 229
Chapter 41: The Pygmalion Effect.. 233
Chapter 42: Mentors.. 238
Chapter 43: Being a Business Leader During a Crisis 243
Chapter 44: How to Guarantee You'll Be Miserable in Business 249
Chapter 45: Marathon or Sprint? 252
Chapter 46: Culture 256
Chapter 47: To Thine Own Self Be True.................................. 263
Chapter 48: Purpose in Business 267
Chapter 49: Personal Purpose... 274
Chapter 50: Perspective 281

Acknowledgments 286
Tom's Favorite Business Leadership and Management Books.... 287
About the Author.. 291
Bibliography.. 292

Preface

The genesis of this book was a series of seminars I presented to the supervisory leaders at Assurity Life Insurance Company, which I had the pleasure to lead for many years. Several of the supervisors who attended these seminars suggested I write a monthly blog on some business or leadership issue. For over five years I wrote this monthly blog. These blogs are the basis for the chapters in this book. The topics came from triggering events in the life of the company over those five years.

Since I began leading in business, I've wanted to continuously improve as a business leader. The practice for my entire business career was to seek out the best thinking and writing on business management and leadership. Additionally, I've read many biographies and autobiographies on business leaders. I've long been addicted to learning and being inspired by other people's lives. In the back of this book I provide a list of the books that had the biggest influence on my approach to business and leadership.

I've distilled some of what I've learned over the years into fifty concise chapters. These are not academic treatises but practical lessons that were honed by the everyday of running or helping govern a variety of businesses. My thoughts aren't original. I'm reminded of a Mark Twain quote:

> There is no such thing as a new idea. It is impossible. We simply take a lot of old ideas and put them into a sort of mental kaleidoscope. We give them a turn and they make new and curious combinations. We keep on turning and

making new combinations indefinitely; but they are the same old pieces of colored glass that have been in use through all the ages.

But it is my own take on these ideas and how they have been helpful to my business career. I know they can be helpful to you as well.

Tom Henning
March 2023

Introduction

Let me give you a competitive advantage. Let me give you a "Boost" by sharing some important lessons I've learned about being a business leader. Success in business requires continuous learning. As I've aged, many times I thought, "I wish I knew what I know now at an earlier age." The thing with wisdom and life lessons is that they generally are learned in retrospect, long after we needed them. Most learn by experience. Learning by experience as you go along is fine, but it's a slow and many times agonizing process.

One of the best ways to improve performance is to change where you start. You don't need to start at the bottom. You can learn from the people who came before you. I realized this fact early in my business career and initiated a lifelong process to be a continuous student of business leadership. An overall goal of mine has been to seek out the best writing and thinking on management, leadership, and investing. To learn from others who have been successful.

Lifelong learning is so important to business success. Most of what you learn in school changes slowly. In the real world, however, a lot of what you need to know changes rapidly. This is why taking in contemporary relevant knowledge is so important.

In fifty relatively concise chapters, I want to give readers the benefit of some of my study of business leadership and real-world experience. You'll see I have a number of business heroes—Warren Buffet, Charlie Munger, Jeff Bezos, Steve Jobs, and many others. I'll be sharing the wisdom I've learned from these business icons throughout this book. Think of the information in this book as a CliffsNotes version of some of the best that has been written and practiced on business leadership. I've curated what I've studied and learned over the years to provide the reader with practical real world advice to gain a competitive advantage Remember, where you end up depends on where you start. This book's objective is to give your business leadership journey a "Boost!

CHAPTER 1
Right People, Right Seat

A business leader's most important responsibility is to be sure she or he has the human resources talent to have their organization perform at a high level. I learned this lesson early in my business career. At age thirty, the CEO of First Commerce Bancshares, James Stuart Jr., asked me to become the CEO of one of our subsidiary community banks, which at the time was in trouble. We were in the throes of the ag financial crisis in the mid-1980s. After our initial discussion, Jim asked me to come back the next day with questions I might have before accepting this important career opportunity. I came the next day with a list of predictable questions: How bad is the asset quality? What is the bank's capital position? Have the regulators taken any enforcement action against the bank?, etc. After letting me go on for a while, Jim interrupted me and said I wasn't asking the most important question. I said I didn't know what he meant. Jim then said to me, "The most important question you should ask me is, 'Can I have the people I need to get the job done?'" I somewhat sheepishly said, "Oh, yeah, that is a great question."

Jim Stuart Jr. often said to me over the years, "I've never seen anything good happen without having the right people in the right spots." He would typically go on to say, "If you don't have the right people in the right spots, you won't accomplish your business goals—it is like pushing string."

"Right people, right seat" is a concept advocated by many successful business leaders. Probably the most famous advocate was Jim Collins in his book *Good to Great*, with the now-iconic mantra,

"Make sure you have the right people on the bus in the right seats on the bus." So, how do you make sure you have the right people in the right seats? It begins with a sound selection process. A sound selection process starts with a comprehensive position description that doesn't just list the skills, knowledge, and experience required but also lists the talents an ideal candidate would possess. Next the candidate needs to complete a number of instruments to better understand their strengths and natural talents. Over the years I've used the Kolbe Index, Myers Briggs Type Indicator, Gallup Strengths Finder, Talent Plus interviews, and others. I find there is value in using more than one instrument. You start to develop a mosaic of the candidate's talents and natural strengths.

Finally, deciding who to employ involves interviewing. Many business leaders think they are good interviewers. I think they are wrong. After many hiring mistakes over the years, I don't believe I'm a good interviewer; I don't believe anyone else is, either. Many believe they can trust their intuition—their gut feeling. Don't believe it. So how do you select for fit and talent?

You start by primarily relying on a structured interview that does not just focus on a candidate's skills, knowledge, and experience but also the candidate's innate talents. A structured interview is the most important tool a business leader has to make a good hiring decision. What is a structured interview?

> A structured job interview is a standardized way of comparing job candidates. Each interviewee is asked the exact same questions, in the exact same order. The interviewer also creates a standardized scale for evaluating candidates. Every interviewee is ranked on the same scale.

A structured interview will always produce a better result over a "wing it" interview.

Here's why I like structured interviews:

1. They're more objective. Each candidate is asked the same

questions by the interviewer that best measures the talents required for the position. This provides candidates with equal opportunity to showcase their talents.

2. They're more predictive. I've found structured interviews are more effective at predicting job performance than unstructured ones. Especially with talent-based structured interviews, the questions more accurately draw out the behaviors needed on the job, and the candidate's responses indicate how they will perform once in the role.

A philosophy I've worked hard to establish in every organization I've led is to be sure that what we ask people to do fits with their natural strengths. I believe people perform best when they work in their areas of strength.

Armed with structured interview results and insights from other instruments, you are in a better position to have an effective face-to-face interview. Here are the steps I take to have a face-to-face interview that allows me to make the best hiring decision.

1. I develop a form with questions customized for the position. I ask the same questions in the same way for each applicant. I've developed an inventory of potential interview questions I've compiled over the years, which I've included at the end of this chapter. These questions come from a variety of sources including human resource consultants we have used. Many came from Talent+. We have used Talent+ selection services over many years. I don't ask all of these questions in each interview. I pick and choose—customized to the position.

2. Try to put the interviewee at ease by developing a rapport with them. After reviewing the advance material, I always pay them a compliment. For example, "In reviewing your background it's evident you bring a great deal of relevant experience for this position," or "I'm impressed with what you

accomplished in your previous role." I try to say something not only positive but sincere and authentic.

3. Keep good notes. When interviewing several candidates, it can be easy for them to become a sort of blur. By keeping notes on each candidate's responses, you'll be in a position to keep the candidates straight and remember the details of their responses.

4. I try and avoid the expected questions (e.g., "What do you consider to be your strengths?"). Rather, "Tell me what you do better than anyone else?" I try to ask meaningful, authentic questions—not strange stuff. As an example, I once heard of a manager who asked every interviewee, "If you were going to be a superhero, would you be Superman or Batman?" Now maybe this manager felt the answer to this strange question uncovered some deep truth; to me it just sounded weird.

   I also have some knockout questions. For instance, I usually ask, "What are you reading these days?" If they say I really don't like to read, that is a knockout question for me because it demonstrates a lack of interest in growing and learning.

5. In the end, let them ask you questions. I always start the interview by saying, "We are going to have some time at the end for you to ask me questions, so be thinking about what you might like to ask me." I've found I usually learn a great deal from this part of the interview. Here is what I usually learn from this exercise:

   - Does the candidate properly understand the position, and have they carefully considered whether their talents, skills, knowledge, and experience are a fit?
   - Have they put forth the work and researched the company?
   - Do they understand our mission and values, and do

their own values align with ours?
- Are they naturally curious?

6. Be a good listener. Be careful to not just hear what you want to hear. Be aware of your own filters, which could impede or distort the interviewee's response.

7. Have a good conclusion. Describe what is going to happen next. Relay how and when you will follow up with the candidate.

Bringing on new associates whose talents are a fit for the position is any business leader's most important responsibility. Remember, nothing good happens until you have the right people in the right seats. A proper selection process can make all the difference in being sure every hire is adding to the company's intellectual capital and ultimate success.

What about existing personnel? One of the commonsense ideas I've found over the years is if I have to manage someone too intently, they are probably the wrong person. Think of those you feel you have to continually coach and monitor. They are probably in the wrong seat on the bus.

Finally, I've never been able to "fix" anyone. Most people become more and more like they really are. Don't try to avoid conflict by rationalizing that by providing additional training or coaching you are going to fix someone. Almost never happens.

I made this the first chapter of this book because the biggest responsibility of any business leader is to be sure you have the right people in the right seats. Only then will you be positioned to accomplish your business objectives.

Tom's Inventory of Possible Interview Questions

1. In your previous work, what did you enjoy the most?
2. Tell me about what you do better than anyone else?
3. In the past, what has held you back?

4. Have you given positive recognition to another person within the past two weeks?
5. Have you developed enthusiasm in other people within the past two weeks?
6. Are you considerate of others' feelings?
7. How do you feel when you are given constructive criticism?
8. Are you positive when others in the company are negative?
9. Do you tend to make friends easily at work?
10. Please describe your career goals.
11. Does it bother you when someone is upset?
12. Are you a perfectionist?
13. Do you enjoy responding to guests'/customers'/clients' requests, then exceeding their expectations?
14. What is the best recognition for you?
15. Tell me about the system you use to keep track of your progress day by day.
16. Do you like working in a fast, intense-paced environment?
17. Do you always keep your promises?
18. Do you directly seek the acceptance of others?
19. Do you work well under pressure?
20. Is your energy level well above average? Tell me about a time you were expected to work long hours. How did you handle the situation?
21. Are you good at creating ways to improve your work?
22. Do you prefer to work within groups rather than working independently?
23. In the past, have you had fun at work?
24. Describe your skills and competencies for this job.
25. Why are you considering leaving your current position?
26. Please describe to me your current supervisory responsibilities.
27. Do you enjoy managing other people? Do you consider managing others a strength?
28. Do you like learning new things?
29. What are you currently reading?
30. If we are sitting together around this table three years from

now, what has to happen in your career for you to be happy with your progress?
31. Tell me about an ethical dilemma you faced in the past and how you handled it?
32. Tell me about a time when you had to resolve a problem with no rules or guidelines in place.
33. What is the hardest thing you've ever done?
34. What is your personal definition of success?
35. Up to this point in your life, what is the professional achievement you are the most proud of?
36. What is it about this position that excites you the most?
37. Tell me about a person or organization who you admire. Why do you admire this person or organization?
38. When working on a team, what's hardest for you?
39. Tell me about the last time you encountered a rule in an organization that you thought made no sense. What was the rule? What did you do, and what was the result?
40. For the last few companies you've been at, take me through why you left. When you joined the next organization, why did you choose it?
41. Tell me about a time you took unexpected initiative.
42. Tell me about your ideal next role. What characteristics does it have from a responsibility, team, and company culture perspective? What characteristics does it not have?
43. Tell me about a time you strongly disagreed with your manager. What did you do to convince him or her that you were right? What ultimately happened?
44. Tell me about the best and worst bosses you've ever had.
45. What's one part of your previous company's culture that you hope to bring to your next one? What's one part you hope to not find?
46. When was the last time you changed your mind about something important?
47. What is the most important thing you've learned from a peer, and how have you used that lesson in your day-to-day life?
48. Tell me about a time when you failed and what did you

learn from that experience?
49. If I were to go and speak to people who don't think very highly of you, what would they say?
50. What do you do for fun?
51. What have I not asked you that I should have?
52. At the end of an interview, I like to ask, "After you leave today, what are the top three things you want me to have heard about who you are?" and "What do you want to make sure sticks with me about you?"

CHAPTER 2
Servant Leadership

In the 1960s, Robert Greenleaf served as director of management development for AT&T. He was noted for establishing the first corporate assessment center and for the first promotions to professional positions of women and minorities at AT&T.

Greenleaf used the term *servant leader* in an essay he wrote and sent to fellow managers in 1966. This essay was the result of Greenleaf's experience as a manager. He was also influenced by the Herman Hesse novella *A Journey to the East*.

The following is from the website of the Greenleaf Center, a nonprofit focused on promoting the concept of servant leadership, named in Mr. Greenleaf's honor:

> "The idea of The Servant as a Leader came to me as a result of reading a book by Herman Hesse, *Journey to the East*. It is the story of a band of men on a mythical journey. They key person in the story is Leo. He is a servant who does chores for the travelers, but he also lifts their morale with his positive spirit and his singing. He is the glue that holds the group together. The travelers all sense Leo's extraordinary presence.
>
> The journey goes well until one day when Leo disappears. Without Leo, the group falls apart and the journey has to be abandoned. They simply can't continue.
>
> The traveler who tells the story goes looking for Leo, and after some years of wandering, he finds Leo. He discovers that Leo, whom he had known first as servant, was in

fact the titular head of the Order that sponsored the journey. Leo is its guiding spirit, a great and noble leader."

In 1977, Greenleaf authored the book *Servant Leadership*. It popularized the concept of a business leader becoming a servant leader. Greenleaf's basic principle was that servant leadership occurs when a leader seeks to serve others first. He distinguished the servant leader from other individuals who seek leadership because of a desire for power or wealth.

Although the modern discussion of servant leadership owes much to Greenleaf, the concept of a leader who puts his followers first didn't originate with him—or with Herman Hesse. Servant leadership is an ancient concept.

Servant leadership is a prominent theme in Christianity. Perhaps the earliest notable reference to servant leadership is recorded in the Biblical teachings attributed to Jesus Christ, when he said to his twelve disciples, "And whosoever will be chief among you, let him be your servant" (Matthew 20:27). A similar passage occurs in the book of Mark, chapter 9:35: "If any man desire to be first, the same shall be last of all, and servant of all." Jesus told his apostles in Matthew 23:11, "Whoever is greatest among you let him be your servant." The concept of the virtues of a servant leader also dates back thousands of years in Eastern and Western secular philosophy.

But Greenleaf's 1977 book ignited the concept of servant leadership in American business. This highly influential book has been embraced by business leaders everywhere. Over the years I've observed many firms when recruiting for a particular executive position list "servant leadership" as a desirable attribute. I've served on the boards of companies where being a servant leader was one of the qualities on which the executives were rated. So many popular and scholarly articles have been written about the attributes of being a servant leader.

So what does it mean to be a servant leader in today's business environment? Here is a servant leader definition I like from the Society of Human Resource Management (SHRM).

"Servant leaders are a revolutionary bunch—they take the

traditional power leadership model and turn it completely upside down. This new hierarchy puts the people—or associates, in a business context—at the very top and the leader at the bottom, charged with serving the associates above them.

That's because these leaders possess a serve-first mindset, and they are focused on empowering and uplifting those who work for them. They are serving instead of commanding, showing humility instead of brandishing authority, and always looking to enhance the development of their staff members in ways that unlock potential, creativity and sense of purpose."

Not everyone is a fan of the concept of servant leadership. Here is what some detractors say:

1. Servant leaders are typically weak leaders because they want to serve. Therefore, they can't handle tough situations or deal with high pressure or conflict.

2. Servant leadership is a religious concept; therefore, it does not have a place in a corporate setting.

3. The concept is difficult to communicate and time consuming for leaders to implement.

4. It can be difficult to attain—it's a constant journey rather than an end goal.

5. It requires a high level of authenticity that can be difficult for most leaders to achieve.

6. Retraining existing leaders to become servant leaders can be daunting and time consuming.

7. The formal authority of the leaders may be diminished, and the speed of decision-making is slower due to higher team involvement.

8. It may be out of sync with corporate performance management and incentive systems.

I believe the potential problems with servant leadership are more imagined than real. I believe servant leadership is more important than ever. Here's why:

1. **A high-performance culture is a byproduct of servant leadership.**
   In a study published in the *Journal of Applied Psychology*, Drs. Linden and Jia Hu found that servant leaders are more successful than others as they promote self-confidence, assertiveness, and building the potential of their team. This results in greater productivity and a high-performance work culture.

2. **Servant leaders develop others.**
   Servant leaders understand that regardless of how skilled they are, they can't go far without the team. A servant leader understands how critical their team is to achieving their business goals. Servant-based leaders empower others to recognize their inner potential and give them space to nurture their creativity and talent.

3. **Servant leaders garner high levels of engagement from associates.**
   Associates who work in an atmosphere of mutual support have greater job satisfaction. Servant leadership builds a growing environment of trust and mutual cooperation. People know that their leaders care about them. A leadership strategy that balances professional skills with personal warmth and empathy will result in highly satisfied associates. It stifles backbiting and unhealthy competition and helps everyone potentially achieve a better work-life balance.

4. **They are winners in the long run.**
   Servant leaders don't manage for short-term results. They

have a long-term perspective and manage for long-term results. Making knee-jerk decisions in reaction to immediate pressures is not the way of the servant leader. Instead, these leaders rise above the short-term noise and cultivate value by thinking long term. A lot of good advice simply boils down to thinking long term.

5. **They are customer focused.**
   These executives look at their companies through the lens of their customers and associates and ask, "How can I enrich their lives?" Servant leaders are givers, not takers.

6. **They are purpose driven.**
   These leaders ask how their actions can serve humanity and not just the bottom line. This approach does not discount the importance of profit, but it puts profit in the context of a more holistic view of what the company accomplishes.

7. **They are courageous.**
   Associates many times come up with better ideas than the boss. Courageous executives adopt a mindset that puts egos aside and allows others' perspectives and ideas to flourish.

8. **They are authentic and trustworthy.**
   Servant leaders show their true selves to others. They are transparent and open. They are adept at discovering and discussing other people's strengths and weaknesses because they have already become aware of their own positive attributes and faults. A servant leader is a confidante. These leaders act as sounding boards for important decisions. Because servant leaders are natural coaches and want the best for others, people turn to them over and over again.

9. **They are approachable.**
   Humility is what makes the servant leader approachable. It's the difference between the executive leader that associates

want to avoid in the hallways and the leader who makes team members feel comfortable and at ease.

10. **They are excellent listeners.**
    Most people don't listen as well as they think they do. Servant leaders are deep listeners. And because they really take in what others say, they are able to ask illuminating questions and provide intelligent and strategic guidance for their colleagues.

So how do you become a servant leader?

Here are four ways to begin to transform into a true servant leader:

Strike a balance between valuing people and results. Research shows that leaders who primarily focus on just one or the other are not viewed as strong leaders. Leaders who are positive and motivational toward associates in addition to being strategic about business goals make the winning combination that produces great long-term results.

Ask how you can support rather than tell people what to do. This approach will leave behind the boss-gives-orders mentality and cultivate the leader who provides vision, direction, and resources.

Discover ways you can give people more power. The best leaders give their power away. In doing so, they earn respect from those who follow them. True power is the ability to empower others to lead and flourish in their own capabilities.

Show associates they are valued through words and actions. Do you express appreciation for associates by thanking them for something specific they accomplished? Are you actively recognizing associates individually or as a team formally and informally? Do you have an associate recognition program? If so, does that program reward only revenue winners, or does it spotlight associates who have exhibited extraordinary teamwork, integrity, generosity, or kindness in the workplace?

Set a great example. A large part of leadership success stems from the ability to set a good example. Subordinates notice what behavior gets rewarded and what standards are set by the person at the top.

Servant leadership has influenced many noted writers, thinkers, and leaders. Max De Pree, former chairman of the Herman Miller Company and author of *Leadership Is an Art* and *Leadership Jazz*, has said, "The servanthood of leadership needs to be felt, understood, believed, and practiced." And Peter Senge, author of *The Fifth Discipline*, has said that he tells people, "Don't bother reading any other book about leadership until you first read Robert Greenleaf's book *Servant Leadership*. I believe it is the most singular and useful statement on leadership I've come across." In recent years, a growing number of leaders and readers have "rediscovered" Robert Greenleaf's own writings through books by De Pree, Senge, Covey, Wheatley, Autry, and many other popular writers.

Dr. Kent Keith, former CEO of the Greenleaf Center, said in a 2010 article in "Inc." magazine, "I think the simplest way to explain it would be to say that servant leaders focus on identifying and meeting the needs of others rather than trying to acquire power, wealth, and fame for themselves."

In countless for-profit and not-for-profit organizations today, we are seeing traditional, autocratic, and hierarchical modes of leadership yielding to a different way of working—one based on teamwork and community, one that seeks to involve others in decision-making, one strongly based in ethical and caring behavior, and one that is attempting to enhance the personal growth of workers.

Be the embodiment of the leadership values all business leaders should aspire to: consistency, reliability and a constant presence all can depend on. Couple these values with a prodigious work ethic and enthusiasm for your organization's success and you'll be on your way to being a great servant leader. Remember, leadership is ultimately about service.

CHAPTER 3
Communication

In 1985, Michael Jordan was named NBA Rookie of the Year, New Coke hit the shelves, and I became the president of NBC Bank— at that time, the second largest bank in Lincoln, Nebraska.

The ag crisis of the mid-1980s had left debt-ridden farmers in dire financial straits, which then rippled through the local economy, causing a lot of other loan problems. Associate morale at the bank was low from dealing with all the credit problems. I thought we should hire an outside firm to do an associate survey to better understand how to reengage team members and build morale.

Shortly after I received the survey results, our seventy-year-old executive chairman of the holding company stopped by my office. I told him about the survey, and before I could share the results, he blurted out, "I bet your biggest problem is communication." I asked him how he knew. He replied, "Because it is always the biggest problem." Over the years I've learned the wisdom of his assertion.

Communication is an issue in most organizations. You would be hard-pressed to find an organization in which communication is not an issue. When people leave organizations they often cite poor workplace communication as a top reason for moving on. So what's the answer? There's a long list of potential solutions. Google "improving communication at the workplace" and thousands of results are instantly at your fingertips.

Transparent, frequent, and authentic communication should be an important focus for any business leader to build trust and engage associates. Transparent, frequent, and authentic communication is like a disinfectant—it dispenses with a lot of politics, bureaucracy, cabals, and other nefarious activities within a business.

Effective corporate communication has changed dramatically since I entered the workforce. Early in my career, most corporate communication could be categorized as centralized, controlled, top-down, and directive. Today, an effective corporate communication program needs to be multidirectional—one in which all associates participate and where questioning, challenging, and listening are encouraged.

Following are some of the most important lessons I've learned about developing and fostering a world-class corporate communications culture.

Communicate in a multitude of ways.

Communication channels can be formal and informal, verbal and written. Communication in person and on demand. Variety ensures that the broadest possible assortment of associates will receive the message.

Listen to Feedback

An important part of effective communication is listening—really paying attention to what associates in your organization are trying to communicate to you. Wisdom is the reward you get for a lifetime of listening when you would have preferred to talk.

Over Communicate

Effective communication needs to be repetitive. One and done is almost never enough. I've found that when I start to tire of communicating the same message, it is just starting to be fully understood by the organization.

Explain Why

If you are communicating any major corporate change or initiative you need to explain "the why". If you struggle to craft this explanation, reconsider whether you have something worthwhile to communicate.

Be Concise
Whenever possible keep your communication simple and direct. We all have so much information coming at us that any communication risks being lost in the flood of information we all deal with every day. Send worthy not wordy communications.

Consistent Internal and External Communications
What you communicate internally and externally should be consistent. Yes, you need to compose different messages for different audiences. But internal and external communications need to work together. Keeping your message coherent and consistent will boost understanding by all of the company's stakeholders.

Avoid Unnecessary Communication
Even though frequent business communication is important to associates, too much irrelevant information can be a huge productivity blackhole. Yet, many associates still receive information that is not relevant to them at all. Remember, it only takes a few one-size-fits-all emails for associates to start ignoring them. We all must do a much better job of making communications more personalized and relevant.

Encourage a Two-Way Channel for Feedback
The days when employers send a company-wide newsletter and believe they have effectively communicated are over. Such one-way communication doesn't allow associates to share their own thoughts. The most important things to remember are to communicate with consistency and credibility and understand the difference between your corporate branding and associate voices.

Communication Expectations
As a top business leader, you must set communication expectations for all your managers. Managers need to understand and believe that effective, authentic and open communication is required, and a key part of what they need to do every day. Associates need to feel they can rely on their company's leaders to keep them fully informed on

all key issues impacting the company. Open and honest communication needs to become a key part of the organizational culture.

Now I want to turn to some thoughts on specific types of communication.

Written Communication
Effective written communication is the foundation of any company's communication program. The primary benefit of written communication is it provides an opportunity to better organize your thoughts. Clear writing produces clear thinking. You'll hear me say this time and again throughout this book. Clear written communication is hard work. It is rare to be able to sit down in one session and produce a communication that will accomplish what you as a business leader want to communicate. I take comfort in the great German novelist Thomas Mann's quote, "A writer is someone for whom writing is more difficult than it is for other people." Effective written communication is hard work.

In planning for an important communication, you need to realize you can't write well without creating for yourself space for good thinking. Good thinking requires time. If you want to write better, you need to think better. You need to have a deep understanding of what you want to communicate. For any important communication, I build in time for multiple iterations. Typically for a communication like this chapter, I would do a minimum of six iterations before I have a piece I would find passable. In the first iteration I try to get down every topic and key points I want to make. At this point I don't focus too much on grammar, sentence structure, phraseology, and so on. I just want to get down on paper the key points. In future iterations I'll clean up grammar, sentence structure, and so on. I also find I do better if I create some space around each iteration. Revisit the communication in a day or two, or go for a walk, a run, or some physical activity and then rewrite. I find my first thought is never my best thought. My first thought is usually someone else's; it's what I've already heard about the subject, usually the conventional wisdom. I find I come up with new insights after an interlude, which allows my subconscious to generate some new ideas.

If possible, once you have what you consider to be a final product, seek out another set of trusted eyes to critique your masterpiece. I've been fortunate to have Susan Becker, vice president of human resources at Assurity, review my internal blogs, which are the foundation for the chapters in this book, followed by Assurity's marketing area. They always provide edits that improved the quality of the communication.

A very important type of written communication is a companywide communication that addresses some key topic. This type of communication needs to be a group effort. One member of senior management needs to author the initial iteration. This individual needs "to own" the communication but will want to run it by other members of senior management for their input. During the COVID-19 pandemic, we had many communications that required a group effort. Susan typically did the initial draft, and the rest of senior management provided edits. In the end, the "owner" of the communication needs to have the authority to accept or reject a suggested edit.

Oral Communication

When surveys are conducted of people's biggest fears, public speaking is always in the top five. For most people, the thought of getting up and talking before a group is terrifying. In my own case, I'm lucky in that I draw energy from giving a talk. I do get nervous, but if I'm prepared, I look forward to a public speaking opportunity. The key is to be prepared.

It's an extremely rare individual who can give an impressive off-the-cuff, extemporaneous speech. Winston Churchill was legendary for his oratorical skills. He delivered so many memorable talks in Parliament that he seemed to deliver impromptu. But Churchill once said it took him an hour of preparation for every minute of an extemporaneous speech. I've also found this to be true. For any important oral communication opportunity I find, I need to allocate an hour of prep time for every minute I plan to talk.

If you want to distinguish yourself and get noticed, work on improving your oral communication skills. There are so many good resources available. Toastmasters was an organization which was very helpful to me early in my career.

Video, Podcasts, etc.
More and more we now communicate via short videos and podcasts. Like with all other forms of good communication, to produce a quality product requires significant effort. A minimum of one hour of work for every minute of a video talk—is the time required to produce the content and then practice your delivery. I use a teleprompter when doing a video. Even with a teleprompter I never go to a videotaping without having practiced delivering the talk multiple times. The same is true with doing a Q&A podcast. Request the questions in advance and have your responses prepared in writing. Now you may think this will make you come off as too scripted. If you really know your material, you will come off as well informed—not scripted.

Social Media
Traditional corporate communication takes place within a clearly defined structure, using channels such as internal emails, telephone calls, memos, press releases, and formal meetings. Social media is much messier, but it needs to be actively used and managed. Social media allows a company to gain better insights and engage with their associates and customers in a method they prefer.

Social media has transformed the field of corporate communication and the way it is practiced professionally. Companies use social media to share information on company events, announcements, products, news, and so on—any information that they wish their associates would know. Social media is now an image builder and key to building the company's brand.

But as a business leader, you have to establish processes and controls to monitor social media and effectively react to what is being said about the company. Today a company's reputation and brand largely depend on the image built by the company in social media.

Facebook, Instagram, Twitter, Glassdoor, and a host of other social media platforms, if properly used, can aid a company in building an effective corporate communication program. But stay on top of what is being said about the company. If you don't, social media posts can spin out of control and cause lasting damage.

Summary

In closing this chapter, here are some summary thoughts on the important topic of communication.

1. Good, clear communication is hard work. For all important communications, you need to allot enough time to do the prep work required. Clear writing reflects clear thinking. This takes time.

2. Communicate in a way that is best understood by the individual or group. The principal reason I've historically asked associates to complete a Myers-Briggs assessment and Gallup StrengthsFinder is to better understand each individual's unique strengths. Using Myers-Briggs terminology, how you communicate with an ISTJ is very different than how you should communicate with an ENFP. Adopt your communication style and approach to your target audience.

3. Don't pass on a required communication in order to avoid conflict. Being afraid of conflict is at the root of many problems and especially so when needing to communicate on a difficult subject. Becoming more adept around handling difficult conversations is an important skill for any business leader to acquire and develop. Remember most of the time it is just a matter of being open and naming a problem. Susan Scott's book *Fierce Conversations* was an important resource for me in learning how to communicate around difficult or contentious topics.

4. Make time to communicate face to face. All your direct

reports crave face time with you. Be careful about hiding behind emails rather than having a face-to-face conversation. Gallup research indicates associates would rather have a difficult discussion with their supervisor than no discussion at all.

5. Aim for clear, concise communication. Writing or speaking clearly and concisely means choosing your words deliberately and precisely. Construct your sentences carefully to eliminate deadwood and use proper grammar. Speak in plain English. Avoid jargon, officious, and bureaucratic speak like the plague. As managers start to climb the corporate ladder, it seems like they begin to lose the ability to talk or write clearly and are caught up in a bunch of corporate speak. When we are undisciplined in our language, we become undisciplined in our thinking and actions.

Being clear and concise displays your clarity of thought. People have more confidence in what you say because it shows that you know exactly what you are doing and what needs to be done. Build trust, strengthen team cohesion, and create a more productive working environment with clear, concise communication.

An effective communication program is a vital component to any organization's success. Whether the communication's purpose is to update associates on new policies, how we are reacting to a pandemic, announcing a corporate reorganization, or something much more prosaic, a good communication program is critical. As Churchill once said, "The difference between mere management and true leadership is communication." If you don't get anything else from this chapter, recognize that communicating effectively is hard work. Most communication problems I've witnessed over the years reflect someone being unprepared—maybe they are lazy, they didn't do the work required to communicate effectively. Do the work—you'll be glad you did.

CHAPTER 4
Trust

In January 2005, I was the new President and CEO of Assurity Life. Assurity came to be by the merger of three life insurance companies all over 100 years old. About a month into the merger, I realized we had major trust issues at the company. As has been my practice when facing a major problem, I started doing research. Fortunately, I found Stephen M.R. Covey's excellent book "The Speed of Trust". This book helped me understand how building a foundation of trust is essential for business success. In fact, I decided we would have a book club which would include all middle managers and above using this book as our primary resource. We hired a facilitator and spent about three months discussing this book and getting things out in the open and building trust among our new team. It was a gamechanger for us and set us up for future success.

If the associates who report to you don't trust you, your days as a business leader are numbered. Unfortunately, many corporate cultures are filled with fear, stress, gossip, and politics. An environment of fear is deeply toxic to our well-being and our capacity to function optimally. The most fundamental, powerful, and enduring fuel for performance is a feeling of safety and trust.

Trust is a precious asset. It's the basis for facilitating almost all business transactions. Charlie Munger has often spoken about a "seamless web of deserved trust" as an important lifelong pursuit. Trust is the most essential form of capital a leader possess.

Trust is hard to build but easy to break. Many of us tend to take trust for granted until it is in short supply. You might be given the benefit of the doubt initially, but abuse of trust is likely to ruin your reputation and severely curtail future opportunities. As an example, a deal with Warren Buffett is a deal you can take to the bank. Barring some egregious instance of fraud or intentional deception, he will not try to back out of an agreement, and not just for acquisitions. Berkshire enters into all sorts of other transactions in which trust is critical. How much money has Berkshire made over the years by operating in the spirit of Charlie Munger's seamless web of deserved trust? For more on the advantage of trust at Berkshire Hathaway, I recommend "The Berkshire Handshake" in the July 14, 2022, issue of *Kingswell*. The article discusses the role of trust in Berkshire's acquisitions and how this has made Berkshire the preferred acquiror for many business sellers.

I've never been able to do business with someone who is fundamentally not trustworthy. I'm reminded of another Buffett quote: "You cannot make a good deal with a bad person." No contract can protect you if you try and do business with someone who is not ethical. Over the years I've been tempted because the deal seemed so good. But it is always the wrong decision because if the individual is dishonest he will try and get out of the contract if something happens. Don't sully your own business reputation by doing a deal with an untrustworthy person.

William Green, in his extraordinary book *Richer, Wiser, Happier*, introduced me to the concept of "the compounding of goodwill." On page 179 in discussing Tom Gayner of the Markel Corporation, he writes, "If your goal is sustainable success, Gayner is convinced that it works better to behave admirably, not least because more people want to do business with you if you're trustworthy."

I hope I have convinced you on the importance of building trust in your organization. But how do we build trust?

First, I should point out that like almost everything worthwhile, building trust takes time. It comes from a consistent pattern of acting in good faith. It's a big mistake to assume too much trust too quickly.

Several years ago I attended the CEO Global Leaders Conference and participated in a session where Bob Chapman CEO of Barry-Wehmiller discussed how he builds trust at his company. Bob had just authored his book "Everybody Matters". Bob introduced to the audience a concept he called "CCCI". CCCI stands for compassion, competence, consistency and integrity. He indicated practicing CCCI is foundational for building trust at Barry-Wehmiller. Mr. Chapman's talk and his book further helped me understand the importance of building trust to having a great corporate culture.

Years ago, I attended a presentation by Dr. Don Clifton, the founder of Selection Research Inc. (SRI), which became the organization we know today as Gallup. In addition to starting SRI, Don was a professor at the University of Nebraska—Lincoln (UNL) and a nationally recognized leader in the positive psychology movement. The talk I heard Dr. Clifton deliver was called "The Theory of the Dipper and the Bucket."

Here is how Dr. Clifton explained it in his book, *How Full is your Bucket*, which he wrote with his grandson bestselling author Tom Rath:

> "Each of us has an invisible bucket. It is constantly emptied or filled, depending on what others say or do to us. When our bucket is full, we feel great. When it's empty, we feel awful.
>
> Each of us also has an invisible dipper. When we use that dipper to fill other people's buckets—by saying or doing things to increase their positive emotions—we also fill our own bucket. But when we use that dipper to dip from others' buckets—by saying or doing things that decrease their positive emotions—we diminish ourselves.
>
> Like the cup that runneth over, a full bucket gives us a positive outlook and renewed energy. Every drop in that bucket makes us stronger and more optimistic.
>
> But an empty bucket poisons our outlook, saps our energy, and undermines our will. That's why every time someone dips from our bucket, it hurts us.
>
> So we face a choice every moment of every day: we can fill one another's buckets, or we can dip from them. It's an important choice—one that profoundly influences our relationships, productivity, health, and happiness."

At Gallup's office in Omaha, you'll find most associates have a physical bucket on their desk where others can put in congratulatory, recognition, or other positive notes to "fill their bucket." I've been in the offices of senior executives of Gallup whose bucket is overflowing with positive notes. Filing someone's bucket is building trust.

Here are my top tips on how to build trust:

1. **Be Honest**
    This is the first step in building trust.
    - Tell the truth. Even small lies and twisted truths are still lies.
    - Share honest information, even if it's to your disadvantage.
    - As a business leader, you need to walk your talk—be an example of doing the right thing. Be on time, protect and honor company resources, and treat everyone with respect.

2. **Use Good Judgment**
    Know *what* information to share, when to share it, and *when not* to share it.
    - Protect associates' personal information and company or competitors' proprietary information as if it were your own.
    - Think twice before sharing a blunt, unsolicited judgment. Extreme honesty may hurt the recipient, ironically destroying trust and the safe environment.
    - Don't expect apologies to erase your wrongdoings. Apologies might earn a forgive, but perhaps not a forget.

3. **Be Consistent**
    The third step is to be consistent in words and behaviors. It's not enough to be trustworthy only on Tuesdays and Thursdays.
    - Show up—every day and on time—and stay at least the

required hours.
- Do the work, and meet or exceed what is expected of you.
- Do what you say you will do. Fulfill your promises.
- Be reliable. Unreliability can cancel out other virtues.

4. **Be Honest in Nonverbal Communications**
   Body language experts tell us that more than half of communication's impact is in nonverbal communications. To increase trust through body language:
   - Look others in the eye with comfortable and direct eye contact.
   - Exhibit open body language with open arms versus closed across the chest or hands clasped together, and keep your hands in sight (not behind you or in your pockets) and open (not in a fist).

5. **Demonstrate You Want the Best from Others**
   - Trustworthy supervisors see people as individuals—not with generational or stereotypical biases.
   - Demonstrate you genuinely care about others and promote we, we, we, *not* me, me, me.
   - Nurture mutually beneficial relationships with open communications.
   - Willingly accept information and constructive criticism.
   - By word and deed, demonstrate to those who report to you that you want the best from them. Help them apply and develop their strengths and reach their career goals.
   - Remember that goodwill is compounding. The more you practice goodwill toward others the bigger "trust bank" you'll build.

6. **Lead the Quest for a Trustworthy Environment**
   Trusted leaders are sorely needed. Leaders should be able to:
   - Ask the hard questions to build and protect the company.
   - Listen and consider others' ideas with an open mind.
   - Focus on issues and solutions rather than personalities.

- Set the example by being responsible and accountable.

7. **Say Thank You**
   Trusted leaders freely acknowledge the efforts and contributions of those they work with. Remember, a good leader takes a little more than their share of blame and less than their share of credit.

I'm going to end this chapter with two quotes, the first from Doug Conant, former CEO of Campbell Soup.

> "As a leader, you've got to live in three time zones simultaneously, the past, the present, and the future. Everything you do has got to honor the past, deliver in the present, set the table for a more prosperous future. And as you think that way, that's why trust building become mission-critical."

The other from Charlie Munger: "To get what you want, deserve what you want. Trust, success, and admiration are earned."

CHAPTER 5
Recognition

Close your eyes and think back to last week. Was it a good week? A busy week? Did you receive any praise, recognition, or appreciation?

This question is vital. It's so important that the question: "In the last seven days, have you received recognition or praise for doing good work?" is one of just twelve questions Gallup asks when evaluating the engagement of a workplace.

Associates want not only good pay and benefits; they also want to be treated fairly and recognized and appreciated for their work. Corporate America believes recognition programs are important. In a January 24, 2018, survey conducted by the Society of Human Resource Managers (SHRM) and the recognition consulting firm Globoforce, 80 percent of organizations reported having a formal employee recognition program.

Although 80 percent of corporate America's companies have a recognition program, they haven't been very effective. According to Gallup, only one in three workers received praise or recognition in the past week.

To solve this dilemma, let's start with some recognition basics.

What is associate recognition? Associate recognition is corporate and area programs and individual acts that help associates know their contributions are recognized and appreciated. Associates want to know how they are doing, and recognizing associates demonstrates what success looks like and encourages more of the same.

Why does associate recognition matter? From a very early age we crave recognition from our parents, teachers, and friends. This need never goes away. As we enter the workforce, our need for recognition does not diminish. It's a lifelong need. I once gave one of my older direct reports some sincere recognition. I saw his eyes light up, and I was surprised when he said to me, "Even an old dog likes to be petted once in a while."

Sometimes we confuse recognition and appreciation. Mike Robbins, an author and consultant who wrote *Bring Your Whole Self to Work*, penned an article in the *Harvard Business Review* on November 12, 2019, titled, "Why Employees Need Both Recognition and Appreciation." Here is how Mr. Robbins contrasts recognition and appreciation: "Recognition is giving positive feedback based on results or performance. Appreciation, on the other hand, is about acknowledging a person's inherent value. In simple terms, recognition is about what people do; appreciation is about who they are." Both recognition and appreciation are important and integral to an overall recognition program.

Unfortunately, effective employee recognition is not as common as needed for optimal associate engagement. Plenty of managers choose not to make it a priority, either because they are too busy themselves, or because they simply don't understand why it's so vital to a thriving workplace.

What are the elements of a good associate recognition program?

1. Specific and relevant—Recognition is always more meaningful when it is tied to a specific accomplishment or the attainment of a particular business objective.

2. Timely—The reward or recognition should be delivered as close as possible to the time of the desired behavior to strengthen the link between the associate's action and what was accomplished.

3. Recognition comes in many shapes and sizes—When thinking of recognition, many managers imagine a corporate-wide program, like an employee of the month program.

Although this kind of programs is important, relying on it is insufficient. There are so many other ways to provide motivation, recognition, and appreciation. I'll provide some less common ideas later in this chapter.

4. Connect to the bigger picture—Recognition helps associates see that their company values them, and their work directly contributes to the success of their area and the company overall.

5. Artfully carried out—The manner of delivery can make or break a program. Recognition should be carried out in an authentic and heartfelt way. Associates will be more motivated by a manager's single act of consideration than by a substantial gift delivered poorly. It should feel personal, not part of a scheme cooked up in the human resources department.

6. Administratively uncomplicated—The entire recognition process should be managed with a minimum of administrative effort. A system that requires excessive management control, complex financial calculations, or exceptional associate efforts to be understood will not likely achieve its desired results. Keep it simple; simple is always better.

7. Regularly evaluated—Corporate-wide programs must be monitored continually for relevance. The evaluation process should be completed after every award cycle so adjustments can be made to improve the program and retain associate interest.

8. Takes effort—The best recognition involves effort. A handwritten note is better than an email, which is better than an algorithmically generated communication.

9. Aligned with Mission Values and Goals—Recognition programs are most effective when they are aligned with the

organization's mission, values, and goals. Associates should see a clear connection between the recognition they or their colleagues receive and the attainment of corporate goals.

Ways to Provide Recognition
You all know the standard ways to provide recognition. These are things like:

1. Companywide awards like an employee of the month program.
2. Expressing appreciation in writing—a personalized handwritten note is best, but an email can also work.
3. Shout-out at a department or company wide meeting.
4. Heartfelt words expressed in person, either individually or in front of coworkers.
5. Spot bonuses for a job well done.
6. Awarding gift cards, tickets, movie passes, and the like for great performance.
7. Length of service awards and public recognition for this service.
8. Recognizing the attainment of certain industry-related educational achievements.

Here are some other less common recognition ideas that I feel are more effective.

1. Ask someone for their opinion You pay people the highest compliment when you ask them for their opinion on some important issue. What you are communicating is that you think they have expertise around the issue and that you value their thoughts. You are making them a thought leader on some particular subject matter.
2. Award top-performing associates with additional responsibility. You are communicating that you recognize their expertise and that you, as their manager, know they can do more.
3. Encourage peer-to-peer recognition. Recognition is great

coming from a manager or the executive level, but it's also appreciated when it comes from peers. Get everyone involved with the recognition process, and give your team ample opportunity and encouragement to recognize one another. I once had a manager who occasionally as an icebreaker asked that everyone go around the room and say something they liked or admired in the other participants. Very effective!

4. Write a letter to an associate's spouse. I once had a manager who sent my wife a letter to our home address and commented on how much he appreciated me and what I was doing for the company. This may be the best recognition I've ever received.

5. Catch people doing something right. If you want to change the culture in your area, catch people doing something right and then publicly recognize the behavior. I've seen how quickly you can get your area moving in a new direction using this type of praise.

6. Have fun. Don't be too serious in dispensing recognition. Deliver positive feedback in a humorous way. Please keep in mind the person you are recognizing; always tailor the praise to what you know the individual receiving it would like. A random pleasant surprise is almost always a hit.

7. Recognize associate "wins" on social media. When an associate has a win, post their accomplishment on the company's social media sites. Sharing their win on company social media will cause the associate to be recognized by a broader audience. Consider writing a LinkedIn recommendation that recognizes your staff member's particular areas of expertise.

8. Provide the opportunity to attend a professional development course. For example, tell an associate you've noticed they are very good at writing. Indicate the company wants to send them to a particular writing course to further enhance their writing skills. This is a very powerful way to recognize someone.

I once had a boss that spewed out recognition continuously—"good job," "you are fabulous," "way to go," "great work"—all delivered in an insincere, rapid-fire way. This type of recognition is not meaningful, and all his direct reports knew he was only being fatuous. Eventually it became an office joke, and behind his back we all mimicked his insincere recognition. One of the secrets to showing appreciation is that scarcity matters. Recognition should be sufficiently rare to register as meaningful: thanking everyone for everything turns gratitude into a commodity.

I like British comedy shows, and the BBC sitcom *Are You Being Served?* is an old but classic British sitcom. The show follows the staff of the men's and women's clothing area in a major London department store. In one scene after a busy holiday season, the department store's elderly owner comes for a staff meeting and only says to the staff, "You've all done very well," before tottering away on the arm of his nurse. No one feels motivated by such bland, indiscriminate praise.

Whatever you do to honor your associates, make sure it comes from the heart. Whether you're recognizing the work of an individual or the whole team, appreciation only works when it's sincere and authentic. Don't offer recognition just for the sake of morale; offer it for a job well done. Giving praise is just what your area needs for a happier, more productive environment. Don't be afraid of flattery. Why? Because it works. There is little danger of ever laying it on too thick. According to a study by Jennifer Chatman at the University of California Berkeley, there is no level where flattery stops working. I've personally experienced this with certain individuals. Over the years I've witnessed certain associates and business partners have an almost insatiable need for recognition. If you effectively scratch that itch, you'll have a very loyal and productive colleague or business partner.

I'm going to conclude this chapter with two of my favorite quotes on associate recognition—quotes I've tried to live by:

> "Always treat your employees exactly as you want them to treat your best customers."
> —Stephen R. Covey, author of *The 7 Habits of Highly Effective People*

"To win in the marketplace, you must first win in the workplace."

—Doug Conant, former President and CEO of the Campbell Soup Company

CHAPTER 6
Ethics

During my long business career, I've witnessed many corporate ethical crises. Here are a few that were memorable to me:

1. Bhopal Gas Disaster—Dow Chemical Company, 1984
2. Lincoln Savings & Loan—Charles Keating Fraud & Racketeering Scandal, 1989
3. Salomon Brothers Trading Desk Scandal, 1991
4. Sears Automotive Service Center Scandal, 1992
5. Enron Corp Scandal & Failure, 2001
6. World Com Inc. Scandal & Failure, 2002
7. Lehman Brothers Collapse, 2008
8. American Insurance Group Credit Default Scandal & Near Failure, 2009
9. BP Deepwater Horizon Oil Spill, 2010
10. Volkswagen Emission Scandal, 2013
11. Theranos Blood Testing Fraud, 2015
12. Wells Fargo Account Fraud Scandal, 2016
13. Equifax Data Breach, 2017
14. Boeing 737 MAX Cover-Up, 2018
15. WeWork IPO Disaster, 2019

I could have named quite a few others—I thought fifteen were enough to make my point that unfortunately, corporate ethical crises are fairly commonplace.

The aftermath of these major lapses in corporate ethics is very predictable: congressional hearings and calls for greater corporate oversight. Perhaps new laws and regulations. More corporate compliance-based ethics programs and a plethora of seminars on developing an effective corporate ethics program. A surfeit of consultants who promote their qualifications to assist companies in developing an effective corporate ethics program will flood corporate America's inboxes.

The frequency of corporate ethical scandals demonstrates the failure of formal corporate ethics programs in preventing these problems. Executive management and their board of directors would be mistaken to regard a formal ethics compliance program as an adequate way to address the full range of ethical issues facing corporate America.

As an example, here is an excerpt from Wells Fargo's ethics statement prior to their account fraud scandal:

> "Wells Fargo's reputation as one of the world's great companies for integrity and principled performance depends on our doing the right thing, in the right way, and complying with the laws, rules and regulations that govern our business. We earn trust by behaving ethically and holding all team members and directors accountable for the decisions we make and the actions we take."

For years, banking industry leaders and analysts viewed Wells Fargo and Co. as the bank with the strongest culture, the highest profitability, and the best reputation among large banks in our country. But the key lesson around the Wells Fargo scandal is no matter how powerful a company's culture, it is still fragile if management doesn't walk the walk. And from Wells Fargo's experience, we learn that corporate scandals seem to never go away.

Almost all major companies have ethics and compliance policies that get reviewed and signed annually by all associates. Here is another example:

> "Associates are charged with conducting their business affairs in accordance with the highest ethical standards. Moral

as well as legal obligations will be fulfilled in a manner which will reflect pride on the company's name."

Guess whose ethical policy this language is from? None other than one of the most infamous corporate scandals in American business history: Enron.

Warren Buffett once said, "I don't believe in putting out a 200-page manual on how we should conduct business because if you put out a 200-page manual, everyone is looking for a loophole." I agree.

Or consider that integrity, ethical behavior, "do the right thing," or some variation is a value espoused by almost all corporations. Having read and researched many vision, mission, and values statements over the years, I think "being ethical" or some variation would be the most common value.

So, if formalistic legal ethical compliance programs don't work, and having ethics or integrity as a corporate value doesn't work, what does?

Before I get to what I believe works, I want to disabuse you of an idea that I believe is held by many business leaders and by many boards of directors: that most ethical failures are caused by one or two bad apples. Executives and boards are usually quick to describe any wrongdoing as an isolated incident, the work of a rogue associate. They believe the company shouldn't bear any responsibility for any one individual's misdeeds.

Here's the unfortunate truth: rarely do the character flaws of a lone actor fully explain corporate misconduct, especially at the level of the major ethical lapses we've been discussing. I believe unethical business practices involve the implicit, if not explicit, values, attitudes, beliefs, and behavioral patterns that define an organization's operating culture. I believe ethics is primarily an organizational issue, not an issue at the individual level.

So what to do? If formalistic, legalistic, compliance-based programs don't work and stating ethics as a corporate value doesn't work, what does? I believe there are four broad things that business leaders and their boards should monitor to prevent most major ethical disasters.

1. **Tone at the Top**

   Tone at the top refers to the ethical atmosphere that is created in the workplace by an organization's leadership. Whatever tone management sets will have a trickle-down effect on the company's associates. If the tone set by managers upholds ethics and integrity, associates will be more inclined to uphold those same values. However, if upper management appears unconcerned with ethics and focuses solely on the bottom line, associates will be more prone to commit ethical lapses because they feel that ethical conduct is not a focus or priority within the organization. Associates pay close attention to the behavior and actions of their bosses, and they follow their lead. In short, associates will do what they witness their bosses doing.

   The tricky part is how you measure tone at the top. Associate exit interviews, whistleblower complaints, social media posts, and associate surveys can all be used to assess tone at the top.

   Here is a powerful way executives can create the proper tone at the top: let associates see executive management making decisions that financially disadvantage the executives. The executive group makes the decision because it is the right thing to do despite how it will affect them. More than anything else, this communicates the importance of ethics in the organization.

2. **Hire and Fire Based on Integrity**

   Of course there are many other factors that come into the hiring decision. But I believe integrity should be the number one thing. Warren Buffett once quipped, "In looking for people to hire, you look for three qualities: integrity, intelligence, and energy. And if you don't have the first, the other two will kill you. Think about it; if you hire somebody without integrity, you really want them to be dumb and lazy."

   So, when hiring, how do you determine a person's ethics? Here are three questions I consider asking during an interview.

- Tell me about a time when you experienced a loss for doing what is right. How did you react?
- When was the last time you "broke the rules?" What was the situation, and what did you do?
- Describe a situation where you saw an associate or co-worker do something you thought was inappropriate. What did you do?

I have to admit I do not ask these questions in every interview, but here is one question I almost always ask in interviewing: "Tell me about an ethical dilemma you faced in the past and how you handled it." The answer to this question will reveal a great deal about this individual.

Firing for ethical transgressions also sends a powerful message across the company. When I reflect on the executives and middle managers I've had to terminate over the years, most were not for performance reasons but for some sort of ethical lapse. I try to live by the Warren Buffett comment to the Salomon Brothers traders when he served as interim CEO: "Lose money for the firm, and I will be understanding. Lose a shred of reputation for the firm, and I will be ruthless."

3. **Be careful of Excessive Pressure to Reach Unrealistic Performance Targets**
   I'm all for stretch goals, but boards and executive management need to be careful that in establishing these goals they don't create too much pressure, which could cause aberrant behavior.

   Early in my career I witnessed this firsthand. I was asked to join the board and serve as chair of the audit committee for a small publicly traded company. My company at the time had a small investment in this company, and the current chair of the audit committee had unexpectedly passed away. Needless to say, I didn't ask enough questions before agreeing to chair the audit committee because at my first meeting a national audit partner showed up and told the committee we had a revenue recognition problem. As chair, I had to hire outside legal counsel and a forensic accounting firm. What we found was there had been tremendous pressure applied to the sales area to hit unrealistic sales objectives. My experience is when you put too much pressure on people, their character tends to come off in shades. We need to have challenging but realistic goals.

4. **Avoid an Absolutist Moral Perspective**

   I currently chair the audit committee of a publicly traded company. Part of my responsibility as audit committee chair is to review all whistleblower submissions. The vast majority of these submissions relate to some relatively minor human resource issues. For example, "Sally in the cube next to mine texts her friends all day and doesn't do any work" or "Johnny is habitually late for work and often leaves early." Not true whistleblower submissions.

   When we were planning our move into the new Assurity Center, a contingent of associates came to see me to express their views that allowing plastic bottles in the Assurity Center would violate our moral responsibility to the environment. When I told them I didn't think this was practical, they were aghast.

   Another example, we have many colleagues who feel very strongly that we need to be in total compliance with every insurance regulation at all times. Given the complexity of state insurance regulation, this is an impossibility.

   I once heard Warren Buffett and Bill Gates speak at a seminar at the University of Nebraska—Lincoln. They spent a good deal of time discussing ethics and integrity. Mr. Buffett said something that initially startled me but on reflection makes so much sense. He said, "At Berkshire, we currently have over 250,000 associates. I can tell you right now somebody is doing something illegal." It made me think with 400 associates and over 30,000 distributors under contract, it is likely someone is doing something unethical and maybe illegal at our company this very moment. If everything is important, nothing is important. I favor focusing on avoiding major ethical lapses as opposed to a perfectionist approach to ethical expectations. Let's be sure we don't have a major ethical lapse.

5. **The legendary value investor Guy Spier, who manages the Aquamarine investment firm, annually publishes his investing principles. In his 2015 annual report, I particularly liked his principle #4, "Play Center Court."** Here is what he wrote:

> "Donald Keough, who was president of Coca-Cola and a board member at Berkshire Hathaway, provided an enlightening discussion of ethics in his book *The Ten Commandments for Business Failure*. One problem with playing the game close to the foul line, he explained, is that the foul line moves around. AIG and the Greenberg family discovered this in the realm of insurance.
>
> Another benefit of playing center court is that it usually doesn't require vast amounts of expensive input from lawyers, accountants, and other high-priced advisers. Accountants and lawyers often don't like it when their clients play center court, since people who push the boundaries tend to generate higher fees."

I want to amplify an important point from Mr. Spier's comments: ethical standards can change. What is acceptable behavior today could be different tomorrow. An important reason to play center court.

6. **Foster a Culture of Goodwill**
As I mentioned in chapter 4, in *Richer, Wiser, Happier*, William Green writes about the concept of compounding goodwill. He indicates that Guy Spier introduced this

BOOST! | 47

concept to him. Mr. Green indicates Mr. Spier puts a lot of energy in helping others. Because of this, he is surrounded by people who wish to help him. Being nice to people pays.

No individual or any business knows what life has in store for them. Being kind and supportive will go a long way in transforming your life. One day, you'll need a kindness from other people. And you'll always get what you give. This is one of the good life lessons to adopt early in life.

I also heard William Green say on his podcast, "When you're taking care of other people, the universe conspires to make you more successful anyway." Fostering goodwill, conducting yourself ethically, and being kind to others will give your firm a competitive advantage.

We need to remember that ethical lapses are very costly to any business.

The Economist magazine in the March 31, 2018, Schumpeter Column wrote the following:

"Schumpeter has looked at eight of the most notable crises since 2010, including those at Uber and Wells Fargo. The evidence shows that these episodes were deeply injurious to the company's financial health, with the median firm losing 30% of its value since the crisis when compared with a basket of securities.

In today's business environment making a good return for shareholders will not be enough. How you make your money is as important as how much you make. Mistrust exacts a price, though sometimes it take a while to manifest itself.

A big scandal distracts management, hurts the company's reputation and usually leads to additional regulatory scrutiny."

I've long tried to live by this quote from the American philosopher Aldo Leopold when he said, "Ethical behavior is doing the right thing when no one else is watching even when doing the wrong thing is legal."

I'm going to end with three additional quotes from Warren Buffett, who I believe for his entire life has been compounding relationships, trust, and reputation. These quotes have guided my own behavior and, I think, can be valuable to you.

> "I want our CEOs to judge every action by how it would appear on the front page of their local newspaper, written by a smart but semi-unfriendly reporter, who really understood it, to be read by their families, their neighbors, their friends. And it has to pass that test."
>
> "We have all the money we need, but we don't have an ounce of reputation beyond what we need. And we can't afford to lose it."
>
> "It takes twenty years to build a reputation and five minutes to ruin it. If you think about that, you'll do things differently."

CHAPTER 7
Conflict Avoidance

Years ago I was fortunate enough to attend the Wharton Effective Executive Program at the University of Pennsylvania, a multiyear program that at the time was focused on the behavioral aspects of management. I've never forgotten a question asked to the lead professor on the last day: "What is one thing you would have us all do to become better leaders and managers?" Without hesitation, the distinguished professor said, "Don't avoid conflict, and learn how to effectively deal with it."

He then abandoned his lecture notes, and we spent the rest of the day discussing conflict. One surprising thing our professor said was that CEOs are typically some of the biggest conflict avoiders in every organization. He discussed the great lengths many CEOs will go to in order to avoid conflict and how this negatively impacts their company's success.

But here's the thing: avoiding conflict doesn't reduce tension. Instead, it escalates it. Issues become bigger, resentment grows, and people become disengaged and then feel powerless to solve their problems.

A reluctance to deal with conflict is hugely detrimental to business. Good ideas remain unspoken, people create silos, and leaders don't get the information they need because everyone is afraid to bring up potentially contentious issues. The postmortem on any business failure almost always reveals critical information went unaddressed because somebody was avoiding conflict.

Many times when I'm facing a difficult business problem,

somewhere, lurking in the background, I'm avoiding conflict. In my own case, becoming aware and calling myself out helps me find a solution. Management, leadership, and conflict go hand in hand. If you cannot or will not address conflict in a healthy, productive fashion, you should not be in a leadership role.

The issues surrounding conflict resolution can be best summed up by adhering to the following ethos: "Don't fear conflict; embrace it—it's your job." While you can try to avoid conflict, you cannot escape it. Conflict in the workplace is unavoidable.

The biggest reason people avoid conflict is because they don't see a clear way to bring up an issue and resolve it peacefully. They assume it's going to be contentious. But disagreements don't mean death; they're just disagreements. You don't have to be afraid of them. Human beings will always be human beings, and there's always going to be conflict.

When you accept conflict as an inevitable part of business and relationships, you wind up dealing with it more effectively. The more confidence you have in your ability to handle disagreements, the quicker you resolve them. Handling a conflict isn't the worst thing in the world. But letting one go unresolved can cause big problems. A common example in any business is dealing with a demanding customer on a difficult issue. Too often we indicate we need to check something out or ask a superior when we already know the answer should be no. Saying no from the start keeps us all from a great deal of wasted effort.

The ability to recognize conflict, understand it, and quickly resolve it will serve you well as a leader. The inability to do so may be your downfall. I hope I've convinced you that to be a great business leader, you have to get better at addressing conflict. Here are my suggestions for handling conflict:

1. **Communication:** If you reflect back upon conflicts you've encountered over the years, you'll quickly recognize many of them resulted from a lack of information or misinformation. Clear, concise, accurate, and timely communication of information will help to ease both the number and severity of conflicts.

2. **Hit Conflict Head-on:** One of the secrets to conflict resolution is conflict prevention (not conflict avoidance). By seeking out areas of potential conflict and proactively intervening, you may be able to prevent certain conflicts from ever arising. If a conflict does flare up, you can minimize its severity by dealing with it quickly.

3. **Understanding the WIIFM Factor (What's in It for Me):** Understanding who you are having a conflict with's WIIFM position is critical. It's absolutely essential to understand others' motivations prior to addressing areas of conflict. Listen more than you talk. Approach conflict from the perspective of taking action that helps others, and you'll likely find that fewer obstacles stand in your way of resolving the conflict. Additionally, don't set up a win-lose situation. Resolving business problems is not about proving someone wrong. Create ways for others to save face and succeed.

4. **The Importance Factor:** Pick your battles and avoid conflict for the sake of conflict. This may seem contradictory to everything else I've said in this chapter. Those of you who are parents understand—with your kids, you have to pick your battles. There is only so much time, and we all only have so much energy. Don't fight every fight; it's not worth your time and energy.

5. **View Conflict as Opportunity:** Hidden within virtually every conflict is the potential for a tremendous teaching-learning-growing opportunity. Where there is disagreement, there is the potential for growth and development. If you're a manager who doesn't leverage conflict for team building and leadership development, you're missing a great opportunity. Divergent positions addressed properly can stimulate innovation in ways agreeing minds can't even imagine. Smart leaders look for the upside in all differing opinions.

In the end, remember running a business isn't a democracy. Although you'll want the best ideas and inputs from your colleagues, you don't need to take a vote. Sometimes as a business leader you just need to decide, recognizing not everyone will be happy.

The bottom line is avoiding conflict won't make the problem go away. Don't be afraid of conflict; it's a natural part of business. Develop a reputation for being a straightshooter. Speak the truth and don't set up win-lose situations. Be known for doing what's best for your organization.

CHAPTER 8
Change

Raise your hand if you like change. My guess is there are not many raised hands. Change is hard. But change is even harder for associates when executive management or supervisors don't embrace it.

So many industries are going through tremendous change. Technological advances, economic challenges, shifting consumer values and preferences, and regulatory changes are all affecting industry after industry like never before. These are just the garden-variety changes. And then bam-slam! A worldwide pandemic and all its aftermath. It is hard to think of a period of modern peacetime history where the scale, intensity, and degree of change across an entire economy has occurred at once. In the business world, sameness and stability are not realistic concepts.

Yet most business leaders resist change. A witty line I heard at an industry conference years ago is that an executive's prayer is said to go, "This change too will pass." I'm here to tell you that waiting for a change to pass won't make the pace of change slow or disappear. Nothing is permanent.

Why do we fear and resist change so much? We fear change for a variety of reasons. These fears are often associated with fear of failure, fear of rejection, fear of criticism, fear of the unknown, and sometimes fear of success.

The growing research in neuroscience is proving the belief that "we are creatures of habit." We like "certainty." Certainty brings with it clarity and predictability; therefore, change may often activate a threat circuitry in the brain. This can trigger powerful effects on our body and emotions, which we refer to as stress. However, change does not always have to culminate in fear and anxiety. How well organizations handle the process of change and transition—and how much we perceive we have control and influence over the change—is the key to managing the fear of change.

Whether you love or hate change, it's here to stay. As a business leader, you not only have to deal with your own reaction to change but your team's feelings on the matter. Years of experience have taught me an individual associate's reaction to change will largely mirror their leader's reaction. If the leader reacts negatively to change, I can guarantee that leader's team will react negatively as well. As Ryan Holiday wrote in his recent book *Courage Is Calling*, "It has been said that leaders are dealers in hope, but in a more practical sense, they are also slayers of fear."

Even more importantly, change and risk-taking are necessary adjuncts of growing any successful business. I've never known of a successful business whose plan was to resist change and embrace the status quo.

How does one best navigate through times of uncertainty? Here is what I've observed the best business leaders do to help themselves and their colleagues adjust to change:

1. **Know You Are Strong.** Top performers cultivate a frame of mind that when conflict, struggle, or change occurs, they believe in their ability to handle whatever comes their way. They have unwavering confidence in their strength to adapt. Adopt this mentality and you will be well-served. You need to remember that the only true security in life is to know whatever comes your way, you will be able to handle it and hopefully exploit it for your advantage. It's important to project a calm demeanor. Assess the situation, form a plan of action to deal with it, and always show an interest in learning from the experience.

2. **Strengthen Your Hardiness.** In turbulent times when change is inevitable, it makes sense to strengthen your

ability to adapt. One way to do this is by increasing your hardiness, or how you remain healthy under stress. Hardy leaders are more open to change and challenges in life. While not immune to the ill effects of stress, someone who is very hardy is strongly resilient. They tend to interpret stressful and painful experiences as a normal aspect of existence, a part of life that is overall interesting and worthwhile. Eat right, get enough exercise, and utilize stress-reduction techniques like meditation—whatever works for you to build your resiliency. Developing your own hardiness as a leader and encouraging a hardy workplace sets the stage for success in your organization.

3. **Fear Not.** One of the most entertaining and enlightening books on dealing with change is Dr. Spencer Johnson's helpful tome titled *Who Moved My Cheese?* This book is a fable about four characters who live in a maze and learn to deal with unexpected change. I consider this book a business classic. What I especially like is how the book deals with the fear that accompanies change. Here are some quotes from this book on dealing with the fear that accompanies most significant change.

"What would you do if you weren't afraid?"

"What you are afraid of is never as bad as what you imagine. The fear you let build up in your mind is worse than the situation that actually exists."

"When you stop being afraid you feel good."

Do not let the fear of change overtake you. If you want to accomplish great things, you must first learn how to conquer fear, or at least rise above it in moments that matter.

4. **Guard Against Undue Pessimism.** Optimists can seem naïve. Looking on the bright side does not have the same

intellectual cachet of forecasting calamity. I think one of the principal reasons pessimism sounds smart is that optimism often requires believing in the unknown, perhaps a future event that seems fanciful and maybe naïve. If you stick to only the known, you will necessarily be pessimistic.

5. **Be a Hopeful Realist.** The business leaders best at dealing with change are not wide-eyed optimists who tell their people everything will always be okay, and neither are they constant pessimists. Rather, they are realists with a hopeful nature. Take, for example, Admiral Jim Stockdale, a United States military officer held captive during the Vietnam War and tortured for eight years. While being held, Admiral Stockdale keenly observed that individuals with high amounts of optimism didn't survive captivity. So he approached adversity with a different mindset. Stockdale accepted the reality of his situation. He knew he was in hell and making it through was going to be tough, but he had faith that he would prevail, regardless of the difficulties. Stockdale is a great example of a realist with a hopeful nature.

6. *Accept* **Rather Than** *Resist.* There are generally two types of coping: escape coping and active coping. Escape coping is a form of coping that involves changing our behavior to try to avoid thinking or feeling things that are uncomfortable. Ultimately the most important thing to do to cope with change in the workplace is to acknowledge it's happening. Recognizing and accepting change is one of the first steps toward managing it. Feel the fear and do it anyway.

7. **Look for the Opportunities.** We need to remember change usually translates to possibility for those who are willing to exploit what change brings. Encourage your people to take on new tasks that might accompany change. Establish a mindset that change is an opportunity. With new doors opening, your team has different opportunities and new

potential to shine. I think many times the reason change is so painful is that we have a failure of imagination. This is the inability to understand in advance the full breadth or range of outcomes. Be wary of binary choices—heads or tails. Be more open to the possibility of a range of outcomes and the opportunities that come with any change. I became much better at handling change when I accepted this mindset.

In his book *Make Change Work for You*, Scott Steinberg states that change can become your secret weapon. If you and your organization get really good at change, you will have a decided competitive advantage. Effectively handling change will become your secret weapon. Focus your team on the positive outcomes of change.

8. **Be Persistent.** With major changes, it can take time before the scope or specifics of what's going to change can be clearly defined. The business leaders best at handling change keep working and maintain their team morale. Get up every day, put on your work clothes, and go back to the office and work. Keeping at it is more than half the battle.

9. **Act Your Way into a New Way of Thinking.** I've observed so many who try to think their way into a new way of acting to deal with change. This almost never works. We rarely think our way into a new way of acting. Rather, we should act into a new way of thinking and being. Act as if you have accepted the change and are already effectively coping and thriving within the new environment.

10. **Overcommunicate.** During periods of great change, good communication is critical. Any communication gaps will instantly be filled by rumors and speculation, which create even more fear and uncertainty around what is changing. Build trust in your team by being transparent and communicating what you can as soon as possible. When asked questions you can't answer, say so, but let them know you will share more

as soon as you are able. Transparency accompanied by good communication will greatly help your team adjust.

Remember, standing still is not an option. Jack Welch, longtime General Electric CEO, once said, "If the rate of change on the outside exceeds the rate of change on the inside, the end is near." The riskiest thing any business can do in the new, uncertain world is to *not* change. We never know what lies ahead, but we can prepare for possibilities and develop a mindset to embrace change—to view change as an opportunity. The best business leaders know this and lead the way through change using it as an opportunity to create a stronger tomorrow. Maybe you'll never learn to love change, but I would encourage you to accept its inevitability and develop the skills and knowledge you need to move your organization forward through the many inevitable changes that will come your way. I'm going to end this chapter with a quote from the futurist Alvin Toffler. "The illiterate of the twenty-first century will not be those who cannot read or write, but those who cannot learn, unlearn, and relearn."

CHAPTER 9
Making Good Decisions

A skill that is highly valued in business is the ability to make good decisions. Exercising good judgment is essential to business success. In fact, Bain & Company research found that decision effectiveness is 95 percent correlated with financial performance. As Euripides said many years ago, "Fortune truly helps those who are of good judgment."

Think of all the bad decisions made in business over the years. If you "google" worst business decisions ever, you'll see a plethora of bad decision lists. Here are some that are top of mind to me:

1. New Coke
2. Blockbuster not acquiring Netflix
3. Kodak not embracing digital photography
4. Excite not buying Google for $750,000 in 1999
5. Selling Instagram to Facebook for only $1 billion

The list could go on and on. And yes, hindsight is 20/20.

So many poor decisions are made—why? Here is what I've observed as some of the most common reasons for poor decisions.

Avoiding Making a Decision

This is the most common decision-making error. Many managers go to great lengths to avoid making a decision. They prefer a ponderous rulebook. They want a rule for everything, so they don't have to exercise judgment and make a decision. But you can't have a rule for everything. The world is too complex to make a 200-plus-page rulebook work. Ultimately, great business leaders practice Gordon Graham's admonishment, "Decision is a sharp knife that cuts clean and straight; indecision, a dull one that hacks and tears and leave ragged edges behind it."

Data Issues
We are simultaneously living in the best and worst times for making data-based decisions. It is the best time because there has never been a time when data is so plentiful, easy to manage, and readily available. It is the worst of times because data may be poorly analyzed, drawing inaccurate conclusions. There is so much data that do not provide an actionable insight—they're just noise. The data can be contaminated and not detected. Too much data can cause paralysis by analysis.

Succumbing to Cognitive Biases
There are a whole host of cognitive biases that can negatively impact the decision-making process. In chapter 21, I discuss the most common cognitive biases affecting a business leader.

Slow Decision-Making
This is a malady that seems to infect many established firms. Typically these firms have become very bureaucratic with management layers and a plethora of standing committees. In today's fast-paced business environment, the competitive landscape changes quickly, and old, plodding approaches are lethal. I started an entity called Assurity Ventures Inc. (AVI), which partners with insurtech firms. Insurtech founders like to work with AVI because we are not bureaucratic and can decide. In contrast, our much larger insurance company brethren struggle in being responsive.

Groupthink
Groupthink happens when dissent is not encouraged. It is the forced manufacture of consent. This problem bedevils decision-makers from the White House to company board rooms. Because of our

overreliance on hierarchy, an instinct to prevent dissent, and a desire to preserve harmony, many groups fall into groupthink. Expert opinions or outside consultants can quickly assume an oversized role. Biases can easily spread across the group and lead to bad outcomes.

Not Making the Decision at the Right Level
McKinsey & Company has identified four broad categories of decisions and where these decisions should be made. Here is an excerpt from research they published on May 1, 2019.

> "Big-bet decisions (such as a possible acquisition) are infrequent but high risk and have the potential to shape the future of the company; these are generally the domain of the top team and the board.
>
> Cross-cutting decisions (such as a pricing decision), which can be high risk, happen frequently and are made in cross-functional forums as part of a collaborative, end-to-end process.
>
> Delegated decisions are frequent but low risk and are effectively handled by an individual or working team, with limited input from others.
>
> Ad hoc decisions, which are infrequent and low stakes. Clearly, it is important that these types of decisions happen at the appropriate level of the company (CEOs, for example, shouldn't make decisions that are best delegated). And yet, just as clearly, many decisions rise up much higher in the company than they should."

So being sure decisions are being made at the right level is very important. There is always a tendency to push a decision up to the next level. I suppose lower-level managers feel they are "off the hook," so to speak, if they bounce a decision up a level or two.

Solving the Wrong Problem
You don't properly assess whether you are solving the right problem. Here are some warning signs you may be solving the wrong problem.

- You let someone else define the problem for you.
- You're far away from the problem.
- You're thinking about the problem at only one level or through a narrow lens.

As you can see from this list, there are a lot of potential pitfalls to good decision-making. As the great American humorist Will Rogers once said, "Good judgment comes from experiences and a lot of that comes from bad judgment." Awareness of these decision-making pitfalls is a good first step. What else?

Here are some techniques to facilitate better decision-making.

Upstream Thinking
Several years ago, our senior management team did a book club on the book *Decisive* by Chip and Dan Heath. It's one of the best books I've read on decision-making. Dan Heath, in an article for the CFA Institute, discusses upstream thinking. Here is part of what he wrote:

> "We're always chasing emergencies; we're always putting out fires. We respond after a bad thing has happened. We rarely make the time and devote the resources to get upstream and solve problems at their root.
>
> We need to get to the root of the problem to understand what decisions we need to make to solve the dilemma we are facing. We need to take the time and go upstream to where the problem starts. Take the broad view. Don't view each problem in isolation. Get to the root of the problem."

I agree with Mr. Heath. To make a good decision you need to get to the root of the problem.

Test for Regret
Ask yourself, *If I make this decision this way and it turns out I'm wrong, how will I feel?* The more potential for regret, the more you need to be certain you are following a sound decision process. Remember, you can't control the result for almost any decision, but you can be sure you have followed a sound process.

Be Skeptical of Model Results
Many believe results coming out of a sophisticated model converts inherent uncertainty into certainty. Nothing could be further from the truth. My experience is that confidence rises when a greater amount of information goes into a model, but the accuracy of the model remains the same. If you're a true believer in models, read *Models Behaving Badly* by Emanual Derman. In this enlightening book, Mr. Derman demonstrates why no model can fully encapsulate human behavior.

Manage Expectations
All success, all accomplishments are a two-part equation: a result relative to expectations. Managing expectations is a big part of making a good decision. Getting the goalpost to stop moving is one of the hardest tricks in life, but it's essential. An insatiable appetite for more will always push you to the point of disappointment and regret. Manage the expectations of all stakeholders for any critical decision.

In concluding this chapter, I want to cover one more important concept around decision-making. As I mentioned in Chapter 7, I participated in a multiyear program by the Wharton Business School called the Wharton Effective Executive program. This program had a course on effective decision-making. Prior to this course I thought there were right decisions and wrong decisions. This course disabused me of this idea. What Wharton research found was that the most important factor for a successful decision is that all the key players believe they have made the right decision. In other words, executive managers should seek commitment, not unanimous approval.

In his April 2017 letter to Amazon shareholders, CEO Jeff Bezos introduced the concept of "disagree and commit" with respect to decision-making. It's good advice that often goes overlooked. Too frequently, executives charged with making decisions leave the meeting assuming that once there's been a show of hands—or nods of agreement—the job is done. Far from it.

Indeed, any agreement voiced in the absence of a strong sense of collective responsibility can prove ephemeral. One of the most important characteristics of a good decision is that it's made in such a way that it will be fully and effectively implemented. That requires commitment—something that is not always present in many firms where after a decision is made some executives and mid-level managers continue to question the wisdom of what has been decided. This continued questioning will almost assuredly result in an ineffective implementation of the decision. As President Lincoln said, "A house divided against itself cannot stand."

I'll end this chapter with a quote from the leadership scholar Warren G. Bennis:

> "In the face of ambiguity, uncertainty, and conflicting demands, often under great time pressure, leaders must make decisions and take effective actions to assure the survival and success of their organizations. This is how leaders add value to their organizations. They lead them to success by exercising good judgment, by making smart calls when especially difficult and complicated decisions simply must be made, and then ensuring that they are well executed."

CHAPTER 10
Delegation

Undoubtedly, some of you feel you have way too much to do. You're buried in work and it seems the piles on your desk and the unread emails in your inbox grow every day. You feel somewhat overwhelmed and see no way out. To use a rural Nebraska colloquialism, "You feel you've been rode hard and put away wet." But there is a solution: delegate some of what you are doing.

Delegation is a critical management skill. Delegation benefits the manager, direct report, and the company. The human resources (HR) community has developed many educational courses devoted on how to do it effectively. It's hard to go to any HR conference and not find a session on effective delegation. It's ironic, but even with all the educational resources on delegation, many managers have real difficulty with effective delegation.

One of the most difficult transitions for leaders to make is the shift from doing to leading. So why do so many managers struggle with effective delegation? Here are some things I've observed which have caused problems for supervisors in effective delegation.

1. **Unnecessarily Hoarding Work**
    You may not realize it, but you may be unnecessarily hoarding work. A classic sign of insufficient delegation is that you are working long hours and feel totally indispensable, while your staff isn't terribly energized and strangely keeps regular hours.

2. **Perfectionist Tendencies**
   You are a perfectionist and truly believe no one can do the work as well as you can. Perfectionists many times feel it is easier to just do things themselves. You'll not get far as a manager if you live by the maxim, "If you want to make sure something gets done, do it yourself."

3. **Lack of Self-Confidence**
   Some managers believe passing on work will detract from their own importance. Others don't want to be upstaged by their subordinates. These managers are confusing being involved with being essential. The two are not the same. Your involvement is a mix of opportunities, requirements, and choices you make regarding your work. How essential you are to the success of your work depends on how you engage those around you.

4. **Fear of Being Burned**
   Some managers fear delegation because they have been burnt in the past where they have delegated an important task and their subordinate failed to come through. They may have lost face or looked bad to executive management.

5. **Wanting to be the "Go-to Expert"**
   This problem is related to unnecessarily hoarding work. For years you may have been considered the company expert in some particular subject matter or discipline. You've received recognition and some prestige from being this expert. You now have broader responsibility but loathe giving up this area where you are an "acknowledged" expert.

6. **You haven't Trained or Communicated Properly for Effective Delegation**
   A lot of managers don't delegate because they haven't come to grips with the reality that doing so will create more work until they properly train and communicate how to do what

is asked *and* why it's important. Get over the idea that "it's quicker to do it myself than to explain it."

7. **You Are a Seat of the Pants Delegator**
Have you ever had a boss delegate something to you but fail to provide any of the important details? Or having delegated something one day, then abruptly change direction on another. If you are this kind of delegator, you are going to sow confusion among your associates and demoralize many.

So what to do about this problem of delegation? You first need to recognize if you want to be a great business leader, you better get good at delegation. It's a critical management skill. You need to avoid the seven problems I pointed out earlier in this chapter.

You also need to inspire commitment from your people. People get excited about their work once you have clearly communicated how their contribution moves the corporate rock forward. It is your job to build enthusiasm.

Additionally, really know your people—their capabilities and expertise. Become deeply committed to their coaching and development. Delegate but trust and verify. Remember, it is one of the highest forms of recognition when you provide an increasing level of responsibility to one of the associates in your area. You are saying, "I trust you and know you can do this additional work."

I'll share with you my own philosophy. I aim to delegate everything but genius. I was first exposed to this concept years ago when I read several articles on delegation by Dan Sullivan, president and co-founder of The Strategic Coach. Mr. Sullivan also provided an additional important concept of "unique ability" where you work in your area of unique ability, it generates excitement, energy and the desire to do more. More about these important concepts in chapter 47.

You should spend most of your time working in your area of unique ability or more commonly called your areas of strength. If you do this you'll have more energy and be happier, which will cause you to be a much better business leader. One of my longtime goals is to work more and more in my areas of strength. I also try to spend little time doing activities which aren't a fit with my Unique Ability.

Remember, great managers and supervisors are extremely skilled at delegating to their entire team, not just the people who have earned their confidence. And they do it in a way that inspires accountability across the board—while also transforming even the most challenging associate's performance.

CHAPTER 11

Leaders Are Readers

In this chapter, I'm going to give you my number one secret to career success: read a lot.

In fact, when Warren Buffett was once asked about his key(s) to success, he pointed to a stack of nearby books and said, "Read five hundred pages like this every day. That's how knowledge works. It builds up, like compound interest."

And Mr. Buffett is not alone. According to an April 14, 2016, article in *HuffPost*, here are just a few top business leaders and entrepreneurs who make reading a major part of their daily lifestyle:

- Bill Gates reads about fifty books per year.
- Mark Cuban reads more than three hours every day.
- Elon Musk is an avid reader, and when asked how he learned to build rockets, he said, "I read books."
- Mark Zuckerberg has resolved to read a book every two weeks.

But successful people don't just read anything. They are highly selective about what they read, opting to be educated over being entertained. They believe books are a gateway to learning and knowledge. Successful people tend to choose educational books and publications over novels, tabloids and magazines. And in particular they obsess over biographies and autobiographies of other successful people for guidance and inspiration.

I personally love to read biographies and autobiographies. I enjoy learning about how great people lived their lives. I've read many biographies and autobiographies on business leaders. I've been inspired and learned a great deal from studying the lives of these successful people. The leadership benefits of reading are wide ranging. Here are some of the principal benefits of a well-thought-out reading program:

1. **Reading Expands Your Horizons:** How many leaders/entrepreneurs/achievers can you connect with and learn from? Books give you an insight into the journeys, learnings, and mindsets of extremely successful people and companies. I've always liked Charlie Munger's comment, "Learn deeply from the eminent dead. Bathe in the wisdom of great people who lived before you."

2. **Reading Gives You Innovative Ideas:** Did you know there are about ten ways in which saying thank you to your teams can boost productivity and morale? Did you know how important trust is to creating a high-performing culture? Do you know how best to conduct a meeting? Well, I didn't either until I read about these concepts in books.

3. **Reading Give Us Perspective:** Leaders sometimes get caught up in linear ways of thinking. Reading helps open up differing viewpoints and fresh perspectives to a subject. Adopt it or not, it makes you understand the customer's or associate's viewpoint.

4. **Reading Makes Us Thinkers and Doers:** In the age of constant consumption in social media, we have forgotten how to "chew the cud"—introspection and thinking is as important as executing the idea. Reading makes us thinkers as we have to visualize the idea/concept in our imagination and then figure how we can act on the idea.

5. **Reading Makes Us Better Communicators:** Reading gives you an amazing vocabulary—three times more than

nonreaders. You use better words, correct words, and quotes in your communication. You are better able to present scenarios and case studies you can use in real life to get your point across.

6. **Reading Challenges Us:** Reading saves us from narcissism and self-absorption. It gives us a macro-view of the world. It challenges our thoughts, feelings, ideas, judgments, biases, deeply held beliefs, and perspectives.

7. **Learning and Growth Culture:** Reading is fundamental to a learning and growth. In this day and age, every successful business needs to have learning and growth as a foundational part of its culture.

8. **The Compounding of Knowledge:** Albert Einstein once said, "The strongest force in the Universe is compound interest." This secret weapon—compounding—can be utilized not just in financial matters but also when it comes to knowledge acquisition and learning. As we continue to read, knowledge builds up like compound interest.

Unfortunately, most of us spend our time consuming information that has a very short life. When you read or watch the news, most of that information decays quickly and is of little value even just a few days later. In this day of information overload, most of us spend too much time consuming information we won't care about next month, let alone next year. Expiring information like social media is sexy, but it's not knowledge. How can you tell the difference? Expiring knowledge lacks detail and nuance, and it's easily digestible. Expiring information is not knowledge; it won't be relevant in a month or a year.

Focusing on accumulating knowledge that will be as useful ten years from now as it is today. Charlie Munger once said, " I constantly see people rise in life who are not the smartest, sometimes not even the most diligent, but they are learning machines. They go to bed every night a little wiser than they were when they got up, and boy does that help, particularly when you have a long run ahead of you."

I feel so strongly about the importance of reading to career success, and I typically conclude an interview with this question: "Tell me what you are reading these days." If the interviewee says, "I really don't like to read or I'm not much of a reader," the interview is over. It's a knockout question for me because it demonstrates a lack of interest in learning and growth. In our fast-moving economy, this is a deadly trait.

So I hope I've sold you on the benefits of reading. Now you are probably thinking, *How do I have time to read?* Here are ways I carve out time to read:

1. I always read something enjoyable to me—usually a biography or autobiography right before going to bed.

2. I usually carve out several hours over the weekend to read.

3. The place I get the most reading done is in the air. When I'm on an airplane, I'm reading. It always amazes me the number of people on a plane staring blankly ahead—doing nothing or playing video games when they could be improving themselves by reading.

4. Audiobooks—I love audiobooks. When I'm working out or driving, I'm either learning Spanish or listening to an audiobook or podcast.

5. I never go anywhere where I might have to wait—doctor's offices, business appointments, etc.—without taking along something to read.

6. When our children were young and I needed to attend sporting events or dance recitals—if they weren't playing or performing, I was reading.

7. Start a book club for your area, and read a book together that

will help the whole team perform at a higher level. I have done this many times with my senior management team.

One last reading concept I want to share with you is the value of spaced repetition. This is where you read or listen to something and several days later you read or listen again to the same material. The spacing effect is a wildly useful phenomenon. We are better able to recall information and concepts if we learn them in multiple, spread-out sessions. We can leverage this effect by using spaced repetition to slowly learn almost anything.

Becoming a reading machine is a super skill that will give you a huge competitive advantage. But like everything worthwhile, it takes time. Start a vigorous reading program tomorrow and get that compounding of knowledge underway.

CHAPTER 12
Clear Writing Produces Clear Thinking

The modern workplace's vogue is informal information exchange. We sit in open floor plan offices so we can spontaneously collide, chat, and collaborate. We also go to a lot of meetings, where we discuss and discuss the problems, challenges, or opportunities we face. During many of these meetings, someone will walk everyone through a PowerPoint presentation. Each slide contains some bullet points. This is easy for the presenter but difficult for the audience. With most of these encounters, I usually find "when all is said and done, more is said than done." The pandemic and the transition to remote work has added to the proliferation of these kinds of encounters.

I've long been frustrated with those kinds of exchanges and meetings. Fortunately, Jeff Bezos of Amazon has provided a better approach. It's called the "Amazon 6 Page Narrative." A lot has been written recently about how Bezos and his senior executives run their meetings. Amazon has made it very public that their senior team has banned PowerPoint. Instead, when dealing with an important issue, someone must write a maximum six-page narrative memo that describes the facts around the problem and offers a possible solution. It's unconventional, tough, and time-consuming, but it does one thing incredibly well. By being forced to use the medium of the written word, the author of the memo must really think through what he or she wants to present. In writing it all down, authors are forced to think out tough questions and formulate clear, persuasive arguments, all the while reasoning through the structure and logic.

Amazon's approach provides credibility to something I've long believed: clear writing ultimately produces clear thinking. Writing, apart from being a communication tool, is a thinking tool. I like to think of writing as focused thinking. An important lesson I've learned during my career is that writing helps me better understand any problem I'm struggling with and helps me reason out potential solutions. In fact, when I'm facing any difficult problem, including personnel problems, I've found great value in "scripting" or writing out how I will respond. If you can't write clearly, it is likely you don't think very clearly. And if you don't think clearly, you're in trouble.

I think we all agree how important effective communication is to business success. But I think too often we only consider oral communication. Being able to effectively communicate in writing is also essential. These days, we use written communication more than ever before—you need to be able to write, and write well. Being able to explain yourself clearly and write consistently can help you to gain credibility and increase the perceived value of your work. This will help ensure your clients or colleagues recognize and value your input. The late automotive executive, Lee Iacocca, once said, "The discipline of writing something down is the first step toward making it happen."

Writing is a core professional skill that must be learned and continually improved. The demands of business writing and rigors of producing professional reports are very different from grammar school assignments.

I hope I've convinced you that "clear writing produces clear thinking." So, how do you become a better writer? Here are some approaches that have helped me become a better writer:

1. Pick a time of the day when you are at your best to do your writing. I'm at my best the first thing in the morning. I try to not schedule any meetings for the first couple of hours of the day so I can think and write.

2. Cut the fat. Don't use three words when one would do. Read

your writing through critical eyes, and make sure each word works toward your larger point. Cut every unnecessary word from the sentence. Short sentences are easier to understand. If you try to pack a lot of words into a sentence, you lose clarity.

3. Avoid jargon and ten-dollar words. Business writing is full of industry-specific buzzwords and acronyms. While these terms are sometimes unavoidable and can occasionally be helpful as shorthand, they often indicate lazy or cluttered thinking. Throw in too many, and your reader will assume you are on autopilot—or worse, they won't understand what you're saying. Jargon doesn't add any value, but clarity and conciseness never go out of style. Some writing experts suggest creating a "buzzword blacklist" of words to avoid. Another helpful thing to do for your board or other outsiders is to develop an acronym list. You should also avoid using grandiose language. Writers often mistakenly believe using a big word when a simple one will do is a sign of intelligence. It's not. I think Winston Churchill said it best: "Broadly speaking, the short words are the best, and the old short words are the best of all."

4. Read what you write. Put yourself in your reader's shoes. Is your point clear and well structured? Are the sentences straightforward and concise? Read your writing out loud. This is where flaws reveal themselves: the gaps in your arguments, the clunky sentence, and the section that's two paragraphs too long. And don't be afraid to ask a colleague or friend—or better yet, several colleagues and friends—to edit your work. Welcome their feedback; don't resent it. Editing is an act of friendship.

5. Shorter is always better. I've always loved the Mark Twain story when he apologized to a friend for writing a long letter. Ostensibly he said, "I apologize for the length of this letter, but I didn't have time to write you a short one." It

is definitely more work to be succinct, but it is better for the reader. Good writing and useful writing share the same essential qualities: brevity and a clear purpose.

6. Don't expect to get it "right" in one sitting. As an example, if I were working on an important communication to our board of directors I would try and start around three weeks prior to when the communication needs to be sent. I would probably complete six iterations until I have a final product. As I stated in chapter 3 on communication, usually after the first draft I set it aside and let my subconscious take over. After a run or another physical activity, I'll have new insights. I almost always discover new things in the process of writing. You need to schedule time for editing and revising. Rewriting is the key to improved thinking. Writing and reworking your own writing is time well spent.

7. Practice every day. Writing is a skill, and skills improve with practice. The more you write, the better writer you'll become. I find reading well-written material every day and being attentive to word choice, sentence structure, and flow are important to improving my writing. Invest in style and grammar guides for reference. Time and again, I turn to the following:

- *The Elements of Style* by William Strunk Jr. and E. B. White
- *The Economist Style Guide* by the editors of *The Economist*
- *Dreyer's English* by Benjamin Dreyer
- *Do I Make Myself Clear?* by Harold Evans

Clear writing does produce clear thinking. Writing is focused thinking. There is a kind of thinking that can only be done by writing. Thinking through writing has given me an edge. One way to raise your profile is to become a good writer. Video is more memorable, a phone call is quicker, but the written word is the best for structured thought. When you write well, you will also become a better oral communicator. When you train yourself to write and ultimately speak more clearly, you're training your brain to think more clearly.

CHAPTER 13
Managing Information

We live in an age of information overload. Most of us find ourselves inundated with vast amounts of general news, social media feeds, specific work information, and other data. According to Daniel Levitin, McGill University psychology professor and author of *The Organized Mind: Thinking Straight in the Age of Information Overload*, "we've created more information in the last 10 years than in all of human history before that."

So information is available in infinite abundance, delivered automatically to our electronic devices or accessible with a few mouse clicks. Many of us feel overwhelmed, but paradoxically, in the knowledge economy, information is our most valuable commodity.

Paul Hemp, director of Global Thought Leadership at Straight Talk Online, in September 2009 wrote an article for the *Harvard Business Review* with the title "Death by Information Overload." In this article, Mr. Hemp makes the point that most organizations unknowingly pay a high price as individuals struggle to manage the information glut. A great deal of productive time is lost as associates deal with information of limited value.

Email is an especially nefarious problem. I know many of you struggle with managing email. There are a lot of different email management systems and theories on how to deal with this problem. In this chapter, I cannot provide a solution that I know will be right for you. It's essential you do research and design an approach that works for you.

In this chapter, I do want to give you some "30,000-foot" ideas on how to deal with information overload. Specifically, I'm going to share with you what I personally do—I need to confess that part of what I'm presenting is aspirational.

1. I'm very selective in my news feeds. So much of the news is redundant. I try to avoid hearing or reading the same thing over and over. I also make sure the news I rely on has been vetted in some way—that is, an editor has been involved.

2. I try to keep things out of my head. In other words, I don't try and remember a bunch of stuff. I extensively use Apple Notes (Microsoft OneNote and Evernote are also good), where I have many folders where I capture things I may want to remember and possibly refer to at a future time.

3. I try not to multitask. I try to focus on one thing at a time. Multitasking costs by forcing you to decide whether to answer or ignore a text, phone call, email, and then thinking about how you should respond. Lots of wasted energy.

4. Decide at what time in the day you are at your best and tackle difficult things at this time. As I mentioned earlier, I'm at my best first thing in the morning, so that's when I work on difficult projects. During this time, I discipline myself to not be distracted by emails, texts, phone calls, and so forth.

5. Successful people simplify their lives by focusing on the facts and actions that matter most. There is always pressure to collect more information before making a major decision. A good question to ask is "Will this new information likely change how I plan to proceed?" If not, it isn't worth the effort. Remember the lost opportunity cost you may incur by waiting to collect additional information.

6. One test for information noise is to ask whether a piece of information will still be useful in a year or so. If not, is it worth

cluttering up your brain? The trickiest part is staying open to new and contradictory information while cutting out clutter.

7. Remember, not knowing something doesn't necessarily equate to ignorance; knowing what to know is true wisdom.

8. I use Microsoft Outlook and attempt to take full advantage of all of its capabilities. I extensively use the ability to convert emails into a "to-do" list or appointment. An important resource for me was Michael Lineberger's *Total Workday Control* book.

9. Set up a time to review articles, research papers, and so on. During your review time, your actions should be:

    - Deal with it now.
    - Add it to your to-do list to deal with it later.
    - Pass it to someone else to act on.
    - File it away as information that is useful to know.

    Remember, if it is not an action item, it's for future reference or should simply be discarded.

10. Don't be afraid to unfollow and unfriend. Quit the social media rat race.

11. Remember, information and data are abundant. Judgment and insight are rare. As a business leader, your most important responsibility is to exercise good judgment.

Information overload is only going to get worse. Most information is irrelevant. Knowing what to ignore saves you time, reduces stress, and improves your decision-making. Develop the techniques and strategies that will help you become a more effective consumer of information. Remember: If you are drowning in information, it's not information overload—it's filter failure.

CHAPTER 14
No

One lesson I've had difficulty learning during my career is the importance of saying no. One of my top five Gallup strengths is Ideation, and one of the "basement" qualities of Ideation is I'm always intrigued by new ideas, approaches, methods, and so on. I'm usually up for trying something new. Fortunately, two of my other top strengths are Discipline and Focus, which serve as a "governor" on my Ideation strength. One of the most difficult things about saying no for me is getting FOMO (fear of missing out). But saying no is key to being an effective business leader. The ability to say no in an inoffensive way is a very important life skill.

I've caused myself more stress, worry, and difficulty by not learning to properly say no. Saying yes to others can have a powerful impact on your career, your reputation, and your professional growth. But saying no—especially when it's uncomfortable to do so—is one of the most powerful steps you can take in your personal growth and ultimate effectiveness. We all have the same number of hours in a week. What separates people is how they use them. For most we have so many possibilities in what we can do that we need to remember we can't do everything.

On January 17, 2012, Tony Schwartz,c CEO of the Energy Project and author of "The Way We're Working Isn't Working" advocated in a post for the *Harvard Business Review* that no should be the new yes for busy executives who don't often have time to be everything to everyone or to be everywhere at once. As Schwartz wisely put it:

"Prioritizing requires reflection, reflection takes time, and many of the executives I meet are so busy racing just to keep up they don't believe they have time to stop and think about much of anything. Too often—and masochistically—they default to "yes." Saying "yes" to requests feels safer, avoids conflict, and takes less time than pausing to decide whether or not the request is truly important.

"No" improves productivity and mental health, none of us can afford to keep saying "yes." In the words of Warren Buffet, "The difference between successful people and very successful people is that very successful people say no to almost everything." I'm not saying you need to say "no" to almost everything, but I am saying that your success rides on your ability to honor your truth."

Very sagacious comments.
Why aren't we better at saying no? Usually two reasons:

1. You may, like me, be intrigued and gain energy from new ideas and experiences.

2. You want to avoid conflict.

Here again, the avoidance of conflict raises its ugly head. I think avoidance of conflict is the principal reason people don't say no. It's a good idea to have criteria for when to say yes and when to say no. This helps decision-making become easier. Here is some criteria I use:

1. Will saying "yes" realistically help my company accomplish its short- and long-term objectives?

2. What would I personally or professionally gain by saying yes?

3. Saying yes creates an obligation. Saying yes requires a commitment. Will saying yes ultimately make my future easier or harder?

4. Does my company or do I realistically have the time, financial or other resources to honor the request?

5. I've learned to almost never say yes right at the time of the request. Make it one of your personal rules. Tell the requester you'll get back to them after you've had time to think about the request.

6. Use the 10-10-10 approach popularized by Suzy Welch in her book *10-10-10*.

    - How will no feel 10 minutes from now?
    - How will no feel 10 months from now?
    - How will no feel 10 years from now?

    More about the 10/10/10 approach in Chapter 50.

7. What would I tell my best friend to do? Or, what would my successor do?

8. Say no for a bigger yes. Anyone can say no to a bad opportunity. It's more difficult to say no to a good opportunity so you have the time and resources to say yes to a great opportunity.

Saying no has a lot of merits. Let's discuss how to say "no":

1. **Be quick and definite.** Tell the person you can't do it and politely decline right away. This allows the party you are saying no to make other plans. When dealing with certain individuals not being definite will usually come back to haunt you. For some people, anything other than a definite no may be interpreted as an implied yes.

2. **Explain why.** As a longtime successful distributor of ours once said to me, I don't mind you saying no when you have

good reasons—I just hate no without reasons. Be honest and explain you have other commitments, priorities, and so on.

3. **Suggest an alternative.** This is not something you need to do in every case, but it can prove helpful and build goodwill with the individual making the request. I recently had to turn down a young friend of mine who wanted me to serve on his startup board. I suggested someone else to him and both appreciated the introduction.

4. **Ask for a raincheck.** Sometimes we really want to do something but just don't have the time or other resources at present. If this is truly the case, make a plan for the future and your involvement at that time.

A thoughtful no, delivered at the right time, can be a huge plus saving time and trouble for everybody down the road. Steve Jobs once said, "I'm actually as proud of the things we haven't done as the things we've done. Innovation is saying no to 1,000 things."

A book that had a beneficial impact on my journey to effectively saying no is William Ury's *The Power of a Positive No*. This book is based on Professor Ury's experience as one of the founders of the Harvard Negotiation Project. This indispensable book gives you effective methods for saying a positive no. It will show you how to assert and defend your key interests, how to make your no firm and strong, how to resist the other side's aggression and manipulations, and how to do this while getting to a positive yes. If you want to further explore the benefits of no, I highly recommend Dr. Ury's book.

I'm going to end this chapter with a quote from Shane Parrish, which he made in his excellent "Farnam Street" blog: "Saying no is like saving your money in the bank, whereas saying yes is spending it. Most of us are on overdraft. Before you say yes, ask yourself if it is necessary?"

CHAPTER 15
Time

What do you think are the primary determinants for success as a business leader? Your natural strengths? The skills, knowledge, and experience you've acquired? Your ability to inspire and motivate your direct reports? Overall business acumen? Arguably, they're all important, but I believe what will determine your success more than anything is how you spend your time. I believe "your time" is your most important resource. Time is the scarcest commodity.

Nobody needs to be told there isn't enough time. We are all dealing with long to-do lists, email overload, and meeting after meeting. Early in my career I complained to one of my mentors that I didn't have enough time to complete everything I felt required my attention. I was expecting some empathy. Instead, he said, "Get used to it; you'll never have enough time. You had better learn to effectively prioritize where you spend your time and don't let others steal your time." Wise words.

A lot of people believe money is their most important resource, but I think they're misguided. Their most important resource is time. You can get more money through various avenues, but once time is gone, it's gone forever. You can't buy more or borrow more, so time is a limited resource that expires every day. As a business leader, you have to be very careful with this precious resource.

A fascinating book I recently read is *Four Thousand Weeks Time Management for Mortals* by Oliver Burkeman. In the introduction to his book, Mr. Burkeman writes the following:

"The average human lifespan is absurdly, terrifyingly, insultingly short. Here's one way of putting things in perspective: the first modern humans appeared on the plains of Africa at least 200,000 years ago, and scientists estimate that life, in some form, will persist for another 1.5 billion years or more, until the intensifying heart of the sun condemns the last organism to death. But you? Assuming you live to be 80, you'll have had about 4,000 weeks."

Four thousands weeks put into perspective the short amount of time we have.

Other people are more than willing to take your time. You've undoubtedly experienced getting stuck on a phone call or having someone drop by your office without an appointment. I'd be a wealthy person if I had a hundred dollars for every time someone popped in my office and said, "Hey, I saw you weren't doing anything, so I thought I'd drop by." The fact is I was busy doing something and this distraction got me off track. Here are some of the biggest time wasters I've witnessed over the years:

1. Email—We're all bombarded with email and it's one of the worst time blackholes. It's easy to develop a habit of constantly checking your email, especially when one of those little windows appears on your monitor telling you a new one has arrived. Who can stand the suspense? But this can be a huge time waster. Consider setting aside certain times each day to read and answer email, and learn to resist the temptation to even glance at your inbox outside those times.

2. Poor-quality meetings—Meetings can get totally out of control if participants are allowed to go down rabbit holes. Not following an agenda and controlling how the meeting progresses will waste everyone's time. Following the Entrepreneurial Operating System (EOS) Level 10 meetings protocol can mitigate the endemic problem of poor-quality meetings. More on EOS's approach to meetings in chapter 28.

3. Smartphone addiction—We live in remarkable times. We have an infinite wealth of information, connections and resources

at our fingertips thanks to the internet and our smartphones. Your time and attention are extremely valuable to marketers and social media platforms. Your phone, the apps you use, and every website you visit are designed to capture and hold your attention. Media companies know this and use it to their advantage. Headlines that trigger feelings of uncertainty make you look. That's why they write them that way. And when they have your attention, they make money. And guess who loses? You because you're not spending your time on what's going to help you accomplish your business goals.

4. Majoring in the minors—Be honest: Are there certain routine things you do just because you've always done them and you like it? An unwillingness to delegate work to others can rob you of time you could spend more profitably elsewhere. It can also steal your personal time by forcing you to work later to get everything accomplished. It's easy to keep busy by just doing routine, everyday tasks. But routine tasks don't usually move the business or your career forward. More about majoring in the minors in chapter 17.

5. Taking on monkeys—A November 1999 *Harvard Business Review* article that achieved cult status was titled "Who's Got the Monkey?" In the article, William Oncken Jr. and Donald L. Wass explain an age-old management problem they refer to as monkeys on one's back.

    Imagine this scenario: An associate drops by your office and informs you of a problem. At that point you have enough information to get involved, but you don't have time to make an on-the-spot decision. So, you tell your associate you'll get back to him or her. Guess what happened? The associate just took the monkey (the problem) off their back, and it is now on your back.

    Now, consider the wider implications. If you have ten direct reports and each of whom transfers a monkey to you every day, by the end of the week you'll have fifty monkeys on your back. You'll spend all of your time juggling these monkeys and ignoring your own responsibilities. Your associates may linger outside your door, perhaps complaining that you're ineffectual because you can't make decisions quickly enough, and your boss will begin to wonder if you can handle your job. Resist taking on others' monkeys!

6. Not understanding the difference between being busy and being effective—If you ask most business leaders, they will tell you how busy they are—they don't have enough time. Many, however, don't understand the difference between being busy and being effective. Being effective means spending your time on things that produce the results you want and work that will help you accomplish your business objectives. Do not confuse effort with results.

There are many other time wasters; the aforementioned are just some of the more common ones. But what should we do about protecting our time?

Wonderful books have been written on time management. I've read and studied many that have helped me immensely during my career. What follows are my key tips for effective time management, which I've learned from a variety of resources over the years.

1. Use a daily to-do list. Taking the time to develop a daily to-do list is a discipline that will provide incredible benefits. With a thoughtfully developed daily to-do list, you'll know your daily activities are aligned with your quarterly, annual, and long-term goals.

2. Years ago I read the book *How to Get Control of Your Time and Your Life* by Alan Lakein. An iconic quote from this book follows: "What is the best use of time right now?"

    I ask myself this question repeatedly during the day. Asking this question pulls me back to what's really important.

3. Use General Eisenhower's Matrix and spend more time in Quadrant 2. Working more in Quadrant 2 will make you more effective and valuable as a business leader. Stephen Covey popularized this approach to time management in his book The 7 Habits of Highly Effective People. Covey advocated utilizing the Eisenhower Matrix as a framework for prioritizing our time and tasks for optimized efficiency and productivity. In chapter 48 I provide a more detailed explanation of this important time-management tool.

4. Say no! The previous chapter in this book was all about the importance of saying no. You can't do everything, so you had better get good at saying no. Warren Buffet, chairman and CEO of Berkshire Hathaway, states that he learned a long time ago that the greatest commodity of all is time. This is why he's very protective of his own time. I'm going to repeat one of my favorite Buffett-isms: "The difference between successful people and really successful people is that really successful people say no to almost everything."

5. Develop a "stop doing list." Most of us are terrible at stopping work even when it is obvious that the work is a complete waste of time and money. One effective way is to look at all our work as if a private equity firm has just taken over our business and is pushing the firm to be more effective. What would they require us to change? Another effective method is if the board or CEO brought in a new senior management team, what steps would this new leadership team probably take?

The Roman Emperor Marcus Aurelius writes in his book *Meditations* the following: "Ask yourself at every moment is this necessary?" "Doing what's essential," Marcus writes, "brings a double satisfaction to do less better." The concept of relinquishment is something I've come to value. We all keep doing things that no longer aid us in accomplishing our goals. Get rid of these things; wear relinquishment as a badge of honor.

6. Overcome FOMO. A lot of our time pressures can be traced back to a fear of missing out. We continue to try and cram more and more into each day. In *Four Thousand Weeks: Time Management for Mortals,* Mr. Burkeman introduces the concept of the "joy of missing out." The joy of missing out is the recognition that you can't do everything, and you need to make choices. In this state of mind you embrace the fact that you forgo certain activities to say yes to activities that are more important to you.

In closing out this chapter on time, I need to address the concept of work-life balance. Many times younger people at Assurity have asked me how I maintained a healthy work-life balance. I think my answer surprises them because I'll say, "I've never been balanced." Okay, maybe they believed that, but not in the context of time.

To me we have it wrong when we talk about work-life balance. Work-life balance means that there is work, the tough part of our lives, and then there is the personal side of our life, which is pleasurable. This is wrongheaded thinking. There are many things I do at work that I greatly enjoy and find pleasurable. Conversely there are things at home I need to do that I don't enjoy at all.

A better approach is to more and more do things you find pleasurable and in your areas of strength whether in your professional or personal life. I've never kept track of the hours I worked. I don't see the point. But a longstanding goal of mine is to do more and more of what I enjoy and in my areas of strength and less and less of those activities that are not pleasurable to me and not in my areas of strength, whether business or personal.

Time is our most important resource. As Benjamin Franklin said, "Dost thou love life? Then do not squander time, for that is the stuff life is made of." You can either master your time or be forever wanting more. You can allow other people to steal your time, or you can be in control.

Time is your most valuable resource and must be guarded carefully, or you won't achieve your personal and professional goals.

CHAPTER 16

Becoming a Humble Narcissist

How can anyone be humble and narcissistic at the same time? When you think of narcissists, you probably think of personality traits like "full of themselves," "self-centered," and "arrogant." We tend to think of narcissism in a pejorative way. The word *narcissism* has its roots in Greek mythology: the hunter Narcissus falls in love with his own reflection in a pool and stares at it until he dies and turns into a flower. So how can humility and narcissism reside in the same individual? How can being a humble narcissist be a winning combination for any business leader?

I first learned of the concept of being a humble narcissist by watching a March 14, 2018 TED talk by the organizational psychologist Adam Grant. Dr. Grant is a professor at the Wharton School and has written a number of New York Times best sellers. Several years ago, I read and enjoyed his book *Originals*. Dr. Grant found that humble narcissists bring the best of both worlds to business. They have bold visions, they are sure of themselves, they believe they will ultimately win, but they're also willing to acknowledge their weaknesses and learn from their mistakes.

Far from a contradiction in terms, *humble narcissism* can prove a powerful leadership formula. Traditionally, leaders are expected to have qualities like being aggressive, confident, competitive, and determined. At the same time, they're tasked with being emotionally intelligent, relationship builders who foster trust by being cooperative, understanding, openminded, and compassionate. In other words, we ask conflicting things of our leaders and offer few frameworks for reconciling those demands. Combining humility with narcissism is a concept that balances the conflicting demands we make on our leaders.

There are a few common ways narcissism tends to be misunderstood. First, certain aspects of narcissism—extreme drive, self-confidence, and a desire to lead—have the potential to bring about productive results. Healthy narcissism, which is about self-belief and ultimately succeeding, usually produces good business results.

Second, narcissism may not be as stable a trait as some think. Recent social science suggests that narcissism may be a fluid quality that can be tempered in order to minimize its toxic potential. Workplace narcissism is something many people can tame or manage by deliberately practicing humility. Humble narcissists are sure of their own strengths but also recognize the value of other people's contributions. They acknowledge that someone else may be better at certain things, and they are open to learning.

Most would agree that one of the most successful business people of this century is Steve Jobs. Mr. Jobs is probably the most successful humble narcissist ever. One of my favorite business biographies is Walter Isaacson's book on Steve Jobs. The subtitle to this book, "Passion, Perfection and Contradiction" says it all about Steve Jobs.

In the early years of Apple, Steve Jobs was humiliated by being forced out of the company he had co-founded. Impacted by this humbling experience when he came back to Apple he retained his intense drive and narcissism but was tempered by the public shaming he had experienced.

Narcissism gives leaders like Steve Jobs the self-confidence to aim high, but it is best paired with humble behavior. Humility is the yin to narcissism's yang.

According to Dr. Grant, there are three kinds of humility that matter. The first kind of humility is humility about your ideas. Over the years I've learned this the hard way. Using Kolbe Index terminology, I'm a big "Quick Start." "Ideation" and "Activator" are also two of my top Gallup strengths. With this combination comes a lot of ideas. What I've learned over the years is most of my ideas aren't any

BOOST! | 95

good. Maybe one out of one hundred are worth pursuing. I've come to understand I need to honestly discuss the risks and disadvantages of my ideas.

The second kind of humility is performance humility. It means admitting that sometimes we fall short of our goals, make mistakes, and sometimes even fall flat on our faces. I've observed over my many years in business that most leaders like to erase their stumbles and struggles. A question I ask almost everyone I interview is "Tell me about a time you've failed and what you learned from that experience." It is surprising to me how many people can't come up with a time that they failed, or if they do, it's a very prosaic example. True humility is living up to mistakes. Remember, the only people who don't make mistakes are the people who aren't doing much. Dr. Grant's third kind of humility is cultural humility. At Assurity, I believe we have a very healthy culture. I've heard some of our managers say we can't hire so-and-so because they wouldn't fit our culture. And in many cases, that statement makes sense. But hiring on cultural fit alone reflects a lack of humility. It suggests that our culture is already perfect—all we need to do is bring in people who will perpetuate it. When we just prize cultural fit, we end up hiring people who are similar to us. This approach weeds out diversity of thought and background, and it's a surefire recipe for groupthink.

Cultural humility is about recognizing that our culture always has room for growth. Great cultures don't stand still, they evolve. Diego Rodriguez, executive vice president and chief product and Design Officer at Intuit, coined the term "cultural contribution" in a September 10, 2015, article published on LinkedIn. He made the point that the corporate goal shouldn't be to find and promote people who clone the culture; it's having the humility to bring in people who will stretch and enrich the culture by adding elements that are absent. This is something every organization needs to revisit on a regular basis to discover what's missing in the corporate culture.

When leaders show more humility, team performance improves. In this age of more and more information, it's difficult for any one leader to figure it all out. Perhaps the greatest advantage of humility is that it can temper perceptions of narcissism, thereby allowing a leader to remain strong without appearing dictatorial.

One thing I've grown to admire during my study of stoic thought is its emphasis on humility. According to stoicism, developing a modest or low view of your importance in the overall scheme of the world is key to achieving personal peace. I think the ancient stoics were right. Becoming a humble narcissist may be the best combination for business leadership success.

CHAPTER 17
Majoring in the Minors

I remember when Microsoft Excel debuted in the mid-1980s (yes, I'm that old). I was running a regional community bank at that time, and Excel revolutionized so many things. It also happened to coincide with a tough time in Nebraska's agricultural economy and we were facing a lot of problem agriculturally related credits.

As we were dealing with all these problem loans, I became very frustrated with what I called the "Excel Wars." Excel caused us to change the format for our credit writeups. Almost everyone on our senior loan committee had a strong opinion on the new format. So as Rome burned—lots of problem credits, we argued about formatting—we were "Majoring in the Minors." Time and time again throughout my business career, I've been a part of (or watched others in senior management) avoiding addressing serious issues by majoring in the minors.

During the pandemic I was copied on an internal memo from the VP of HR from another company. The VP of HR was asking the other members of their senior management team to comment on a comprehensive communication she planned to send regarding a return to their offices. Later she shared with me that one of the more analytical members of this senior management team completely reworked the format of the memo but not the content. Now I'm all for striving for excellence in everything we do, but in my opinion this revision only slightly improved this communication. He did not revise the contents, only changing the format. He was majoring in the minors.

Sales is an area that seems to lend itself to "majoring in the minors." If you ask most salespeople how they are doing, almost inevitably they will say they are very busy—I mean really busy. Somehow being busy has become synonymous with being of value. The busier you are, the more important you must be.

But the reality is that there's a lot of busy, busy salespeople out there who are spinning their wheels and not accomplishing much. Yes, they're putting out fires as they hastily make their way from one activity to the next. But at the end of the day, quarter, or year, they don't have much to show for their efforts because they are majoring in the minors.

So why do people waste time and resources majoring in the minors? Here are five broad reasons:

1. The first problem is all of the minor stuff tends to feel major at the time it's happening. You need to keep perspective, keep your eyes on the prize. I mentioned earlier to keep in mind what Alan Lakein wrote in his timeless book *How to Get Control of Your Time and Your Life*. Continually ask yourself, "Is this the best use of my time right now?"

2. It's hard dealing with difficult problems. It's a lot easier to edit a memo, revise the format of a spreadsheet and fool yourself into thinking you are making progress. You are just avoiding the tough issues in front of you. Majoring in the minors is usually an unconscious avoidance tactic.

3. Believing only you can do certain things and not being willing to delegate. If you are trying to do everything, then chances are you are not focused on your longer-term objectives. If you are a business leader you better be focused on achieving your longer-term goals.

4. Being busy and working on many projects can give you a false sense of accomplishment. You fool yourself into thinking you are making progress, while in truth you are only

getting a respite from the huge problem or reality you must ultimately face. You may just be rearranging the deck chairs on the Titanic. You get a buzz or satisfaction from dealing with the extremely urgent. Your direct reports give you their "monkeys" and now their monkeys are on your back. David Allen, author of another timeless book, "Getting Things Done," calls this activity the "curse of the eternally urgent." Sure, it is an adrenaline buzz, but it doesn't propel you along to accomplishing your ultimate goals. It reminds me of a Yogi Berra quote: "We have no idea where we are going, but we're making great time."

So, how can you avoid majoring in the minors? Here are some ideas.

1. Remember that you cannot be successful in the long run if you are ten miles wide and an inch deep. You need to stay focused on your long-term business objectives. Stay focused on what needs to happen to make these goals a reality. As a business leader, you always need to remember to "keep the main thing, the main thing."

2. Give up on some of the details. Life is full of details, but how many big things will you get done if you spend all your time on the small things.

3. Remember it is not enough to be busy. You need to be busy for a purpose. That's because in our age of hyper-distraction, one of the biggest challenges many people face is staying focused on what matters most. If you're like me, you've probably often felt pulled in multiple directions, regularly juggling (and dropping) balls in your efforts to manage conflicting commitments, responsibilities, and expectations. However, unless you're careful, you can easily find yourself spread very thin and majoring in minor activities—super busy but not particularly effective. Sound familiar?

4. Schedule your priorities. Before you fill up your calendar, make a conscious decision on each appointment. What you're committing to needs to reflect your priorities. You can do many amazing things, but you can't do everything. Put aside time on a regular basis to review your long-term goals and clarify the "most" important things you want to accomplish in the various aspects of your work or business, family, health/well-being, finances, and other areas of your life.

   Unless you've got your "vital few" activities scheduled into your calendar, the "trivial many" will crowd into your day and overtake it. Often what you don't do is just as important as what you do! So be sure to block out chunks of time in your calendar to ensure the important things get done.

5. Outsource. Just because you can do something well doesn't mean you're the person to do it. Think about the things that take up your day that could be done just as well (or nearly as well) by someone else, freeing up your time to focus on even more valuable things. Ask yourself, "Is this the best and greatest use of my time right now?" and if the answer is no, then consider who could do it for you.

6. Compromise. Every choice you ever make involves a tradeoff. Sometimes they're easy to accept. Other times, less so. The truth is that you can't be in two places at once or do multiple things with 100 percent attention. You have to make tradeoffs. Accept that and then make them intentionally. One of my most important mentors use to say all the time, "Don't sweat the small stuff and remember, most things are small stuff."

So don't major in the minor things. As I've gotten older, I have realized that, in life, there are matters of great importance, and then there's everything else. And it's these important things, whatever they may be, that are the "majors" in life that require our attention, efforts, and focus. The trap is letting the "minor things" distract us and ultimately betray us and lead us to failure. The trick is letting go of the minors and focus on the things which will make a true difference in your life.

CHAPTER 18
Lies, Damned Lies, and Statistics

This now-famous phrase is derived from the full sentence "There are three kinds of lies: lies, damned lies, and statistics." Most historians agree this phrase was popularized in the United States by Mark Twain. Twain and others attributed the original progenitor of this well-known aphorism to British Prime Minister Benjamin Disraeli, although many Disraeli scholars are less certain that the great man ever uttered this truism. In any event, it has become a famous quote that is often cited by those who are dubious about the reliance on a certain set of statistics.

But being data driven is now widely accepted as the most sensible way to manage a business enterprise. Being a data-driven company is a moniker many business leaders fondly bestow upon their organizations. Developing a data-driven culture is also advocated by many consultants and business thought leaders. In simplest terms, a data-driven company is a company whose implicit hierarchy of values leads individuals within the company to make decisions using data. Data-driven companies use data to transform business models and improve performance in many areas. Companies that effectively use data can derive a significant competitive advantage.

Every massively successful tech company from Google to Facebook to Apple to Netflix believes the foundation of their phenomenal success is the effective use of data. No thinking person can effectively argue against being data driven and the value of using data to drive better business outcomes.

But I do believe there is a dark side to this enthusiasm for being data driven, and that is what I want to explore in the balance of this chapter. Here are some of the hazards we should keep in mind.

Too Much Data
Annie Duke, the author of *Thinking in Bets*, and Morgan Housel, a partner at the Conservative Fund and the author of *The Psychology of Money*, spoke at the 73rd annual Chartered Financial Analysts (CFA) virtual conference in 2020 and said the following:

> "Another problem with data: There's too much of it. When there is so much data around us, whatever you want to prove, you can prove it with data, not just dogma, which means conformation bias is easily fed. More data increases our confidence, but not necessarily our ability. There's a great quote from Nassim Taleb that we love when he said, "Big data brought cherry picking to the industrial level.""

With an abundance of data, everyone can have their own version of the truth. Through data mining you can find data that supports your viewpoint. David Patrick Moynihan famously said, "You are entitled to your opinion. But you are not entitled to your own facts." Now through carefully selecting the data you want to support your view; you can have your own set of facts.

The Tyranny of Averages
Repeatedly during my career I've come across an analysis or rationalization based upon the average—or more precisely, "the mean." But it is common in any data set for there to be outliers. These outliers skew the average of the data set to "pull" it in their direction. It gives the misimpression that the data points cluster around a point that is higher or lower than where they truly cluster. In these scenarios, it is often best to use the median to represent central tendency measurements instead of the average or mean because it's less impacted by outliers.

Second, many people tend to think of "average" as "typical"; the problem with that assumption in many data sets is there are many, many exceptions to "typical." One could even argue there is no such thing as "typical." For example, one commonly misused statistic in the life insurance business is the average mortality of a company's life block. This aggregate statistic is not very meaningful. Mortality varies greatly between the methods of distribution—that is, individually sold and underwritten, final expense, and worksite life all would have very different mortality rates.

It displays a lack of thoughtful analysis to apply the average of a group of data points to a single point and assume it to be true. Even assuming data is normally distributed (a "bell curve"), the probability that any one data point will be the same as the average is 50 percent—the same as a random guess. Averages conceal a lot.

Garbage in, Garbage out
Making decisions based on a set of data is only as good as the inputs that created the data. As an example, it's no secret that most customer relationship management (CRM) systems are often stuffed with bad data. I think the root cause is that sales management typically hasn't done the arduous work of clearly defining what will be inputted into the CRM system and standardized that approach for all sales personnel. Additionally, audit procedures are not in place to ensure compliance. Also, companies often put in place monitoring that only measures the volume of data entered but not the quality. With only a volume metric, sales management can happily declare that the sales force is fully utilizing the CRM system. Decisions are ultimately made based on data that are fundamentally flawed. This problem not only plagues CRM systems but many others as well.

Take the 2020 U. S. elections. Some of the most sophisticated and highly skilled data scientists in the country designed the approach to polling and reporting the data. But the polls in 2020 were egregiously inaccurate, as in 2016. Why? My guess: garbage in, garbage out. The polling methodology was fundamentally flawed. And perhaps there is no practical way to make it better.

The late George Box was a British mathematician and professor at the University of Wisconsin who once famously said, "all models are wrong, but some are useful". I agree with Professor Box's observation. I've recently started to read a book by Erica Thompson a statistician and a fellow at the London School of Economics. Her book has the alluring title "Escape from Model Land". Among many good observations Dr. Thompson makes this cogent point, "The forecast is a part of a narrative…An engine, not a camera; a co-creator of truth, not a predictor of truth." The phrase a "co-creator of the truth, not a predictor of the truth" largely reflects my real world experience with most models.

Uncertainty to Certainty

Most management teams come to believe that information coming out of their models converts inherent uncertainty into certainty. Modeling is based on data, which results in a projection. But projected data by its nature will not ultimately reflect reality. Results from modeling give the illusion of truth and certainty.

Rather than demand certainty, most management teams would be better served to look at model results in a probabilistic way. We need to remember any modeling is flawed because the information on which it is based is imperfect, and any model cannot factor in all the unknowable turn of events that will impact the final result. Most management teams are reluctant to acknowledge the role luck or chance plays in business outcomes. Models should be based on a range of outcomes and individuals should think probabilistically about outcomes. Instead, most thinking is black and white, or binary. When results are inevitably different than what the model produced, some assume the fundamental data wasn't properly collected, or the modeling methodology was in error. Modeling is always flawed because the data are imperfect—and more fundamentally, no model can account for the many exogenous factors affecting business outcomes.

I've found Nassim Taleb's quote on models to be so true: "A model might show you some risks, but not the risks of using it. Moreover, models are built on a finite set of parameters, while reality affords us infinite sources of risk."

Being an economics major and observing economic models over many years causes me to be skeptical about all economic models. Economic models rarely reveal the future. These models fail because they try to measure incredibly complex systems, which change in ever-changing ways.

Data Illiteracy

Years ago, John Allen Paulos authored a book I liked with the title "Innumeracy." It discusses a topic that is still important today, and that is the widespread lack of understanding of basic mathematical concepts. Innumeracy impacts the proper consideration of any data set.

We've entered a golden age of data availability. But while we have all this data, and it's becoming more influential than ever, most of us are not very good at interpreting and making sense of it. I do believe we have a data illiteracy problem.

Over the years, here are some common data illiteracy problems I've observed:

- Not asking the right questions about the data presented
- Not bringing a level of professional skepticism to any set of data
- Not understanding which data is relevant and how to test the validity of the data they have
- Interpreting data in a binary way rather than probabilistically
- Not advocating for testing hypotheses using A/B tests to see what results pan out
- Mistakenly believing without challenge that correlation is causation
- Not communicating the data set in a way that helps decision-makers see the big picture and act on the results of analysis

Okay, so much for identifying some of the problems. But in this day and age, all businesses need to more effectively use data. How do we deal with the inherent problems of being data driven?

- First, we need to approach every data set with skepticism. You have to assume that the data have inherent flaws and that just because something seems statistically right, doesn't mean it is. Again, judgment needs to come into play.
- Second, you need to realize that data are a tool, not a course of action. You can't let the data do the thinking for you, and you can never sacrifice common sense.
- Third, be sure the data you are collecting will produce actionable insights.
- Remember that every business decision does not require a sharp pencil and an abundant data set. Many times "crayon math" is good enough.
- Remember that a statistics-driven strategy won't help you if all your competitors are using similar data. It is rare to truly have an analytical edge.
- Think probabilistically about any model results. Remember there is never just one outcome but a range of outcomes.
- Get comfortable with uncertainty and the role luck plays in any business result.

In closing, I will leave you with a quote from the late Aaron Levenstein, who was a business professor at Baruch College in New York City: "Statistics are like bikinis. What they reveal is suggestive, but what they conceal is vital."

CHAPTER 19
Relationships

I once heard a new manager say, "I don't want to be liked or have a relationship with the associates I manage, I just want to be respected." Although "being liked" shouldn't be a primary objective of any manager, this comment indicated he was probably not going to sincerely value the associates he managed. This attitude will definitely limit his effectiveness and ultimately his career progress.

Why work on establishing and building relationships? Human beings are naturally social creatures—we crave friendship and positive interactions, just as we do food and water. So it makes sense that the better our relationships are at work, the happier and more productive we're going to be. Our work is more enjoyable when we have good relationships with those around us, and if they feel the same, those people are more likely to go along with changes needed to improve business in the future.

What's more, good relationships give us freedom; instead of spending time and energy overcoming the problems associated with negative relationships, we can instead focus on opportunities. Good relationships are also necessary if we hope to advance in our careers. After all, if your boss doesn't trust you, it's unlikely he or she will consider you when a new position opens up. Overall, we all want to work with people we like and where we have a healthy relationship.

We also need good working relationships with others in our professional circle. Customers, suppliers, and key stakeholders are all essential to our success. So it's important to build and maintain good relations with these people. Although we should try to build and maintain good working relationships with a variety of business colleagues, it is even more important with the associates we manage.

In a recent podcast on the *Investor Podcast*, William Green was interviewing Guy Spier of Aquamarine Capital. Guy called building relationships "The Killer App." Here is what he said: "But my point to you, the listener, is if you come across somebody who you think is a positive influence, make that extra effort, send them a holiday card. Make that extra effort to invite them to a dinner that you're having. It doesn't mean that you have decided upfront that this person's going to have this key role in your life. Just draw those people a little bit closer to you. Yes, put forward the effort to build a relationship with that person."

So what can you do to build better relationships with those who report to you? Here are some ideas I've used over the years:

1. **Build Trust**

    Trust is the foundation of good relationships. There are many things managers can do to establish trust with their associates. Being open and honest about changes that will impact them; effectively communicating by talking to them, not at them; having an open-door policy, following up; and being willing to pitch in to help. Sometimes the smallest gesture of kindness goes a long way, such as taking someone to lunch. Go reread chapter 4 on Trust.

2. **Ask Your Associates What's Most Important to Them**

    I have found the most overlooked strategy for building relationships is the most simple: ask! Inquire what is most important to your associates. Ask how they prefer to be recognized, find out how they like to receive feedback and prefer to communicate. Acknowledging and acting upon their preferences will demonstrate you care about what's important to them.

3. **Listen Effectively**

    Managers need to ask effective questions and then really

listen to associates' answers. The technique of "drilling down" with questions can take a surface-level conversation to a meaningful dialogue. Following up with action in a manner which supports associates' ideas and concerns and reinforces the manager listened.

4. **Save Surprises for Birthdays**

    Associates typically do not like surprise announcements, news or anything serious in nature from managers. Managers need to provide regular communication and scheduled updates like a quarterly conversation and scorecard review. They also need to be transparent about the health of the organization. When an associate knows they can rely on their manager for the truth, it really deepens relationships.

5. **Show Them You Aren't Afraid of Failure**

    Every associate is a threat to an insecure leader. Any mistake or struggle in performance will make the leader look bad, so every associate is seen as a threat. This drives selfish, bad behavior and creates an unsafe place for the team. Relationship can only develop in a fear-free environment. Every leader needs to work on their own fear issues so they can focus on building the team instead of their ego.

6. **Lead with Integrity**

    You can demonstrate you are worthy of leading by keeping your word with your associates. Let them see your integrity. Say what you'll do, and then do what you say. Show them you are leading in alignment with the values of the organization. Reward others who act with integrity. Remember the maxim: "How you achieve your results is as important as the results themselves."

7. **Let Them Manage Their Day-to-Day Routine**

    Offer freedom by not micromanaging associates. Provide the opportunity to manage their own activities. This behavior creates leaders within our organization organically and develops a sense of personal accountability.

8. **Build People up in Any Situation**
Your team members' personal lives matter, and bad times at home can often affect performance at work. Effective managers prioritize taking a genuine interest in their associates and providing support during rough patches. In the same way, when times are good, managers should celebrate victories with the whole team. Build people up in any situation and you'll foster a deep level of loyalty.

9. **Don't Have All of the Answers**
Who do you really value? Typically, it's someone who allows you to be yourself and who encourages you to continuously learn and grow. It is also someone who asks others for their opinion. As Benjamin Franklin once said, "We all admire the wisdom of those who come to us for advice."

10. **Great Communication**
We communicate all day, whether we're sending emails, texts or meeting face-to-face. Get personal. Be efficient with emails and texts, but don't let them replace talking. Walk across the hall to give a compliment. Let people know you care by interacting directly with them.

11. **Appreciate Others**
Show your appreciation whenever someone helps you. Everyone, from your boss to the office cleaning crew, wants to feel their work is appreciated. So genuinely compliment the people around you when they do something well. This falls into the category of reinforcing good behavior. Practice gratitude for what others do for the company. Develop an authentic attitude of gratitude.

12. **Be Positive**

    Focus on being positive. Positivity is attractive and contagious, and it will help strengthen your relationships with your colleagues. No one wants to be around someone who's negative all the time.

13. **Lecture Less—Listen More**

    There's so much temptation to lead in a strong, authoritative way because historically that's what many have done. But the one-dimensional bully leader is dead. Even though 80 percent of people in a Pew Research Center survey cited decisiveness as an essential leadership trait, today's smart leaders understand what precedes decisiveness is equally important—the ability to admit you don't know everything and the willingness to defer to others' opinions. Lecture less—listen more.

14. **Be Humble**

    When leaders show more humility, team performance improves. One reason: In the information age, it's increasingly difficult for any one leader to figure it all out. But perhaps the greatest advantage of humility is it can temper perceptions of narcissism, thereby allowing a leader to remain strong without appearing dictatorial. Go back and read chapter 16. Remember, your ego is not your amigo.

15. **Don't Try to Make Everyone Happy**

    The make-everyone-happy approach actually does the opposite—it makes everyone upset. And it's counter to what groups want and need from the top. Over the long term associates will most value honest candor.

As CEO I spent a minimum of 30 percent of my time on building and fostering customer relationships. I never felt it was enough. I then read a quote by Simon Sinek, the author of *Start with Why*, who said, "The CEO is not responsible for customers. The CEO is responsible for the people responsible for the customers." I don't completely agree with this concept relative to customers, but I do agree the business leader's role is being responsible for the company's associates who take care of the company's customers. "Substitute any business leader for CEO and you understand how important your role is and how important it is to build strong relationships with those you supervise."

Years ago I learned of a Turkish proverb: "No road is long with good company." The essence of life is to surround yourself with good company. Having great business and personal relationships has greatly enriched my life.

CHAPTER 20
Persistence and Resiliency

My first boss after I graduated from college and an important early mentor of mine was smart and insightful. Although he had an outstanding educational background—he had an MBA from Wharton with high distinction—he repeatedly said, "GPA scores don't matter much in the real world." Typically he would go on to say, "I would rather hire a 'C' student who was very persistent than someone with a 4.0." He would usually conclude with this aphorism, which I think can be attributed to President Calvin Coolidge: "Unrewarded genius is almost a proverb."

Why is persistence so important? Success in business is never a straight line up and to the right but rather invariably a messy pattern of ups and downs. It's when the inevitable "downs" happen that persistence becomes so important. Major success as a business leader seldom comes easily or without a great deal of effort. Often the only difference between those who succeed and those who don't is the ability to keep going long after many have given up. Throughout my forty-plus years in business, I've faced a number of very difficult periods—times when I had sleepless nights, high levels of stress, and in many cases no clear solution. What I learned during these difficult times was the importance of being persistent. As Winston Churchill said, "Success is stumbling from failure to failure with no loss of enthusiasm." Remember, a river cuts through rocks not because of its power at any given moment but because it has persistence over time.

Generally people give up too soon because they have the wrong expectations of themselves and the outcomes. They expect the way to be easy, and when they find the reality to be the opposite, their enthusiasm quickly melts, and they lose heart. Remember, there is no such thing as cheap success. Expect a hard path, not an easy one, and you will be mentally prepared when you encounter difficulties. As Charlie Munger said about investing, "It's not supposed to be easy. Anyone who finds it easy is stupid." The same can be said about being a business leader.

Remember at first all-important problems seem to be insolvable. I've always liked the phrase, "When the going gets tough, the tough get going." So, what does persistence look like on the ground?

1. Hard work—An important part of persistence is to work harder. Every difficult challenge required me to redouble my efforts. I've always liked the quote, "The harder I work, the luckier I get," or Thomas Edison's quote, "Genius is 1 percent inspiration and 99 percent perspiration." More on this important topic in chapter 26.

2. Ingenuity—Ingenuity is one of the core values I helped ingrain at Assurity. Getting out of a difficult situation often requires a new way of doing or thinking about things. Another important quote: "Insanity is doing the same thing over and over again and expecting different results." Successful persistence usually requires doing things in a different way. Persistent people realize that any major problem will probably require learning new skills and thinking patterns. They welcome change and new ideas, and are continually looking for better ways to do things.

3. Self-confidence—Have confidence that in the end you will succeed. You will be blown away by what you can achieve if you don't lose hope in yourself. Another mentor of mine used to say, "The only true security in life is to know whatever comes your way, you'll be able to handle it." It's okay to get discouraged—it happens to everyone. It's not okay to

quit. But discouragement should not immediately equate to quitting.

4. Have patience—Difficult problems don't arise overnight, and they won't be solved overnight. You must understand that solving difficult problems takes time. You will need to break down the problem into manageable parts and tackle those parts one step at a time.

5. Embrace boring—being persistent can sometimes be considered boring. What's boring doesn't get attention and what's exciting doesn't always drive results. Most people are so focused on optics they forget that it's the repetition of the boring basics that will ultimately make a difference.

6. Keep going—Champions keep playing until they get it right. As the famous clergyman Dr. Norman Vincent Peale said, "It is always too soon to quit." An important mentor of mine was Hugh Hanson, who was vice chairman of First Commerce Bancshares. Hugh had been "First Commerce's fix-it man"—during his career he was president and CEO of several problem banks. Around the time he retired, I asked him to what he attributed his success. Without missing a beat, he said, "Getting up every morning, putting on my suit and tie, and going back into battle—no matter how difficult the battle." In other words, persistence.

The harsh reality is that the world is full of "could've beens"—people who have wonderful ideas and aspirations but didn't have the stamina, desire, or knowhow to make it happen. Many give up too fast because it seemed too hard, too daunting, or too scary.

I've long loved another quote from President Calvin Coolidge: "Nothing in this world can take the place of persistence. Talent will not; nothing is more common than unsuccessful men with talent. Persistence and determination alone are omnipotent."

To close out this section on persistence I'm going to briefly discuss a paradox around persistence. More on paradoxes in chapter 34. Here is the paradox: it is not always the right thing to do to persist. If you are dealing with a longstanding unsolvable problem, you should probably quit. In chapter 40 I discuss the concept of "Too Hard." Certain business problems just aren't solvable. You need to stop wasting time and resources trying to turn around something that cannot be fixed. I've just started reading a book by Annie Duke titled *Quit: The Power of Knowing When to Walk Away.* Ms. Duke lays out some compelling reasons on when quitting makes sense. Again, whether to persist or quit requires you, the business leader, to exercise good judgment.

I'm going to close out this chapter by discussing a key component of being able to be persistent, and that is resiliency.

In order to be persistent you have to build up personal and corporate resiliency. Resiliency is the ability to overcome challenges of all kinds—unexpected accidents, sickness, financial reversals, and attempts to capitalize on the misfortune. The goal is to come back stronger and better. One of the many Warren Buffett one liners I like is "Predicting rain doesn't count. Building arks does." When you build an ark, you build your resiliency.

Consider personal resiliency. The foundation of personal resiliency is good health. I'm reminded of the oft-quoted maxim "if you don't have your health, you don't have anything." So all the activities and disciplines that drive good health outcomes need to be practiced by those who want to be personally resilient—eat right, regular exercise, properly manage stress, restful sleep, you all know the list.

A great example of being personally resilient involves a mid-sixties-age friend who was diagnosed with stage-4 lung cancer. He had never smoked and never had a major health problem until this lung cancer diagnosis. Fortunately, throughout his whole life he had followed the discipline of a regular exercise program and sensible eating regime. He had a strong social support network, including a very close and supportive family and many friends.

Not that many years ago a diagnosis of stage 4 lung cancer was a death sentence. Not now. Due to major advancements in lung cancer treatment and his fundamental good health, he had a rapid recovery. He only had about six weeks of feeling poorly, and after that he was back to his old self. Now three years later he's completely cancer free. A great example of personal resiliency.

None of us know what tomorrow may bring. You can improve your personal resiliency by controlling stress, getting a good night's sleep, eating healthy, and following a regular exercise regimen.

In addition to good health, a sound financial position allows for personal resiliency. Building wealth, controlling expenses, and properly insuring against loss position an individual for personal resiliency. Many times a financial setback is an opportunity in disguise. If you have structured your financial life in a sound way, you'll be in a position to overcome initial misfortune and instead capitalize on what for the less prepared may represent a major financial reversal. Having a strong personal financial foundation positions you to weather the storm. Be financially unbreakable.

Cohesive family ties and other personal relationships are also important pillars in personal resiliency. If you have built a supportive family unit where each family member supports each other, this foundation assists greatly in overcoming any adversity. A select group of personal friends are also key to personal resiliency. These critical individuals can provide trusted advice, counsel, and a sympathetic ear. When we engage in the messy, unpredictable business of making friends, we are strengthening our resilience.

Corporate resiliency has many parallels to personal resiliency. It starts with a healthy corporate culture. A strong corporate culture allows a company's management to weather adversity. Think of it as a bank balance that has been built over the years. During times of trial you'll need to make withdrawals.

It is especially important to have a cohesive management team—a team that will not disintegrate into blaming politics and bureaucracy when trouble begins. Instead they will rally together and work as a team to turn lemons to lemonade.

Finally, a corporate resiliency's foundation is a strong financial position. A strong financial position not only allows a company to survive difficulty but more importantly capitalize on tough times.

Resilient companies have the intellectual and financial capital not only to survive but to thrive and to turn misfortune into opportunity.

One last point on resiliency is the value of redundancy. Redundancy is having multiple backup systems. Let me tell you about a small business acquaintance of mine who operates a transportation service in the Colorado Rockies. He has to contend with heavy I-70 traffic, adverse weather conditions, and longstanding clients who change their plans last minute and repeatedly. He has a stellar reputation among his clients and would attribute his good reputation to his business philosophy of redundancy. He always keeps at least one large vehicle in reserve to respond to a longtime client's last-minute request. He maintains an inventory of tires for all his vehicles so that a flat or blown tire won't impede service to his clients. And for his drivers he focuses on multiple ex-military personnel who he compensates very well and lavishly during holidays. So when he calls they will positively respond. Some may feel he's negatively impacting his profitability with this built-in redundancy. He will concede he is impacting short-term profitability, but he strongly believes his redundancy positively impacts his long-term profitability. I'm convinced redundancy helps individuals and businesses be optimally resilient.

Every individual and business should have backup plans and escape hatches to protect against the inevitable reversals in life. Good positioning allows you to better control your circumstances. Poor positioning lets your circumstances control you.

CHAPTER 21
Behavioral Biases in Management

I've long been interested in and studied behavioral finance. I'm a chartered financial analyst, commonly known as a CFA. A favorite part of my CFA studies was behavioral finance. It has always been interesting to me how behavioral biases negatively impact investment decisions. In fact, I've long believed the only advantage I've had in investing is behavioral. But through this work, I've also become aware of cognitive biases and blind spots that limit our effectiveness in being a business leader.

A book I particularly found helpful in this area is *The Art of Thinking Clearly* by Rolf Dobelli. Cognitive biases are the focus of this book by Mr. Dobelli. I like Mr. Dobelli's writing and would also recommend another of his books, *The Art of the Good Life*.

Beyond Mr. Dobelli's work, many other authors have influenced my thinking on how cognitive biases impact our decision-making. Other authors who have had an influence on my thinking on cognitive behavioral traps include:

- Daniel Kahneman, *Thinking, Fast and Slow*
- Michael Lewis, *The Undoing Project,* which is about the relationship between Daniel Kahneman and his colleague Amos Tversky
- Dr. Adam Grant at the Wharton Business School, *Think Again: The Power of Knowing What You Don't Know*

- Mervyn King, former head of the Bank of England, *Radical Uncertainty—Decision-Making Beyond the Numbers*
- Dr. Robert J. Shiller, *Narrative Economics: How Stories Go Viral and Drive Major Economic Events*
- Phil Rosenzweig, *The Halo Effect*
- Nassim Nicholas, especially his best seller *Fooled by Randomness: The Hidden Role of Chance in Life and in the Markets*
- Leonard Mlodinow, *The Drunkard's Walk*

We like to think, as business leaders, we are rational human beings. In fact, we are all prone to many biases that cause us to think and act irrationally. Haven't you known business leaders who acted irrationally? Yet individually we believe we are always rational. If you believe that statement, we just identified a bias you might have known as a blind spot bias, one of the many biases that affect us as business leaders.

A behavioral trap or bias in management is the irrational manner in which the human brain usually works, resulting in the inability to make sound business decisions even when we've accumulated abundant work experience and knowledge.

There are many, many behavioral or cognitive biases. In fact, if you google "cognitive biases," you will find a Wikipedia report that lists almost 190 cognitive biases. Some are bizarre, like the "IKEA effect," which is the tendency for people to place a disproportionality higher value on objects they partially assemble themselves, such as furniture from IKEA, regardless of the quality or the end result. Having assembled some IKEA furniture for one of our daughters, I can confidently state this isn't one of my biases; I'm terrible at it and will go to great lengths to avoid doing it in the future!

Although there are many cognitive biases that affect a business leader's effectiveness. I'm going to focus on what I consider the top dirty dozen of cognitive biases.

1. Anchoring—A cognitive bias that describes the human tendency to rely too heavily on the first piece of information

offered (the "anchor") when making decisions. Anchoring is among the most prevalent and impactful cognitive biases that we encounter in our daily lives, particularly when making decisions under uncertainty. We tend to place too much weight on an initial piece of information—the reference point to which we attach (or "anchor") our thoughts. This causes the way in which we assess probabilities to become distorted. Anchoring is most common when we deal with new concepts or objects, and most people struggle to overcome its effect, even when given incentives to do so.

When I was President of NBC bank, our CFO proudly told me he had negotiated a 25 percent discount off a piece of software we wanted to purchase. I know I surprised him when I asked, "How do you know this is a good deal? Maybe everyone got 25 percent off or maybe the asking price was already too high." Our CFO did some additional research and found out we weren't getting a special deal at all.

Beware of anchoring; it is a pervasive cognitive bias.

2. Availability Heuristic—A mental shortcut that relies on immediate examples that come to a person's mind when evaluating a specific topic, concept, method, or decision. People tend to heavily weigh their judgments toward more recent information, making new opinions biased toward the latest news or information that is readily available.

   The words "well, that's what we did last year" are frequently heard in the business world and provide a clear example of the availability heuristic in action. What we did last year is much clearer than the unknown.

   The availability heuristic is also why we see a lot of resistance to change in the business world. What we know is far more certain than what we don't. In other words, we have been working in a certain way for years, and it works. Why change it to something we have no idea about?

   We tend to give greater weighting to the process we know than that we don't. In turn, the likelihood of a new process being successful is seen as highly unlikely, usually more so than the true odds. This is because the value of recent memories (the old process) is greater than the value of the unknown. Therefore, we skew the odds of success to what we know.

Managers conducting annual performance appraisals often fall victim to the availability heuristic. Managers give more weight to performance during the three months prior to the evaluation than to the previous nine months of the evaluation period because it is more available in their memory.

The availability heuristic helps people make fast but sometimes incorrect assessments.

3. Attribution Bias—Attribution bias refers to the tendency of people to attribute their success to their own ability and their failures to external unlucky forces. It also involves attributing other people's actions to their competence or character as opposed to underlying situational factors.

Attribution error is so pervasive I guarantee you will see it in action over the next week if you keep your eyes open. In the workplace, it leads to unfair judgments of people's performance and motivations. Typical behaviors that trigger these judgments include errors, missed deadlines and perceived impoliteness. Our typical inclination is to blame our colleague and believe their behavior is simply a manifestation of a character weakness. Conversely, when we are the party that has committed the error, missed the deadline, or "snubbed" someone, we have a ready defense. We say that we were "overloaded" or insufficiently trained or some other external factor caused our underperformance.

Attribution bias is particularly useful for whittling negative events into neat little packages. When a company has good performance, many times people will characterize the company as having a visionary CEO, great corporate culture, and a disciplined financial process. Here's the true reality: Economic success depends far more on the overall economic climate and the industry's attractiveness than it does on brilliant leadership. Sorry, but this is true.

4. Confirmation Bias—The tendency to search for or interpret information in the way that confirms one's preexisting beliefs. In my CFA studies, this was called "data mining." Data mining is searching for information or data that confirms what we already believe to be true. We automatically, systematically filter out evidence that contradicts our perceptions in favor of confirming evidence. So many management teams are guilty of this, which produces group think.

When people would like a certain idea to be true, they end up believing it to be true. There are so much information and data available these days it's not difficult to carefully select information that will prove what you believe. To combat this bias, I would encourage managers to invert. Look for information and data that are exactly the opposite of what you believe to be true. I do this in making an investment. After becoming interested in a particular investment, but before investing, I'll search for information that contradicts my investment thesis. I always learn a great deal by seeking out countervailing opinions.

Another important way to avoid confirmation bias is to keep learning. Because the world is changing so quickly, you have to keep taking in new information. If you aren't learning, you won't adapt.

5. Consistency Bias—According to Robert Cialdini, author of *Influence: The Psychology of Persuasion*, "Consistency bias is simply our nearly obsessive desire to be consistent with what we have already done and/or said. Once we have made a choice or taken a stand, we will encounter personal and interpersonal pressures to behave consistently with that commitment. Those pressures will cause us to respond in ways that justify our earlier decision."

Robert Cialdini does a great job discussing this tendency in *Influence*. What we are largely unaware of, and what makes this tendency so powerful, is the actions we have taken in the past are subconsciously affecting our self-image, and it is the defense of this self-image that can influence our decision making. As Charlie Munger states, "Wherever you turn, this consistency and commitment tendency is affecting you."

But the world is changing so rapidly, you need to take in new information that could and perhaps should cause you to change your mind. Ralph Waldo Emerson said it so well years ago: "A foolish consistency is the hobgoblin of little minds." I also love this quote attributed to John Maynard Keynes: "When the facts change, I change my mind. What do you do?"

The real and only defense against the consistency bias is awareness about the phenomena and the harm a certain rigidity in our decisions can cause us.

6. Halo Effect—It is the phenomenon whereby we assume because people are good at doing *A* they will be good at doing *B*. The halo effect is also highly influenced by first impressions. If we first see a person in a good light, it is difficult subsequently to darken that light. The old adage that "first impressions count" seems to be true. Much of our thinking about any company's performance is also shaped by the halo effect. When a company is growing and profitable, we tend to infer it has a brilliant strategy, a visionary CEO, motivated people, and a vibrant culture. When performance falters, we're quick to say the strategy was misguided, the CEO ineffective, the people complacent, and the culture stodgy.

GE's performance under Jack Welch is a great example of the halo effect. When he was CEO of GE he was lauded by many as a business genius. And maybe he was. The consistent performance of GE under his leadership is now suspect. No business's top or bottom line marches higher in a predictable and consistent way unless you are cooking the books. The nature of business is to have volatile results, and you then hope the trendline is positive. Anything else and you are probably being fooled by the "Halo Effect."

Watch out for the Halo Effect. Be sure to take into account external factors.

7. Herd Behavior—The tendency for individuals to mimic the actions (rational or irrational) of a larger group. Individually, however, most people would not necessarily make the same choice.

For example, in the late 1990s investors were investing huge amounts of money into internet-related companies, even though most of them did not have a successful business model. Their driving force was the reassurance they got from seeing so many others do the same. Now we have the Robin Hood effect or the digital currency craze: groups of investors piling into bankrupt companies, pushing their prices unrealistically high.

Unfortunately, we are all susceptible to "herd behavior." We all pile into the "got to have" new product or "new technological approach." Some also refer to this as the "school of fish" bias.

8. Blind Spot Bias—I earlier mentioned this bias. Blind spot bias is the failure to notice your own cognitive biases. You may be drawn to a particular style or way of working without being aware of it. For instance, we tend to hire those who match our own ways of seeing the world and are unaware we are doing so. We are more likely to notice bias in others than ourselves because our own biases are so ingrained in our world view.

Bias blind spots may be caused by a variety of other biases and self-deceptions. Self-enhancement biases may play a role in that people are motivated to view themselves in a positive light. Biases are generally seen as undesirable, so people tend to think of their own perceptions and judgments as being rational, accurate, and free of bias. The self-enhancement bias also applies when analyzing our own decisions, in that people are likely to think of themselves as better decision-makers than others.

People also tend to believe they are aware of "how" and "why" they make their decisions and therefore conclude that bias does not play a role. Many of our decisions are formed from biases and cognitive shortcuts, which are unconscious processes. By definition, people are unaware of unconscious processes and therefore cannot see their influence in the decision-making process.

Watch for blind spot bias in yourself and others in your management group. Try inverting as a means for revealing the blind spots.

9. Hindsight Bias (I-Knew-It-All-Along Effect)—This is the tendency of people to overestimate their ability to have predicted an outcome that could not possibly have been predicted. This is a psychological phenomenon in which people believe that an event was more predictable than it actually was and can result in an oversimplification in cause and effect. It is one of management's oldest canards.

For example, after the great recession of 2008, many analysts explained that all the signs of the financial bubble were there. If the signs had been that obvious, why did virtually no one see it coming in real time?

Don't overlearn from your own or others' good or bad experience. The same action under other conditions may cause different results. Hindsight bias may damage people's foresight because it makes people wrongly expect that the future can be easily predicted. One of my recurring themes in this book is that we all underestimate luck and randomness in outcomes

10. Overconfidence Effect—We systematically overestimate our knowledge and our ability to predict. Overconfidence

measures the difference between what people really know and what they think they know. Overconfidence becomes especially bad if you've had some success. There is nothing like success to blind one to the possibility of failure.

Daniel Kahneman once said in a CFA article, "Over confidence is a curse. It's a curse and a blessing. The people who make great things, if you look back they were confident and optimistic. They take big risks because they underestimate how big the risks are."

Examples of the overconfidence effect is everywhere. As an example, studies have found that over 90 percent of US drivers rate themselves above average, and 68 percent of college professors consider themselves in the top 25 percent for teaching ability.

Overconfidence especially manifests itself during the planning process for about anything. Assurity would be over a billion dollars sales company if all the initial projections on new products and distribution approaches I've witnessed over the past thirty-one-plus years would have come to fruition. Someone should ask, "What is our history in making a new product or distribution approach successful? What is our base rate?"

Anytime anyone states something very emphatically to me, my skepticism antenna kicks into high gear. Given all the uncertainty in the world, it is better to consider most things in a probabilistic format rather than in absolutes.

11. Survivorship Bias—This is the mental error of concentrating on the people or things who made it past some selecting process and overlooking those who do not. Take the popularity of investing in startups, which I personally enjoy. Potential investors think this or that startup could be the next Google or Facebook. Maybe they'll be lucky, but the more likely scenario is the company will never get off the starting line. The second-most likely outcome is that it will shut down in the next three years. Of the new companies who survive

the first three years, most never grow to over ten associates. Survivorship bias means people systematically overestimate their chance of success.

12. Sunk Cost Fallacy—The tendency of managers to irrationally follow through on an activity that is not meeting their expectations because of the time and/or money they and the company have already spent on it.

The logic form:
X has already been invested in project Y.
Z more investment would be needed to complete project Y, otherwise X will be lost.
Therefore, Z is justified.

The sunk cost fallacy explains why people finish movies they aren't enjoying, finish meals in restaurants even though they are full, drink bad beer or wine, hold on to investments that are underperforming, and keep clothes in their closest that they've never worn. Get over it and move on. Don't be dragged into this sophistry.

Not all biases result in negative behavior. Some, like optimism, have a mixed impact. Optimism has both benefits and drawbacks. Unrestrained optimism tends to lie on the negative end of the behavioral continuum for business leaders and can morph into a bias toward overconfidence. An unrealistic positive outlook will inevitably contribute to suboptimal and sometimes disastrous management decisions. An abundance of optimism helped create the 2008 financial crisis. But there is an optimism paradox. This bias has major benefits, too, spurring investment in new corporate initiatives and start-up ventures—the sort of enterprises that can catalyze transformative growth and the associated returns.

One bias that is almost always positive for any management group is skepticism. Skepticism is the ability to doubt, to question, and—hopefully—to investigate. By definition, skepticism is on the opposite end of all belief perseverance and information-processing biases. Skepticism helps to keep emotions on a tight leash. Skepticism, to the extent it contributes to inaction, can be a negative management trait. While an abundance of skepticism can lead to paralysis, healthy and consistent skepticism is largely beneficial. I've heard a number of regulators when doing a post-mortem on a failed financial institution say that the management team or board lacked professional skepticism in how they viewed a new product or market which ultimately got them into trouble.

Conclusion
The irrational manner in which the human brain often works influences people's decisions in ways they and others around them fail to anticipate. Charlie Munger appropriately states, "If you want to avoid irrationality, it helps to understand the quirks in your own mental wiring and then you can take appropriate precautions." One of my personal goals is to be the most rational business leader I can be. I think an overarching goal of "rationality" is important for all business leaders.

CHAPTER 22

Bureaucracy / Corporate Politics

In this chapter I want to discuss the problems with bureaucracy and its evil twin, organizational politics.

In preview, a bureaucratic culture is deadly for most companies in today's fast-moving environment. Bureaucratic cultures are hierarchical and compartmentalized. There are clear lines of responsibility and authority. The work is rigid and inflexible; these cultures are usually based on control and power. A high score on bureaucracy means the organization is power oriented, cautious, regimented, regulation driven, uncompromising, and hierarchical. It is a great culture for a company with a large market share in a stable market. Who has this anymore? Today I can't come up with an industry who benefits from a bureaucratic culture.

Bureaucracies form gradually, quietly, and often for reasons that seem sensible at the time. But a close examination of bureaucracies shows that they're often a response to fear of loss, resulting in attempts to regain control, regardless of overall strategies or needs. These barriers are usually created with the best of intentions, which is what makes them so difficult to spot and combat.

So what are the signs of bureaucracy? Here are a few of the most common:

1. Associates are fearful of suggesting anything which doesn't conform to an established rule or procedure.

2. More time is spent completing required reports—an expense report, time sheet, balanced scorecard update—than is given to getting a new customer or serve an existing customer.

3. Overdependence on meetings. *Collaborative* and *inclusive* are corporate buzzwords, but productive teamwork does not require meetings for every single action or decision. Calling a meeting to coordinate a response or respond to an inquiry is a very unproductive use of time.

4. Including a large group of people in email chains so everyone is informed, but less directly, so the senders can cover themselves for any action that might be controversial. "What do you mean you didn't know? I copied you on an email."

5. Hiding behind rules and regulations as an excuse to not challenge the status quo or suggest another way.

6. Wanting black and white answers to a world which is increasingly gray.

7. Parochialism and territorialism. Many times, out of necessity and in response to pressures for results, the leaders of departments start to focus much more on their functional goals than on the organization's overall goals. When this happens, making sure their part of the process is done correctly may become all that really matters, even at the expense of the overall organization's success. The group may not only lose sight of the connection between its work and organization outcomes, but it may also even stop caring about what happens outside its silo. It defines its world by the piece, not the puzzle.

Parochialism develops when a group views the world strictly through the lens of its functional goals, and it judges the relative importance of other activities by the way they affect the group's objectives. Parochialism limits the group to a narrow reference point—ultimately, everything is viewed from that filtered local perspective.

8. Empire building is also a problem. Increased business complexity tends to increase the interdependency between departments. Groups become much more reliant on shared services, such as human resources, IT, or marketing support. They may become more and more dependent on how quickly other departments complete their part of the process. In an environment where one group's success is limited by another group's constraints, a manager may feel compelled to begin empire building—the attempt to gain control over functions or responsibilities that are controlled by another group—either by asserting control over that group or creating a duplicate function.

I also recognize highly regulated industries are more susceptible to forming bureaucracies to force compliance with the myriad of regulators under which they operate.

Here are some steps a business leader can take to combat the evils of bureaucracy:

1. Look for opportunities to empower associates to better serve your customers.

2. Don't hide behind a rule or process. For example, I would never say to a customer we can't do something because it is against our rules. Instead indicate it wouldn't be good for the customer or the company long term.

3. Be careful about calling meetings. Bureaucracies set up regularly scheduled meetings in order to get people together, but there is often a misalignment between the established meeting time and the work that needs to be done. Challenge others who want you to attend a meeting as to the necessity of the meeting. Insist on an agenda and know in advance

what should be the outcome of the meeting.

4. Break the email chain. Get up, go see someone, and work it out.

5. Recognize that not every new or unfortunate situation calls for the development of a new policy or rule that could be limiting and have unintended consequences. Remember, the success of any company will never be measured by the size of its policy manuals. Ponderous rulebooks only encourage people to seek ways to work around the rules.

6. Encourage a culture of transparency. This will not only help with bureaucracy, but it is one of the most effective ways to reduce corporate politics.

7. Within your area, start a "stop doing list." Bureaucracies perpetuate forms, processes, and procedures which at one time made sense, but are now continued out of tradition and inertia.

It's much easier to build bureaucracies than to dismantle them. But rooting out entrenched parochialism, territorialism, and empire building—though it is arduous and unpleasant—needs to be done if the organization is to thrive. Remember, bureaucratic processes, procedures, and rules were created internally. And if they were created internally, they can be torn down internally, and the potential of the entire enterprise can be unleashed. Remember, the lack of bureaucracy can be one of your firm's competitive advantages. Strive to be nimble, fast, and responsive.

Let's turn to corporate politics.

Corporate politics takes many forms. Here's a list of some things I consider the worst:

1. Individuals participating in a "meeting before the meeting." Meetings before the meeting occur to attempt to insure an

outcome in advance of the main meeting.

2. Someone or a group tried to push through a decision on something controversial while someone else was out of the office so they wouldn't be able to participate.

3. Participate in a cabal which informally organizes to speculate on a particular corporate direction, which the members of the cabal fear will be negative for them. This is similar to office gossip except there is typically an unofficial objective of influencing company direction.

4. Grandstanding (aka brown nosing). People pay lip service to the leaders' ideas to curry favor but have no real commitment to implementing anything which changes the status quo.

5. The two-faced two-step. People say what they think the people they are talking to at the moment want to hear. In their hearts they don't believe it, and there is no follow through.

6. Gridlock. Major decisions just can't seem to get made. People can't reach a consensus on how to move forward, so nothing happens.

7. Indirect Communication. Instead of talking to coworkers directly when they have a problem, associates complain to other coworkers and their supervisor and talk about people behind their backs.

8. Passing the buck. No one takes responsibility for anything; people are quick to assign blame to someone else or some other area of the company.

This is just a partial list of the pejorative aspects of corporate politics. Office politics is a major issue in business because the individuals who manipulate their working relationships consume time and resources for their own gain at the expense of the team or company.

The practice of office politics can have an even more serious effect on major business processes such as strategy formation, budget setting, performance management, and leadership. This occurs because when individuals are playing office politics, it interferes with the information flow of a company. Information can be distorted, misdirected, or suppressed in order to manipulate a situation for short-term personal gain.

During my career I have tried to beat down corporate politics at every opportunity. If you see some corporate politics going on in your business don't assume it's an isolated instance. There is never just one cockroach in the kitchen. What follows are my suggestions on the best way to minimize and root out negative office politics.

1. Great communication. Open, authentic, and consistent communication is the best way to minimize negative office politics.

2. Transparency. Be an open book—no hidden agendas. I have said many times in a number of different venues to various associates individually and in a group—"If you are worried, anxious or concerned about something at Assurity—just ask me and I will tell you what I know." Many associates believe that their supervisor or senior management have some big inside information. I can tell you I have virtually no knowledge I wouldn't share with anyone in the company. Transparency is the most effective disinfectant for office politics.

3. Force people to talk to each other. When someone comes into my office to complain about someone else, the first thing I say is "have you spoken directly with this person about your thoughts or concerns?"

4. Be upfront and honest. Create an atmosphere in your area where associates can feel comfortable being upfront and

honest. Encourage an atmosphere where associates are comfortable bringing up and discussing problems. Remember—"don't kill the messenger."

5. Hold people accountable. People need to be held accountable for results in their area of responsibility. Don't allow them to blame others or another area of the company.

6. Avoiding conflict. It is easier to gossip about others than to have an honest straightforward conversation. Be careful about conflict avoidance.

As a leader, you are the first line of defense in stomping out office politics. In summary, do the following:

- Elevate communication to an artform.
- Be radically transparent.
- Reinforce your corporate and area goals, and be sure each associate knows how what they do every day contributes to achieving long-term corporate objectives.
- Don't shy away from conflict and call people out when they are practicing devious behavior.

CHAPTER 23
Accountability

I've found the balanced scorecard (BSC) process developed by David P. Norton and Robert S. Kaplan to be very valuable. A similar program for smaller companies was developed by Gino Wickman and is known as the "Entrepreneurial Operating System" or EOS. One of the many things I like about BSC and EOS is that they naturally foster a culture of accountability.

In fact, in all of their writings on the balanced scorecard, Kaplan and Norton extensively discuss the importance of accountability in executing strategy. For any company to achieve its strategic objectives, supervisors must hold associates accountable for their respective parts in achieving company objectives. Accountability and alignment must link enterprise strategy to personal performance. However, in many organizations, "accountability" is a pejorative term. Associates view accountability as being held responsible for an area or company objectives over which they feel they have little control.

In contrast, the best business leaders foster a culture where accountability is celebrated. Everyone in the organization understands their important role in achieving area and corporate goals. Everyone from the top down must be accountable for completing specific tasks. So how do we foster a culture of accountability?

It is not through a traditional performance appraisal process. I've never liked the traditional performance appraisal process. Rather I'm an advocate of using a quarterly balanced scorecard session as a much better alternative. At Assurity we called it "the quarterly conversations." It's a great substitute because it focuses on goals. It is always much easier to get someone to go toward something positive (achieving goals) than away from something. We all need to remember associates need regular feedback and frequent communication to keep on moving toward the achievement of company goals. Effective business leaders use the scorecard sessions to coach high performance. When people can regularly and easily see whether or not they are on track to reach their goals—and if their rewards are dependent on achieving these goals—they apply the effort needed to succeed.

So here are the key elements I feel a supervisor needs to do in order to foster a culture of accountability:

1. **Communicate the goals of the company and those of your area or strategic business unit.**

   There's an old adage that "if you don't know where you are going, any road will do." Said differently, "The first step in an important journey is deciding where you want to end up." As a supervisor your first responsibility is to make sure all of your direct reports are crystal clear on the overall company and your area goals.

   And the goals need to be "SMART." SMART stand for specific, measurable, attainable, relevant and timebound. Additionally, each associate should have key performance indicators (KPIs) by which the individual and their supervisor can monitor progress. Remember to discuss poor or failing performance before it gets out of hand.

2. **Alignment**

   A key part of the balanced scorecard process is connecting the dots between what an individual does every day and the achievement of area and corporate goals.

   In all the travails the University of Nebraska's football program faced in recent years, many knowledgeable football experts laid a big chunk of the blame on the fact the coaching staff did not connect the dots for the players. Players did not fully appreciate how their individual performance contributed to the team's performance. I've had several former

Cornhusker players indicate this was a big part of legendary Cornhusker football coach Tom Osborne's genius. He let each player know how important their individual efforts were to the overall success of the team.

Lead your people toward something big and be sure to explain to each and everyone their important part in making corporate and area goals a reality.

3. **Provide training and other resources.**
   Associates need to have the proper skills, knowledge, and experience to get the job done. Associates should be provided the necessary training to carry out the duties. This is so fundamental, but too many times in doing a post-mortem on an unsuccessful effort it becomes clear that associates were not properly trained.

4. **Provide motivating recognition.**
   I would always rather catch people doing something right and reinforce this behavior than point out how they missed the mark. Be creative in how you dole out recognition, and be sure it is authentic. Empower people to succeed by providing sincere recognition. Celebrate area and individual successes.

5. **Take action when individuals and teams do not meet expectations.**
   In giving honest feedback, be careful of an old nemesis: conflict avoidance. This is the place where you can't avoid calling out poor performance. You have to tell it straight and suggest action the associate can take to get back on track. Don't avoid the difficult conversations.

6. **Don't instill fear in your workplace.**
   Developing an environment of fear might give you success in the short term, but it will not establish long-term accountability. If associates are afraid of their managers' criticism, they will hardly look for any support when they feel they

need to be supported in order to achieve their objectives.

7. **Be a model.**
Finally, lead by example. Make sure associates understand what you expect of them and that you're holding yourself to the same high standard. Follow through on your promises, own up to your mistakes, and give feedback even when it isn't easy. That's how to create a culture of accountability.

Business leaders can't impose a sense of responsibility on their associates. What they can do is build conditions that support personal engagement by creating a culture of accountability.

CHAPTER 24
The Virtuous Cycle

In so many aspects of life, I've long appreciated the value of creating a "virtuous cycle of events." Merriam-Webster's online dictionary defines a virtuous cycle as:

> "A chain of events in which one desirable occurrence leads to another which further promotes the first occurrence and so on resulting in a continuous process of improvement."

In contrast, a vicious cycle is the opposite. This is Merriam-Webster online dictionary's definition of a vicious cycle:

> "A repeating situation or condition in which one problem causes another problem that makes the first problem worse."

Virtuous and vicious cycles are commonplace in so many aspects of life. Here is an example from the world of wellness: Someone starts on a regular exercise program, and because they are exercising they start to lose weight, which encourages them to adopt better nutrition, which causes them to lose more weight, which leads to better results in their exercise program.

Another example from the business world involved Amazon. In 2001, Jeff Bezos sketched one of the most influential business models ever devised on the back of a napkin. Bezos called the idea the "Virtuous Cycle." The whole thing starts with an exceptional customer experience, which attracts more customers.

More customers attract more third-party sellers, and more third-party sellers drive greater product selection. More product choice usually lowers the cost of goods and attracts even more customers. All this creates an ascending spiral of benevolence that uplifts all that it touches.

Feed any part of the circle, Bezos believed, and it will immediately accelerate the rest of the loop. This helped him understand the core of his business model, which allowed him to build the ecommerce behemoth we see today. Amazon has reaped all kinds of benefits from its savvy implementation of the virtuous cycle.

You get the picture: one good behavior encourages another, which reinforces the first good behavior.

Unfortunately, a vicious cycle can also easily occur—someone stops exercising for whatever reason, gains weight, starts eating the wrong things and gains more weight, and so on.

I've experienced firsthand the danger of a vicious cycle. Shortly after completing the merger of the three companies that formed Assurity, we were in trouble. Service levels to our policyholders and distributors were abysmal, and almost everyone was most concerned about protecting their turf from any changes. I knew I needed to get things turned around quickly. What did I do to get things turned around? An emphasis on first principles. I define first principles as the most fundamental truths.

Principle 1—Nothing good happens until you have the right people in the right seats. I knew I had some mid-level and senior people who shouldn't be leading certain areas of the company. I had planned to eventually address these individuals. I realized I didn't have the luxury of waiting. So I moved quickly to move these individuals out of their roles and replaced them with people who I knew would get the job done.

Principle 2—Effective communication is essential. I redoubled my efforts to provide authentic, open communication. Frequent and authentic communication clears away corporate politics and acts like a disinfectant.

Principle 3—Ensure a fair process is in place on how key decisions are being made. I made sure we had a sound and transparent approach on how we would make key decisions. Key decisions like what will be our surviving IT operating system, our imaging system, and so on.

Principle 4—Create a compelling vision of what could be. After a merger, it's a leader's responsibility to lead the other senior officers and mid-level managers through a process to develop a comprehensive vision of what the new entity can become. A compelling vision of the future needs to be developed and then effectively communicated to all the company's stakeholders. Remember that it's always easier to lead others toward a compelling vision of what could be than away from something else.

Guided by these four principles, we were able to move from a vicious cycle to a virtuous cycle—a virtuous cycle we built for many years.

I've seen business leaders facilitate a virtuous cycle in their company, and I've also seen them initiate a vicious cycle. Here are some of the elements that are common to business leaders who initiate and maintain a virtuous cycle.

- Are great communicators
- Consistently build trust
- Provide continuous sincere recognition
- Model exemplary behavior
- Provides opportunities for growth
- Create high expectations for performance

In previous chapters, I've discussed the need for great communication, the importance of building trust, and the magic of sincere recognition. I won't repeat my comments from those chapters but would encourage you to give them another look. In the balance of this chapter, I want to briefly discuss the last three.

Model Exemplary Behavior

As a business leader, you have to "walk your talk." If you show up late to work, leave early, abuse paid time off (PTO), and surf the internet or text most of the day, what do you believe associates in your work group think is appropriate behavior? Having the privilege of managing other people requires you to model exemplary behavior. A mentor of mine once said, "As a manager you don't have the luxury of doing what you want to do; you have to conduct yourself beyond reproach and be an example to others."

Provide People Opportunities for Growth

Recent research indicates this is the most important thing to millennials. Millennials are now our largest demographic group. They are our current workforce and the workforce of tomorrow. They're very interested in opportunities for growth and development. A key part of your responsibility as a business leader is giving people opportunities to enhance and build their knowledge, skills, and experience. Is there a special project they can take on? How about rotating into a different position? Suggest a book they should read or a seminar to attend. Most importantly, develop a comprehensive personalized development plan for each high potential associate.

Create High Expectations for Performance

What business leaders expect of their associates and the way they treat them largely determines their performance and progress. A unique characteristic of superior managers is the ability to create high performance expectations, which causes subordinates to stretch to fulfill. In short, if you treat your direct reports as stars, they will work to fulfill that expectation. Take a look at chapter 41, "The Pygmalion Effect."

In summary, every business leader has a choice: you can create a virtuous cycle, employing the six things I listed, or you can slip into a vicious cycle of negative reinforcing behavior. My message in this chapter is surprisingly simple, yet powerful: Create a virtuous cycle of positive expectations, which then becomes a self-fulfilling prophecy.

CHAPTER 25

Creating a Great Place to Work

One of my longstanding goals when I was CEO of Assurity was for Assurity to be a great place to work. Taken as a whole, we've done fairly well. We consistently had very high associate engagement scores, for many years in the top 10 percent of companies Gallup surveys worldwide. But creating a great place to work requires ongoing effort. It is something a business leader can never take for granted. Like a beautiful garden, it needs to be continuously tended. Those of you who are gardeners know you can't just plant a garden and consider your work done. The same continual attention is required for a great place to work.

In this time when we have so many associates working remotely, all of us who supervise others must put in more effort to ensure associate engagement. Also, remember we can have great programs at the corporate level, but if an associate doesn't feel good about their immediate supervisor and the area they are working in, that associate will not have good feelings about the company.

I've long loved reading the writings of Charles Handy. Now in his late eighties, Mr. Handy has been an oil executive, an economist, and a professor at the London Business School. I've read many of his books but particularly liked his book *21 Letters on Life and its Challenges*. The book is organized in the form of letters to his grandchildren. One of my favorites is letter eleven, "You are not a Human Resource," which contains this excerpt:

"I found that if you choose the right people to start with, and if they know what they are meant to do, they just get on with it without any checking or fuss. I call that leadership: creating the conditions for good work, choosing the right people and setting them standards of achievement that they can understand, and rewarding them when they meet them. You may say that I am just playing with words, but words describe the world, even the local world of the organization. I now believe that WORK needs to be ORGANIZED, that THINGS should be MANAGED, but that PEOPLE can only be encouraged, inspired and LED."

Mr. Handy's comments totally reflect my feelings.

A recurring theme in this book is if we want great performance, we need to be sure we have the right people in the right spots. You can't have high engagement if you are asking people to do something that doesn't fit with their natural talents.

So, "right people—right fit" is the foundation for having a great place to work. Beyond this foundation, here are the key things to creating a great place to work. You'll see as you review this list that most of these items go back to topics I've covered in previous chapters.

Great Communication

The most important thing after having the right people in the right seats is authentic, honest communication. What are the key aspects of authentic, honest communication? Here's my list:

1. Frequent and timely. Whenever, as a leader, you feel you are over-communicating, you're probably communicating the right amount. Remember: your associates crave direction from you. Don't get behind the curve. Your people should not learn about key things from other sources. They should hear first from you. Use all the methods available—in person meetings of course, but also Zoom, text, Jabber, Microsoft Teams, Webex, email, and an old-fashioned phone call.

2. Be careful of distortion and spin. Particularly in volatile times, don't try and create certainty when there isn't any. Practice "radical honesty." Don't feel an obligation to put a positive spin on the most negative situations. Be honest, open, and straightforward.

3. Be aware of nuancing what you need to communicate to avoid conflict. If something tough needs to be communicated, you need to do it—even if it causes conflict.

4. Although I'm generally in favor of more communication, not everything should be communicated. Jason Fried and David Heinemeier Hansson, who run the Chicago software company Basecamp, authored a delightful book titled *It Doesn't Have to Be Crazy at Work*. One practice they advocate is called "JOMO: Joy of Missing Out." They go on to state, "All workers do not need to be kept abreast of every corporate development." JOMO should happen so employees can concentrate on their own work projects. It is an important responsibility for every business leader to use judgment in determining what to communicate.

5. Be disciplined in your communication. Not every thought should be expressed. Good leaders stick to the script and avoid undisciplined communication.

Develop People

Companies with a great work environment help their associates become better. High potentials want their companies to help them with professional development. The best development plans are customized to the individual and don't usually involve companywide training programs. We need to have professional development plans customized to the individual. When you focus on their professional development, you are demonstrating to them you are interested in their careers and ultimate professional success.

A number of years ago we started requiring that all managers complete a written development plan on all the "high potentials" in their area. I cannot adequately express how important this turned out to be to the retention and career progress of these individuals.

Another powerful idea is to ask some of your people to experiment and solve problems that really matter. Give them a special project—something where they can demonstrate their expertise. Doing this is also an important way to provide recognition—"I'm giving you this special project because I have a lot of confidence in you."

Trust

More than foosball tables and free caffeinated beverages, there is a fundamental emotion that must be in place for employees to be happy: trust. Trust needs to be the common element between supervisors and associates in companies that are great places to work. Associates must trust each other and their supervisors to have a world-class working environment. Trust is built brick by brick; one bad move can negate years of built trust.

Recognition

Sincere, authentic recognition is essential for any company that wants to foster a great work environment. Every human being wants to be recognized and appreciated for the work they do. However, managers often wait until a quarterly or annual conversation to give their feedback and show recognition. Managers shouldn't wait for that one day of the year or quarter to recognize their employees. Instead, they should recognize them every day. This is only possible if associate recognition becomes part of a company's culture. I recommend you make associate recognition an essential part of what you do every day. Here is a novel idea: send a handwritten note to them via USPS. I bet they'll never forget this gesture and will probably keep your handwritten note forever.

Focus on Timely Feedback

Many years ago, we abandoned the traditional performance appraisal system. At the time, the idea of abandoning the traditional appraisal process—and all that followed from it—seemed heretical. But now, by some estimates, more than one-third of US companies are doing what we've done for years. From Silicon Valley to New York and in offices around the world, firms are replacing annual reviews with frequent, informal check-ins between managers and employees.

Traditional performance appraisal is incompatible with the mission-oriented, participative work environments favored by forward-thinking organizations. It is an old-fashioned, paternalistic, top-down, autocratic mode of management.

We have embraced the Entrepreneurial Operating System (EOS) concept of a "quarterly conversation." I believe one of the highest-impact disciplines you can practice as a leader/manager is the quarterly conversation. It is simply a one-on-one meeting with each of your direct reports every ninety days. It's an opportunity for each of you to share what's working and what's not. It's not a performance review; it's an important communication opportunity.

Gallup surveys have found that associates are more likely to be engaged with their work if they get frequent feedback from their bosses and if they are involved in setting these work related goals.

Little (or No) Politics and Bureaucracy

The two twin poisons of politics and bureaucracy will kill all best-place-to-work initiatives. Office politics foster a culture of distrust. In its worst form, it manifests itself in a manipulative culture where individuals do nefarious things that may advance their personal careers or causes but damage the whole organization.

Bureaucracy is an organizational disease that no amount of incremental therapy can solve. Bureaucracy is gripped by the ideology of controlism and worships at the altar of conformance. It cripples organizational vitality. It's a business killer.

Encourage Fun Camaraderie

Gallup found that close work friendships boost associate satisfaction by 50 percent, and people with a best friend at work are seven times more likely to engage fully in their work. Camaraderie is more than just having fun. It is also about creating a common sense of purpose and the mentality that we are in it together. In short, camaraderie promotes a group loyalty that results in a shared commitment to each other and the organization's success.

One of the most essential steps a manager can take is to structure ways for associates to interact socially. In this era of more associates working from home, we need to be creative in making that happen. What about encouraging "coffee break" discussion between associates? Or an online "lunch and learn" on some topic that would benefit everyone? Another idea I know many are already doing is to have Zoom FACs with other departments. Be creative—think outside the box.

Focus on Purpose

People want to be a part of something bigger than themselves. Individuals want to work for a company that is about more than top-line revenue growth and bottom-line profitability. It starts with an inspiring mission statement. At Assurity, we have a simple but elegant mission statement to "Help People through Difficult Times." As I said many times to our associates, "not only do we have a great place to work, but we have good work to do." I believe our mission statement is inspiring to all of our associates. Reinforce your company's mission, purpose, and values every chance you get. More on purpose in business in chapter 48.

Provide People Opportunities for Advancement

Associates need to know they are going to be provided professional opportunities. A key part of our culture is that we would always prefer to internally promote someone. In most cases this creates a virtuous cycle. One internal promotion begets more internal promotions.

As a top leader you've got to be aware of "talent hoarding." This happens when certain managers try to keep high potentials on their team because they don't want to train a new associate or fear losing the top performer's expertise on their team. A culture needs to be fostered where managers are rewarded and recognized for building the company's intellectual capital.

Treat People Well

A key business philosophy of mine is to be sure we treat each other well. I feel we need to acknowledge our duty to one another. I view that duty as helping our associates to grow and thrive. You will get asymmetric returns from being polite. Treat everyone the same until they prove otherwise. Seneca once said, "Wherever there is a human being, there is an opportunity for a kindness."

As I stated at the start of this chapter, creating a great place to work requires continual attention. In this time of managing a hybrid workforce, creating a great place to work requires more effort and new approaches. Remember, like a beautiful garden, creating a great place to work requires continuous attention.

CHAPTER 26
Initiative and Hard Work

Would you rather have an associate who:

- A. Does their job well as long as they're told exactly what to do and when to do it; or

- B. Someone who understands the wider purpose of their role and who thinks of ways they can improve their work and puts those ideas into practice?

I think we would agree we would prefer an associate with the attributes of the latter. We all like to see initiative in the people we work with every day. We know those who exercise initiative will strive to do their work better by thinking of new and creative approaches.

Initiative is a crucial skill that can serve you well in both your personal and professional life. If you wait to be told what to do, then you have waited too long. Initiative is not something you have or don't have. Usually, initiative comes more easily to areas of life that involve using an associate's inherent talents. This is another reason it's important for all of us to work in our areas of strength. Associates will naturally perform better when working on something that engages their natural talents.

Unfortunately, it has been my experience that initiative is too rare. But initiative is more important than ever. In the very competitive environment most industries are operating in, we need associates who can think on their feet and take action without waiting for someone to tell them what to do. Initiative is required to unleash ingenuity and innovation, which are critical for almost all companies.

What does taking initiative mean? Taking initiative means going the extra mile or going above and beyond your normal day-to-day to make things happen. Taking initiative means the ability to see something that needs to be done and deciding to do it without someone else telling you to do it. It means being proactive instead of reactive, thinking ahead and taking action.

As a business leader, what can you do to create an environment that will foster more initiative? Here are some practical ideas:

1. As mentioned earlier, be sure you hire for the right fit. Meaning that the associate possess the natural talents required for the position. You'll see more initiative from those who are working in their areas of strength.

2. Let your work colleagues know that initiative is important. Explain how being proactive will be good for the company and for them. Connect the dots between taking initiative and achieving long-term business objectives.

3. Recognize efforts even if they fail. As Bill Gates once said, "How a company deals with mistakes suggests how well it will wring the best ideas and talents out of its people." Supervisors should provide recognition to associates who try new things even if they didn't work out. This will show your whole area that trying new things is not just okay but encouraged. Be slow to correct and quick to commend. You need to help associates understand that the habit of taking initiative strengthens their personal brands. We all have known individuals who are known for taking initiative. They are always well regarded.

4. Reward successful initiatives. Recognition is a powerful force. Showing appreciation for an associate's initiative in front of senior leadership or during a staff meeting will likely

cause a virtuous cycle of more initiative.

5. Create an environment where associates are encouraged to share their knowledge and insights. As an example, when an associate attends a professional development course, they organize a brownbag lunch to share what they learned.

6. Encourage associates to work with different teams and departments. Create an environment where associates are encouraged to pitch in and help during times when a particular area is overloaded.

7. Thinking ahead should become a key part of the company's culture. Has your organization become good at thinking ahead, anticipating and preventing problems before they occur? Draw on your past experience and knowledge of where mistakes usually happen in certain types of projects and help your organization avoid these errors. Foreseeing challenges is greatly aided by good planning upfront. When working on an activity, set aside some time at the beginning to plan it well.

8. Create an organizational culture that is action oriented. I'm not for jumping off the cliff, but taking action is almost always better than inaction.

9. Become a goal-oriented organization. If an organization is goal oriented, it will naturally encourage initiative. Achieving an associate's personal goals and the area and corporate goals will require initiative.

10. Be a role model. Set a good example by demonstrating initiative in your own work. Become the type of person who spots and acts on opportunities. Always be on the lookout for ways to do things better.

A healthy, forward-looking organization will always choose action over inaction. I know some will disagree, but I think your organization will be healthier if you make more "go" errors than "no go" errors. Nothing significant has ever been created by playing it safe.

I'll conclude my comments on initiative with a quote I like from Mary Kay Ash:

> There are three types of people in this world: those who make things happen, those who watch things happen and those who wonder what happened.

Be the kind who makes things happen.

Hand in hand with initiative is the requirement to work hard in order to accomplish great things.

I was born into a German immigrant farm family and having a strong work ethic was a key family value. From an early age I was expected to help my maternal grandfather with various farm chores. Rightly or wrongly, from this early in life inchoation, I've always found idleness distasteful. I've never been happy sitting at the beach or engaging in mundane small talk.

When I entered the formal workforce after college, I didn't think I had much to learn about the importance of having a strong work ethic. I was wrong. Here are some of the key things I've learned:

To accomplish great things you'll have to work very hard. Harder than you ever imagined. In recent years I've been an active angel investor; watching startup founders and what they need to do to succeed is a revelation. They need to operate with their hair on fire most of the time. Extraordinary effort is the cost of entry for accomplishing anything significant.

Working smart is another important lesson. It is not enough to just work hard; you have to work smart. You have to apply your strong work ethic to those activities that will move the corporate ball forward. Be careful about just being busy. Don't confuse activity with results. If you talk to most corporate executives they will talk about how busy they are—but busy doing what? We can work very hard and fail because we are not working on the right thing. For most business leaders there are never enough hours in the day to accomplish what they feel they must. This is why we need to manage our work life to focus on the most essential.

You should also not confuse effort with results. Just because you put in the effort you still may not achieve your personal and organizational goals. Over the years I've seen a fair amount of effort be undone by countervailing forces. You work hard to secure a new client but find that your operational systems are not prepared for the new business, and you ultimately deliver poor service and lose the new client. Or you work hard at the gym but don't adopt a healthy diet. It is like what one of my personal trainers has said many times to me "you can't out exercise a bad diet."

If you are a business leader, you'll need to have an opinion on a variety of issues. Will you have done the work to have an opinion? Doing the work is the hard part. You'll have to do the research, do the reading and deep thinking to have an opinion. As Charlie Munger once said, "I never allow myself to have an opinion on anything that I don't know the other side's argument better than they do."

Here is another important work concept: Do the hard thing first. This approach to work became my style of prioritizing what needs to get done after reading Dr. Scott Peck's iconic book *The Road Less Traveled*. In this book Dr. Peck discussed the merits of delaying gratification. I too have become a fan of delayed gratification. Do the hard thing first.

If you want an easier future path, do the hard things first. If you want a hard path in the future, do the easy things first and put off addressing the difficult work. The difficult work won't go away if ignored. In many cases the difficult work probably involves some conflict. As I stated in chapter 7, conflict avoidance is at the heart of many interactable business problems. The author and athlete Jerzy Gregorek once said, "Easy decisions, hard life. Hard decisions, easy life." My own experience confirms the wisdom of this quote. Do the hard thing first.

I once heard Chris Davis, who heads up the eponymous Davis Funds, make the following comment: "We won't get every investment decision right, but it won't be because we didn't do the work."

Wise words—do the work to deserve success. I'm going to end this chapter with one of my favorite Teddy Roosevelt quotes: "There has never yet been a man in our history who led a life of ease whose name is worth remembering."

CHAPTER 27
Innovation

Businesses grow and succeed for many different reasons. Some are known for their exceptional products, others for their level of service, financial discipline, acquisition strategy or brilliant marketing. However, if you were to look at the organizations that truly stand out from their competitors, it would be clear that they all have one common factor: they all embrace innovation.

These innovative businesses include relatively new organizations such as Square and SpaceX, which are upending the payments industry and space exploration, respectively. Many established firms have implanted innovation into their corporate DNA. Long-established companies like Microsoft and Apple owe their ongoing success to constant reinvention and innovation. I think it is accurate to say no matter the industry, an organization cannot expect to maintain a competitive edge if innovation is not part of the overall business strategy.

All sagacious business leaders acknowledge the importance of innovation to their ultimate business success. But I think there is a lot of confusion around what innovation means. I expect if you ask ten business leaders to define innovation, you are likely to get at least seven different definitions.

If you google "innovation in business," the number of articles and white papers from both the popular press and academics are endless. All these writers and researchers bring a slightly different take on the importance of innovation and what it means.

There's a lot of debate around the topic, but at least in my opinion, most of it is just academic differences. Let me demystify the word and clarify what I think is a workable definition. My personal favorite is the definition by Merriam-Webster's online dictionary. They simply refer to innovation as "the introduction of something new." Now, this definition isn't just about inventing some new physical product. This definition also covers improvements in many other areas, such as business processes or business models, which are key sources of innovation.

Why is innovation important for business success?

We've all heard the phrase "adapt or die," and for businesses to achieve success in today's ultra-competitive environment, this is a universal truth. Simply put, companies today will not flourish if they do not embrace innovation and change. Here are three critical reasons why innovation in business is so important.

First, innovation helps companies grow. As mentioned earlier, if you want to grow your business in order to become more successful and profitable, there are a few ways you can go about achieving that goal. You might choose to plod along your current path, growing incrementally as you perfect your existing products and business models. This is a tough path and for many may not be realistic. Instead, you might choose to grow your business by merging or acquiring others, which is faster, but also typically a much more expensive and riskier avenue for growth. We need to remember the vast majority of acquisitions never achieve their preannounced objectives. Or you might choose to evolve by rethinking your products or business model—or both—which is a process that can lead to rapid expansion and allow you to scale your business very quickly. In other words, innovation.

Secondly, innovation keeps organizations relevant. The world around us is constantly changing, and innovation allows us to remain relevant and profitable. Just as a business startup has to offer something innovative in order to break into an industry, established organizations need to innovate in order to fend off competition and remain relevant in this changing environment.

Finally, innovation helps organizations differentiate themselves. At the core, innovation is about doing something differently from everyone else operating in the space. Innovation helps an organization differentiate itself and its products from the competition, which can be particularly powerful in a hypercompetitive industry or market. While delivering value to your customers should always be a company's main focus, doing so in a way that is memorable and different from everyone else can become a standout element of your brand identity and business strategy.

So, innovation is very important to business success, but most companies have not experienced any value creation from their innovation efforts. Why? Here are some common problems I've observed in implementing an innovation effort.

Establishing a Separate Innovation Area
Many businesses have set up a separate innovation area and given someone the title of "chief innovation officer." These businesses usually establish a separate physical space with cool-looking furniture, and the associates in the innovation are many times known for their creativity. This effort usually starts with a lot of fanfare and high hope. As the months go by, reality starts to intrude. The innovation area doesn't produce anything significant. Detractors in senior management continually point out the cost of this unit. Typically twelve to twenty-four months into the effort the area is either significantly downsized, dispersed into certain operating areas, or shut down altogether.

Now to be fair, some companies have done well over the years with a separate innovation area—think 3M. These companies have successfully institutionalized their innovation efforts. But these companies are rare and are typically large enterprises.

Not Thinking Long Term
Innovation that results in a competitive advantage takes time. It is never one thing or one event. Most businesses tend to focus more on short-term goals and results rather than thinking from a long-term perspective. In this process of achieving short-term targets, many management teams struggle with supporting a unit that is only an expense center and hasn't produced any meaningful revenue or bottom-line results.

Lack of Innovation Mindset

Another reason why innovation fails is due to the associate mindset within the organization itself. Associates need to have an innovative mindset to create something new. The culture for this mindset has to be cultivated within the organization itself, starting from the top and permeating to every level. Companies need to boost creativity, brainstorm new ideas, and nurture their associates to go one step beyond and think out of the box. Easy to say—very hard to do.

Fear of Failing

Let's say your organization tried to come up with a very innovative product to solve a user's problem. You have spent a considerable amount of money and resources on research and development, sales and marketing costs. But down the line, the product turns out to be a failure. What impact does it have on your associates for future breakthroughs? Associates tend to be more afraid of failing at something that they decide not to even try anything new at all. A sense of low confidence can develop among associates, manifesting as a reluctance to try new things or get involved in new challenging projects. An organization needs to be tolerant of failure.

Senior Management's Commitment

Many times, when an innovation effort fails, it reflects a lack of true commitment by senior management to advocate for and protect the innovation process. Innovation often starts strong and fades because it has no real continuous support. It is an expense center that typically produces little initial revenue and seldom profits. It takes a committed senior team to stay the course. This is why I had the head of Assurity Ventures Inc. (AVI) report directly to me, in effect protecting AVI from the rest of the company.

Relying on an Outside Consultant

Several years ago, Assurity worked with an innovation consulting firm in a year-long project to help us become more innovative. Although there were many good learnings from this effort, it became clear to me that an outside consultant will never magically implant the innovation gene into an organization's DNA. You won't become an innovative company by using an outside innovation consultant.

One of the key learnings I had from this work is the incredible difficulty in making breakthrough innovation happen in a 132-year-old, highly regulated firm like Assurity. We can do incremental innovation all day long, but breakthrough innovation is another matter. To participate and benefit from breakthrough innovation, I think it is better for established firms to partner with startups. This is why we formed Assurity Ventures. Over the past 5 years, Assurity Ventures has evaluated more than 1,000 insurtech and fintech firms. It's been a great experience, and organizationally we learned a great deal. There are a lot of smart, interesting people trying to disrupt almost every industry. For breakthrough innovation, consider partnering with startups.

So what does work? For most established firms, I believe in ingenuity over innovation. This is more than just semantics. There is a real difference. Ingenuity differs from innovation by focusing on solving problems by using the most efficient and effective resources readily available.

Ingenuity is the ability to come up with solutions that are original and clever given the constraints every organization faces. The lightbulb was a forty-year-old invention when Edison found a way to make it a commercial success. Google was not the first search engine. Amazon's Kindle followed a decade of electronic book readers. Apple's iPod was released five years after the first MP3 player hit the market. As technologies and markets converge, ideas appear to many people at the same time. At first, those ideas are out of reach, but gradually the gap between what's possible and what's practical gets smaller. Ingenuity enables a company to jump the gap before its competitors do.

Companies that embrace the value of ingenuity will definitely have a competitive advantage. So how do we foster more ingenuity? Here are some ideas:

1. Business leaders should encourage and enable their colleagues to think and act differently. Don't be bound by the

statement "this is the only way we do things around here." There are a lot of ways to do things.

2. Encourage A-B testing experiments. As a rule, companies should always run the inexpensive experiments first. Business leaders need to be thoughtful and ingenuous while encouraging experimentation.

3. When discussing new ideas and approaches to work, we need to move away from a culture of "no, but" to a culture of "yes, and." We need to create a safe place for ideas to be shared, discussed, and tested.

4. Too often in our business, we want things to be like they always have been. But that is not today's reality. In business today, virtually nothing remains fixed, and value propositions need to evolve. So not only is it important to launch an ingenious idea but also to constantly monitor the market and be prepared to revitalize the experience customers have with your brand to meet the changing competitive landscape.

5. In almost all cases, ingenuity is a team sport, not an individual activity. Get your whole team focused on fostering ingenuity.

6. Encourage a culture of an idea meritocracy. This is a culture where the best ideas win—regardless of where they originate in the company. I first read about an idea meritocracy in Ray Dalio's book *Principles*. Not all good ideas come from the top. I've always believed the best ideas come from those who are closest to doing the work.

7. Don't be afraid of failure. "Try, learn, and adjust" can be a very effective corporate mantra.

I love innovation, but I like ingenuity even more. Two quotes to end this chapter.

"Never tell people how to do things. Tell them what to do and they will surprise you with their ingenuity." —General George S. Patton

"Ingenuity, plus courage, plus work, equal miracles." —Bob Richards, two-time Olympic gold medalist pole vaulter, author of *The Heart of a Champion*

CHAPTER 28
Meetings

I feel corporate America has always loved meetings a little too much. Scheduling a meeting seems to be the answer to addressing almost any corporate problem or opportunity, and the COVID-19 pandemic has accelerated this problem as managers schedule more meetings to supervise their direct reports, which are now working remotely. A surfeit of meetings for sure with all the attendant grievances and complaints of "death by meeting."

Much has been written and said about the evils of business meetings. Here is a list of typical meeting problems:

1. Lack of a clear purpose. The meeting is ad hoc without a written agenda—or with a poorly constructed agenda.

2. Unprepared participants. This usually manifests itself in a meeting where the end result is "when all is said and done, more is said than done."

3. Meeting participants go down rabbit holes. The meeting leader allows "scope creep."

4. Presentation, not conversation. Reading bullet points off a PowerPoint slide rarely encourages authentic, genuine conversation to solve problems.

5. The wrong people are in the room.

6. Too many people are in the room. Unless the purpose of the meeting is to exchange information, having more than eight people in the room impedes worthwhile discussions.

7. Failing to document the action points; develop "to-dos" and appropriate follow-up.

8. Allowing meetings to go on too long. I've seldom seen a meeting that goes beyond ninety minutes to be of any value.

9. The sheer quantity of meetings crowds out solo work and disrupts critical deep thinking.

10. Meetings are too frequent. Regularly scheduled meetings are held whether they are needed or not. The meeting leader doesn't exercise judgment on whether a meeting is necessary.

11. The meeting leader allows certain individuals to dominate the meeting.

12. Conversely, the meeting leader doesn't encourage participation and doesn't attempt to draw out thoughts and ideas from all participants.

Unfortunately, this is just a partial list. Poking fun at meetings has become de rigueur among critics of modern business life. I wonder how many *Dilbert* cartoons were spawned by bad meetings.

Most of us dislike meetings because they are boring, frustrating, and, most importantly, don't help accomplish corporate objectives. The sad reality is having a bad meeting is just normal. I once believed the answer to all the problems with meetings was to have fewer meetings. In fact, I know of one respected business leader who banned all meetings at his company for a month. After that month, the idea was to add back only essential meetings. I don't think this is a bad idea, and I'm always in favor of fewer meetings. Unfortunately, it was reported to me that this experiment was only partially successful.

Reading the book *Traction* by Gino Wickman changed my mind on meetings. Here is what Mr. Wickman wrote:

> "For now and forever, let's dispel the myth that all meetings are bad. That meetings are a waste of time, and that there are already too many of them. The fact is that well-run meetings are the moment of truth for accountability."

After embracing the meeting concepts in the Entrepreneurial Operating System (EOS), I became convinced the answer wasn't to ban most meetings but instead to insist they have the proper structure. Two concepts from EOS—the "Level 10 meeting" and "meeting pulse"—are the primary reasons I'm an advocate of EOS.

Through painful experience in participating in more meetings than I can remember, I have learned the best meetings have a few common characteristics whether in person or virtually. Here is what I feel are the key elements of a great meeting:

1. A great meeting starts on time and is not scheduled to go beyond ninety minutes.

2. A great meeting has a clear and well-organized agenda.

3. The right people are in attendance.

4. The issue(s) to be resolved are clear and appropriate background information has been provided in advance.

5. The meeting leader doesn't allow the group to head down rabbit holes.

What follows is additional background on these key elements of a great meeting:
1. **A great meeting starts on time and is not scheduled to go beyond ninety minutes.**
   It is important a company's culture doesn't tolerate

individuals wandering into meetings five, ten, or fifteen minutes late. In organizations where I have been the leader on time was being in the meeting room ready to go five minutes before the scheduled start time.

Most meeting should not be scheduled to go beyond ninety minutes. If you have brought in people from the outside, it may be necessary for the meeting to exceed ninety minutes. If this is the case, after ninety minutes, schedule a break. Most people cannot stay focused beyond ninety minutes.

We need to also remember in most situations, discussions expand to the time allotted. An important cultural norm to foster is that meetings don't need to run for the fully scheduled time. I often close meetings early with the following, "We are all going to get a bonus today in the form of the gift of time."

2. **A great meeting has a clear and well-organized agenda.**
It is the leader of the meeting's principal responsibility to be sure a well-thought-through and organized agenda is provided in advance to all meeting participants. In addition to having the right items on the agenda, I like to provide a suggested time for each agenda item. I usually don't feel the need to slavishly adhere to the allotted time if the conversation is worthwhile.

3. **The right people are in attendance.**
To have an effective meeting, the right people need to be in the room. When dealing with important topics, it is important all affected areas of the organization are present. A key meeting result is to build consensus for a future direction. This can only happen if all affected areas are represented and participated in making the decision.

4. **The issue(s) to be resolved are clear and appropriate background information has been provided in advance.**

Using EOS terminology, "Identify, Discuss and Solve (IDS)" is the most important part of any meeting. This is where the real work gets done, but so often it is poorly done. Why? It is almost always a waste of time to just get together and talk about an issue. Somebody has to do the hard work of researching the issue and proffering a solution in order to have a worthwhile discussion. This is why I like the Amazon 6-Page narrative. I first discussed this concept in chapter 12, "Clear Writing Produces Clear Thinking." As a reminder, this is a well-researched, detailed memo or white paper that someone or a team has produced regarding a particular problem or opportunity. In the memo, the authors discuss the problem or opportunity and propose a solution.

Developing a good six pager is hard work but incredibly effective. Doing a PowerPoint presentation is much easier for the presenter but much less effective. Remember, clear writing produces clear thinking. With the appropriate background information, you can have an effective discussion.

5. **The meeting leader doesn't allow the group to head down rabbit holes.**
   Going down rabbit holes by raising tangential issues is a common meeting problem. It is the responsibility of the meeting leader to not allow this to happen. A good way to avoid this problem is to maintain an issues list. When a new problem or opportunity comes up, rather than take time at this meeting, it goes on the issues list. You can then decide to perhaps deal with this issue at a future meeting.

6. **All meeting participants should understand that not every thought they have should be expressed.**
   Remember, in most meetings silence can be golden. Silence gives you time to think and reflect on what has already been said. In many meetings I remind myself of the quote attributed to Abraham Lincoln: "Better to remain silent and be thought a fool than to speak and remove all doubt." Or

the oft quoted proverb, "Speech is silver, silence is golden."

I'm convinced good meetings are the lifeblood of any organization, but you need adherence to some fundamental tenets to make a meeting worthwhile.

CHAPTER 29
Benign Neglect

Here is my definition of "benign neglect."

> An attitude or policy of noninterference or neglect of a situation, which may have a more beneficial effect than assuming responsibility; well-intended neglect of a problem or issue.

Benign neglect has always been difficult for me. One of my Gallup Top 5 Strengths is "Activator." This means I have a strong proclivity for action. It's difficult for me to ignore or not act on every problem that comes my way. But experience has taught me that it's not wise to try and solve every problem or issue that comes my way.

I've come to understand good leaders practice benign neglect. They don't try to solve every problem or issue. They aren't fussing around in their direct reports work probing and digging into every real and potential issue and generally interfering with letting others do their jobs. Good leaders are likewise parents with their children: they pick their battles.

Hasty action can make matters worse. We can fall victim to Forrester's Law, which states that "in complicated situations, efforts to improve things can make them worse, sometimes much worse, and on occasion calamitous." Forrester's Law is based on work done by Dr. Jay Forrester, who was a professor of management at MIT. His research demonstrated we can often expect surprising and dismaying results from hasty actions—especially when dealing with complex problems. Many times it is just better to leave things alone, and often the problem resolves itself without any outside action.

This is critically true in medicine. I've received advice from physician friends that many illnesses will solve themselves without medical intervention—they go on to say in most cases with better results than medical intervention.

The late Dr. Otis Young, the longtime senior minister at First Plymouth Church—Lincoln and a mentor to me, wrote the following in his excellent book *Reach Out and Live* when discussing the attributes of leadership.

> "The fourth principle of leadership is the art of knowing what to overlook. This is true in all parts of life: parenthood, marriage, and especially in the leadership of an organization. Determine what's important and needs your attention and what does not. Some items which you might at first think need your attention will improve if you do nothing. It's what I call "benign neglect." Every good physician knows this. Not every symptom needs to be treated. A wise physician once said to me, "Don't let us doctors do too many tests on you because they'll find something wrong and want to fix it. No one has perfect health. There are some things that do not need to be fixed. The first principle is "do no harm."

Masterly inactivity is a concept made famous by British Prime Minister Benjamin Disraeli. He popularized this concept in dealing with certain foreign relationship issues. "Masterly inactivity" is often called wise letting alone. It is just another form of benign neglect.

When I was young and trying to solve every problem that came my way, another mentor of mine advised me

"Remember, more problems are lived through than solved."

So true and very wise counsel. A large part of wisdom is knowing what to ignore. A large part of expertise is knowing where to place your attention.

In most business there are many areas where benign neglect can prove helpful. Examples include one-off customer complaints and associates lobbying for exceptions to existing rules or established processes. Early in my career as a business leader, I would try and react to all those events. Almost by accident, I found out that many of these issues disappeared if I did nothing. Not every articulated issue requires immediate action.

I hope I've convinced you of the merits of benign neglect. But one warning: don't use benign neglect to justify conflict avoidance and not addressing problems or issues that need to be addressed. Don't use the concept of benign neglect to hide behind because unconsciously you want to avoid addressing a festering people problem or other difficult issue. As a business leader, first and foremost you are in this role to exercise good judgment. Use good judgment to discern what needs to be addressed and what is better left alone.

Choosing your battles is an important competency. Business leaders who are good at this ask themselves two key questions:

1. Do I need to address this issue to achieve our long term objectives?

2. If so, is this the right time?

In deciding what to address, it is important to keep your corporate values front and center. Violation of corporate values requires immediate action. Many other things may benefit from benign neglect. I'll end this chapter with a quote from the great American philosopher and psychologist, William James: "The art of being wise is the art of knowing what to overlook."

CHAPTER 30
Narratives

I'll start this chapter with my definition of a narrative.

> A narrative is a way of presenting or understanding a situation or series of events that reflects and promotes a particular point of view.

In essence, it's the stories we collectively tell ourselves and others about some issue, problem, challenge, or opportunity. During my business career, I've come to appreciate how the right narrative can propel a company forward while the wrong narrative can cause a downward spiral and may result in the total failure of the business. The best story always wins. Great ideas explained poorly can go nowhere while old or wrong ideas told compellingly can lead a company down the wrong path.

There are numerous examples of companies and industries that suffered and failed because they embraced a false narrative. Here are a few:

Company	Summary of False Narrative
Kodak	Digital photography will never catch on
Blockbuster	Consumers won't adapt to streaming technology
Blackberry	Consumers will never want a touch screen on their smartphone

Almost every industry has a narrative or two that is not based in reality, and as a result, poor decisions are made. A negative narrative in the life insurance industry is "the big opportunity for our industry to serve the vast underserved middle market." Part of this narrative is true—unlike previous generations, the percentage of US households that own life insurance is at an all-time low. Additionally, it is a well-known fact that many US households are underinsured compared to the past. Both of these facts are true. Many in our industry extrapolated these facts into the "big opportunity narrative." What they failed to consider is that changing consumer preferences and values have fundamentally changed the demand for life insurance. Unlike previous generations, younger people do not value the protection life insurance provides. Embracing the big opportunity narrative caused many life insurance companies to believe they would ignite demand if they only came up with better marketing or a more contemporary way to interact with the ultimate consumer. Many companies in my industry have spent millions and millions of dollars trying to make that happen. But yet life insurance sales growth over the past ten years has been less than 2 percent annually.

It is like a men's tie manufacturer believing if it only came up with better fabrics, designs, or methods of distribution, this would reignite the demand for men's ties. Recently I was at a formal board meeting where only two out of twelve men were wearing a tie. As recently as a few years ago, every man there would have been in a suit and tie. There is not a realistic narrative on how the sale of men's ties will again flourish.

An alluring but false narrative driving consolidation in the financial services industry is that only the biggest players have enough scale to compete in the digital era. Not true. You do need to be of a certain size to have the intellectual capital and afford new technology, but the biggest players' bureaucracies greatly hinder their effectiveness. Many small- and midsized companies are in a better position to compete in the current environment.

In contrast to a false narrative, a positive narrative can propel a company forward. Microsoft had been moribund for many years when Satya Nadella took over as CEO in 2014. The company was at risk of becoming technologically irrelevant and viewed as spiraling toward obsolesce. Before Mr. Nadella's arrival, Microsoft had missed almost every significant computing trend of the 2000s—mobile phones, search engines, social networking—while advocating a narrative of protecting and milking its main source of revenue, the Windows operating system. When Satya took over, he first set to dramatically alter its corporate narrative from a "fixed mindset" to a "growth mindset." He embraced innovation, and one result was Microsoft's enormous cloud computing business. Mr. Nadella also started an acquisition campaign, bringing on great brands like LinkedIn.

In his insightful book *Thinking Fast and Slow*, behavioral economist and Nobel Laureate Daniel Kahneman explained that narrative fallacy arises from our efforts to make sense of the world. Our bias toward sense-making leads us to weave isolated facts into explanatory patterns, jump to conclusions, and infuse experience with logic and causation that are often false. Don't design a false narrative to make yourself feel better. Remember Kodak. Even though a Kodak engineer invented the digital camera, the company embraced a false but comforting narrative that the market for film would stay robust—but failure followed.

What can an individual business leader do? First, be sure you immediately kill any false narrative that may start in your area of responsibility. Usually these narratives are "tribal"—our area against some other part of the company. You can't allow that narrative to get started in your area. Second, promote a positive narrative about how your area and how what you do supports the accomplishments of the company's long-term corporate objectives. Remember, being a business leader involves a lot more than just setting targets and entering numbers into a spreadsheet. It requires an understanding of human nature and an appreciation for the power of stories. You need to be certain the stories told in your area are helping your company achieve its long-term objectives.

Former Herman Miller CEO Max De Pree once said, "The first responsibility of a leader is to define reality." Mr. De Pree's important insight is that reality does not define itself. Experienced leaders recognize that truths obvious to them may not be widely understood throughout their organizations. Reality requires interpretation, and narrative work animates that effort.

One of my longstanding goals as a business leader is to be as rational as possible—not to be too pessimistic or optimistic. As the late, great investor John Templeton once said, "I want to be known as a realist with a hopeful nature." This has been my goal as well: to be truthful and transparent about any situation.

Every organization's culture contains diverse narratives that compete for dominance. Effective business leaders develop consensus for stories that motivate and inspire while remaining grounded in reality. It is no coincidence that market-leading companies like Apple, Microsoft, Walmart, and Starbucks have powerful narratives. We need narratives grounded in reality that propel work toward the achievement of our long-term objectives. We can create narratives that energize and inspire associates, excite partners, and attract customers. Remember that the stories we tell ourselves and others will largely create our future results.

CHAPTER 31
Strategic Planning

I've long been a student of strategic planning; volumes have been written about the development of corporate strategy. I believe an effective planning process is foundational to future corporate success. All business leaders know strategy is important. Yet for many companies their annual planning process isn't producing the desired result. Many view their company's annual budgeting and planning process as a necessary evil. In fact, one year a new manager said to me, "I can't wait for this planning and budgeting work to be done so I can get back to my real work." This is probably an unspoken sentiment by many in American business.

Planning is a major concern to corporate America. The National Association of Corporate Directors (NACD) completes an annual survey of its members with a list of twenty common board agenda items and asks them to identify the top three for the coming year. Invariably, year after year, strategy heads the list. Strategic planning is top of mind for most corporate leaders and their boards.

Although boards are very interested in strategic planning, there is a great deal of frustration and tension between most boards and their executive teams over the strategic planning process. Here is a typical scenario—the CEO or owner hires an outside consultant. The consultant helps the company develop a comprehensive situational analysis in an effort to get the whole executive group and board on the same page. Later, the consultant serves as a facilitator for the CEO and the executive group in an offsite meeting where they jointly develop the annual strategic plan. In days past, the plan was typically housed in a thick black binder and ultimately adorned the shelf of each executive's office. Unfortunately, it was only rarely referred to as the year went by. Now it's a "document file," which is rarely consulted after being disseminated. A great deal of work and effort, but really nothing to show for it. Nothing really changed for the company as a result of all this work.

There is a plethora of reasons strategic planning has failed for so many companies. Here are some common problems I have observed over the years:

1. Having a homerun mentality. Too often, top business leaders expect an immediate and big payoff from planning. In reality, the payoff usually comes gradually as a result of avoiding serious blunders, developing consistent strategies, and clearly communicating the corporate strategy throughout the organization. It is the exception when planning produces immediate measurable results.

2. Not having approaches which encourage growth. To achieve growth, companies should make generating new opportunities a major corporate objective. Executive management need to encourage all managers to be on the outlook for growth opportunities and must establish the principle that achieving high returns without growth is not enough.

3. Not tailoring the plan to the situation. Effective planning can't be a cookie-cutter approach; there is no single right way to do it. A company facing tight financial constraints will want to use planning to identify expense savings and to maintain tight control of resource allocation. In contrast, when a company is most concerned about growing—the identification of new opportunities is most important. In short, planning should serve the company's current needs and be consistent with the company's financial and organizational capabilities.

4. Executive management fails to articulate a vision and the fundamental values of the organization. No amount of planning can substitute for leadership and the establishment of a healthy corporate culture. Senior leaders must define annual, intermediate, and long-term corporate goals. They need to make the connection between the company's mission and values and its corporate objectives. Establishing the company's mission and values is the foundation on which great companies are built.

5. As McKinsey consultants Chris Bradley, Martin Hirt, and Sven Smit relayed in their book *Strategy Beyond the Hockey Stick*, "Through the planning process most managers will try to secure resources for the coming year while defending accountability for the returns on these investments as far as possible into the future." Business leaders need to be on guard for this tendency.

6. Another villain identified in *Strategy Beyond the Hockey Stick* is that the strategy process is loaded with individual and institutional biases, and group dynamics in the strategy room often distort results. I've previously witnessed this time and again. In a respectful way, institutional biases and negative group dynamics need to be called out.

7. Most management teams' planning will be focused on incremental change, but success usually requires bigger moves than most companies are willing to make.

8. Confusing strategic thinking with strategic planning. The purpose of planning is to create winning strategies, not thick planning books. In companies where strategic thinking is prevalent, strategies deal with the realities of market and competitive conditions. New opportunities are pursued aggressively, strategies adapt to external events in a timely and coherent fashion, and planning focuses on substance,

not form. Strategic planning can play a key role in making strategic thinking a way of life.

9. Overly optimistic forecasts result in something called the *planning fallacy*. This term was first coined by behavioral psychologists Daniel Kahneman and Amos Tversky. The planning fallacy occurs when plans and forecasts assume the best case and ignore the base rates of similar cases in the past.

10. The board of directors feels it is their responsibility to be very involved in developing the company's strategy. Boards cannot develop the company's strategy. The boards responsibility is to challenge and critique the strategy management has developed. They have ongoing oversight responsibilities to monitor management's implementation of the agreed upon strategy.

This is only a partial list; there are many things that can go wrong with strategic planning but the number one reason I've seen for failure is viewing the planning process as an annual one-time event. As such, the process is completely at odds with the way most of us actually make important strategic decisions, which are not constrained by the calendar. We make decisions that shape our company's strategy and determine its future—decisions about mergers and acquisitions, product launches, corporate restructuring, and the like—outside the planning process typically in an ad hoc fashion, sometimes without rigorous analysis or productive debate. Critical decisions are made incorrectly or not at all. More than anything else, this disconnect— between the way planning works and the way decision making happens—explains the frustration, if not outright antipathy, most executives feel toward strategic planning.

We live in a time of rapid change, and firms that will ultimately succeed need to adopt an entrepreneurial mindset and foster a culture that is able to take advantage of opportunities as they come about. A plan is only useful if it can survive reality. Every companies' reality is a future filled with unknowns. An annual plan cannot contemplate all the things which will happen in the year ahead.

So here is the paradox of planning.

President Dwight D. Eisenhower said it best: "Plans are nothing, but planning is everything." I couldn't agree more. The discipline of going through an annual planning process is very important, but strict adherence to a plan developed once a year makes no sense. An important reality of every plan is to plan on the plan not going according to plan.

What I think should be the most important results for any planning process is to establish a strategic direction. I like what Nick Tasler, an organizational consultant psychologist, author and speaker, wrote in a May 7, 2014 *Harvard Business Review* article titled "3 Myths that Kill Strategic Planning": "Decide on which broad opportunities to focus your time, people, and money, and which opportunities to starve." The tradeoffs companies make are what distinguish them strategically from other firms. This discipline helps establish the firm's strategic direction. After establishing an overall strategic direction it positions the firm to take full advantage of "strategic opportunism."

The next chapter in this book is about this important concept.

Strategic thinking means deciding not to pursue some initiatives in order to concentrate the bulk of your resources in other areas. Strategic thinking is about getting the right things done well. The corollary of this truth is that strategy requires leaving some things undone. As Peter Drucker famously said, "There is nothing quite so useless as doing efficiently that which should not be done at all." An effective strategic planning process should establish the company's overall strategic direction and put management in a position to develop and capitalize on opportunities consistent with their strategic direction.

So here again is the paradox of planning: the annual plan is close to worthless, but the process and discipline it brings are invaluable. Remember, strategic planning can't have an impact if it doesn't drive decision-making. A strategic plan is not a set-it-and-forget-it document. To be effective, it has to be a living and breathing document that guides decision-making and allocates resources. Done right, strategic planning can have an enormous impact on a company's performance and long-term value. I'm an advocate of effective planning but not of plans. I'll close with a Charlie Munger quote on planning:

> "At Berkshire there has never been a master plan. Anyone who wanted to do it, we fired because it takes on a life of its own and doesn't cover new reality. We want people taking into account new information."

Over the years, my view of strategic planning has changed rather dramatically. I'm now solidly in Mr. Munger's camp.

CHAPTER 32
Strategic Opportunism

In the previous chapter I mentioned the concept of "strategic opportunism." This chapter will provide more information on this important concept. Business today is characterized by volatility, uncertainty, complexity, and ambiguity (VUCA). Under such challenging conditions, it becomes questionable whether long-term plans, objectives, and systematic analysis still serve a useful purpose.

The 2021 fourth quarter issue of *Bank Director Magazine* contained an article titled "The Dinsdales and the Chandlers." The article profiled these two preeminent family banking dynasties and shared some of the wisdom they accumulated over generations. Here is what Sid Dinsdale, CEO of Pinnacle Bank, said about strategic planning,

> "We don't believe in strategic planning. We think it's the dumbest thing anybody could do. Our strategic plan is simple: We want to make really good earnings, we want to have really good asset quality, and we want to have enough capital so we can do whatever we want when the opportunity rises."

I've come to agree with Mr. Dinsdale's sentiments about traditional strategic planning.

One big misconception shared by many management teams is that in building a strategy you turn inherent uncertainty into certainty. Many management teams feel because they have developed a comprehensive strategic plan with all the accompanying metrics that they have a game plan which won't be subject to the vicissitudes of the economy, competition, changing consumer preferences, etc. Management teams should be watchful of pursuing the illusion of certainty.

Recognizing this reality, Roger Martin, dean of the Rotman School of Management at the University of Toronto, and A. G. Lafley, former CEO of Procter & Gamble, coauthored the book *Playing to Win: How Strategy Really Works.*

Here are four overarching themes from *Playing to Win:*

1. **Understand that there are no guarantees.**

    As mentioned earlier, a common misconception is that strategy is about "turning uncertainty into certainty." But it isn't true. The world is inherently an uncertain place, and no choices made today can make future uncertainty go away.

2. **Define strategy.**

    The purpose of strategy is to deal proactively with inevitable change. A strategic plan cannot anticipate all the change that will come. So, think of a strategy as an outline that will help you make good decisions as you move forward, and react to various issues as they arise. Strategy means making the best possible choices you can make today and then being responsive when things change, both good and bad.

3. **Prepare to be flexible.**

    Be prepared to make revisions to your strategy as conditions change. Strategy should be flexible and responsive to changes in outcomes and environment. Be comfortable with editing your strategy to properly react to changing conditions.

4. **Appreciate the value of strategy.**

    After emphasizing fluidity is necessary for a comprehensive strategy, you might be pondering, what is the value of a strategic plan? While you shouldn't expect strategy to eliminate uncertainty, developing a formalized strategic direction is most of all an important discipline. Through this process management and the board should understand the company's strengths, weaknesses, opportunities and threats (SWOT Analysis). From this background work, a strategic direction can be developed on how to improve the business.

Let me provide a little more background on the concept of a strategic direction. A strategic direction refers to the plans that need to be implemented for an organization to progress toward achieving its annual, intermediate, and long-term goals. This strategic direction should allow the company to fulfill its mission and be consistent with the company's values. Going through an effective planning process, a management team should establish an overall strategic direction—for example, "we hope to grow sales by 8 percent a year and achieve this by 4 percent organic growth and 4 percent by acquisitions when measured over any three-year period." Notice that in setting strategic direction, you don't say how many acquisitions or when. You leave this open to react to what becomes available on appropriate terms. I've always liked Warren Buffet's comments about acquisitions: "In looking for acquisitions we adopt the same attitude one might find appropriate in looking for a spouse: It pays to be active, interested, and openminded, but it does not pay to be in a hurry."

So much is uncertain but with a sound strategic direction the management team can then be watchful for opportunities consistent with their strategic direction. In other words, strategic opportunism.

More and more I've come to embrace "strategic opportunism." Strategic opportunism is the ability to remain focused on long-term objectives while staying flexible enough to recognize and capitalize on new opportunities or better unplanned pathways to achieve them. This approach to planning proves difficult for individuals who want everything meticulously planned with accompanying rigid timetables and budgets.

But this rigid approach to planning doesn't work in the face of VUCA. Thinking both strategically and opportunistically is not easy. It requires a tolerance for ambiguity and a vigilant eye for new ideas. It requires, in other words, a toughminded approach to an inherently messy process—the ability to take action in the midst of uncertainty. In its inherent disorderliness, strategic opportunism requires a great deal not only from senior management but also from middle management, who must be able to tolerate working with a fluid set of agendas. Business leaders with a high need for following a preset schedule and budget will likely find strategic opportunism frustrating.

So how do we balance or reconcile the need for flexibility and being opportunistic with the potential danger of reacting to and chasing every whim and new idea that may come along? First, we all need to remember strategy at its core is about making choices. It is important to establish a well-thought-through strategic direction that will allow management to say no to opportunities that don't fit with the company's strategic direction. Conversely it allows management to jump on opportunities consistent with the company's strategic direction. How do we make choices on which opportunities to pursue? To help make these choices, I like filters.

Filters are a great way to avoid expending time and energy on things that should never happen. Here are some filter ideas:

1. Is this opportunity consistent with the company's strategic direction?

2. Does this opportunity fall within the company's overall risk tolerance?

3. Does this opportunity have an acceptable level of complexity? What is the administrative or operational lift?

4. Will this opportunity, if successfully implemented, improve our business profile and differentiate us from our many competitors?

5. Using realistic assumptions, will this opportunity meet our return expectations?

A winning combination in today's unpredictable business world is establishing a strategic direction and then pursuing strategic opportunism with the appropriate filters. Look for opportunities which can propel the company forward. Try to only pursue unfair fights where it's almost assured your company will win.

CHAPTER 33
Luck

What role does luck play in business and personal success? I do believe luck plays a large part in determining business and personal success. Baseball player Lefty Gomez famously said he'd rather be lucky than good. Yet as a society we tend to downplay the role luck plays in success, instead preferring to apportion success to our own hard work and aptitude.

Acknowledging the part luck plays in their lives isn't easy for most people. It's tempting to take full credit for our own successes, especially if we've had quite a few. Acknowledging the role luck plans in our careers or business would oblige us to accept that we have less control over what happens in our lives than most of us want to admit. Randomness can play out in subtler ways, causing us to resist explanations that involve luck. In particular, many of us seem uncomfortable with the possibility that personal success might depend to any significant extent on chance. As E. B. White once wrote, "Luck is not something you can mention in the presence of self-made men."

It's hard to determine what is dumb luck and what is unfortunate risk. Take investing. Investing is a game of probabilities, and almost all probabilities are less than 100 percent. You can make a good bet with the odds in your favor and still lose, or conversely you can make a reckless bet and still win. It's difficult to judge others' performance—lots of good decisions end up on the unfortunate side of risk and vice versa.

Alex Lieberman is the cofounder and chair of the *Morning Brew* newsletter. Mr. Lieberman has some interesting thoughts on luck. On the March 19, 2022, podcast, "We Study Billionaires," he describes the difference between controlled and uncontrolled luck. Mr. Lieberman indicated with controlled luck you actually had a hand in the luck that occurred. You did something which when lady luck smiles on you, you are in a position to capitalize on the lucky circumstances. Uncontrolled luck in contrast is when you haven't done anything to cause your lucky circumstances. An example would be being born into a good family in the USA.

Many people believe their success is solely due to talent and hard work, but "this is because most people underestimate the role of chance." Says psychologist Dr. Elizabeth Nutt Williams, "We do a lot of work to prepare for our careers—education, training, putting in long hours—all of which tend to be in our control." "People don't like to acknowledge the role of luck in their work, as it undermines this feeling of being in control," adds Williams.

Psychologists have found that people tend to estimate the likelihood of an outcome based on how easily they recall similar circumstances (by a process called "the availability heuristic"). This means that when talented, hardworking people think of their success, the first thing that comes to mind is the hard work they put into the task, not the fortunate circumstances that enabled them to succeed, explains psychologist Daniel Kahneman in his book *Thinking, Fast and Slow.*

Even harder to recall is the remote, abstract idea that they may not have prospered in different circumstances. Studies show events that work to our disadvantage are easier to recall then those that affect us positively—meaning we are again, less likely to feel lucky. Everyone remembers working hard, so people are more likely to overestimate how much of their success is due to hard work rather than something much more slippery like luck.

Because of the role luck plays in business success, I've always been skeptical about business gurus. The business world can often be gripped by the cult of the guru, whereby prominent thinkers proclaim to have found the secret to success in this or that field. They make their career out of informing the rest of us how to go about replicating such success.

I believe luck plays a large role in individual and businesses success. If this is true and luck is so important, how do we get to be luckier? Is creating luck even possible? Yes, I think to some extent you can. Here are some ideas:

First, no matter how powerful and successful you become, retain a measure of humility. Individuals who acknowledge their own vulnerability sometimes seem able to miraculously summon those who can help them achieve their goals. All of us have chance encounters, but luck-oriented people are humble enough to believe that in some cases, they have to seize these encounters as they happen, as the world won't easily offer up such opportunities again. In sum, they intuitively understand where their personal control ends, and the rest of the universe begins.

Second, be driven by a profound intellectual curiosity. Be genuinely interested in the lives of others. Constantly seek to improve yourself and your business. Again and again, question the norm. People who create more personal luck read, explore, reframe, discuss, argue, sample, and discard, all with an internal resolve to better themselves and challenge, inflame, and expand the perspectives they bring to their lives and businesses. Their eagerness to question their surroundings increases the likelihood that they can grab an opportunity as it swoops past.

Third, have an optimistic attitude—believe in opportunity. Be a giver of energy rather than a taker of it. How we perceive our own luckiness can become a self-fulfilling prophecy.

Learn from your mistakes. Fool me once, shame on you, fool me twice, shame on me. The same can be said for mistakes. The only people who don't make mistakes are people who don't do anything. People who improve their luck learn from their mistakes and never make the same mistake twice.

Perseverance. Being persistent is important in not allowing bad luck to overwhelm us. It's hanging in there no matter how tough the circumstances. Remember the old adage I shared in chapter 20: "When things get tough, the tough get going."

Be grateful for the luck you have experienced. An experiment by David DeSteno, a psychologist at Northeastern University, offers evidence that gratitude many times leads to a greater willingness to support the common good. In an unexpected twist, we may find that recognizing our luck and being grateful for our luck increases our good fortune.

Finally, deserve luck. You have to be prepared to be fortunate. This means having put in the hard work, developing the skills and knowledge to capitalize on the luck when it comes your way. Remember, "little is achieved without talent, and nothing is achieved without hard work." In David McCullough's excellent biography on James Adams, titled "John Adams," he shared a quote from a letter John Adams wrote to his wife, Abigail, during a difficult period in the revolutionary war: "We can't guarantee success in this war, but we can deserve it." This means doing the hard work so when lady luck shines on you, you are in a position to capitalize on it.

I'm going to end this chapter by introducing the concept of return on luck. Jim Collins in his book *Great by Choice* discusses the concept of "return on luck." Here is my summary of this concept. Great companies are able to capitalize on lucky events through preparation and execution. What that means is that the companies prepared by setting aside reserves of cash, building financial and intellectual capital, constantly evaluating their situation, and keeping their eyes open for any potential changes on the horizon. And when a lucky event happens they are in a position to capitalize on the fortuitous event. Through discipline, anticipation, creativity, and ambition, these companies position themselves to leverage their good fortune to the max.

Conversely, when bad luck happens, these companies have a fortress balance sheet and the intellectual capital to quickly deal with the misfortune and return to focusing on the entity's long-term objectives. Business success will be determined by how well your organization responds to luck.

As the author and entrepreneur Vivian Greene states, "Life isn't about just waiting for the storm to pass. It's about learning how to dance in the rain." Wise words on how to conduct yourself regardless of your luck.

CHAPTER 34
Paradox

I've witnessed many business leaders struggle with the concept of paradox. Business is permeated with paradoxes. What is a paradox? The word comes from the Greek words *para* and *doxos* and means "beyond belief." A simple definition from my Merriam-Webster dictionary app follows: "Any person, thing or situation exhibiting an apparently contradictory nature." Once you start paying attention, you'll see paradoxes pop up everywhere in business, from human resources to operations to sales.

It is hard to find a definition of a paradox that doesn't imply that it's an unsolved problem. But this view of a paradox is wrong. There are problems, and then there are paradoxes. It is a mistake to treat paradoxes as problems that need to be solved. The trouble is when we treat paradoxes as problems, our decision-making process can become paralyzed and inflexible. Remember, by their very nature, paradoxes are not solvable.

Most organizations today are familiar with these recurring issues:

- The conflicting needs of purpose and profit
- Achieving short-term goals vs. long-term goals
- The need for a flatter, more nimble organization that still executes with discipline
- The fact that usually scarcity ultimately creates a surplus
- Paradox of time. We are aware of the incredible value of our time but many times take actions that violate this value.

Paradoxes deal with uncertainty and ambiguity. They take us away from the familiar, the control, consistency, and closure we seek. If you crave control, you won't handle paradoxes well.

But yet paradoxes are rife in today's business world. Here are a few more that may sound familiar:

- As a leader, should I be directive or democratic?
- The need to empower people to make their own decisions, but at the same time keep everyone moving in the same direction
- Giving customers good value while making enough profit to sustain and grow the company
- Should our bonus plan reward individual achievement or only team results?
- How can I excel at work and also maintain a strong family life?
- Associates are at the same time individuals and are also part of the organization.
- Should I push for incremental or radical change?
- What's more important: the people involved or adhering to process?
- Stressing continuity while simultaneously stressing change
- Maintain and grow current company profitability and yet keep investing for the future

The ability to manage paradoxes begins with understanding their nature. It is no easy task, as the presence of paradoxes can initially be difficult to detect. Paradoxes have these characteristics, or principles, in common:

- They are not problems that can be solved, as they are unsolvable.
- They are many times of a cyclical or recurring nature.
- They can polarize individuals into groups, e.g., "I believe x," or "I believe y."

A paradox is a situation that has at least two competing sides and may appear as a contradiction. It has two polarities that can be both right and wrong at the same lime. Treating a paradox like a problem to be solved—one way is right, and one way is wrong—is usually the wrong way to deal with paradox.

As a business leader, you will need to get comfortable in dealing with paradox. To effectively tackle a paradox, you'll need to wholeheartedly embrace and understand both positions. Charlie Munger once famously said, "You need to do the work required to have an opinion." While we hold an opinion on almost everything, how many of us have done the work required to have an opinion? Mr. Munger is also famous for advising us to invert—to take the other side. He once said, "I never allow myself to have an opinion on anything that I don't know the other side's argument better than they do." To effectively deal with a paradox, you need to have done the work to understand both sides of a paradox.

Recognize the validity in more than one viewpoint. A favorite bromide of mine is "reasonable minds can differ on this issue." You can go on to say in this particular situation at this time I believe "x" rather than "y" because of . . .

To deal with paradoxes, ask yourself these questions:

- What is the strength of the other point of view?
- What are the deficiencies in my own point of view?
- What can we do to accommodate the most critical needs of both sides?
- Which side is more consistent with our mission and values?
- Which approach is most consistent with what the business needs right now?
- Which approach is more likely to help us achieve our annual, intermediate, and long-term objectives?

To effectively deal with paradoxes, you need to give up the illusion of control, consistency and closure. You need to embrace and get comfortable with ambiguity. Remember, today's decision may be different at some point in the future. Finally, as a business leader, recognize your biggest responsibility is to exercise good judgment in solving paradoxical situations to the long-term benefit of your organization.

CHAPTER 35
Achieving a Competitive Advantage

For any business leader, achieving a competitive advantage is like the search for the holy grail. In this hypercompetitive environment it is a very difficult and never-ending quest. An important book for me on the quest to find a competitive advantage was *Blue Ocean Strategy*, written in 2004 by INSEAD professors W. Chan Kim and Renée Mauborgne.

Blue Ocean Strategy has been published in forty-six languages, made more than three hundred bestseller lists around the globe, and has received numerous distinguished awards from the Nobel Colloquia Prize for Leadership on Business and Economic Thinking to Fast Company's Hall of Fame. *The Financial Times* called it "one of the bestselling business books of the century."

In its essence, here is the blue ocean concept:

The business universe consists of two distinct kinds of space, which the authors refer to as red and blue oceans. Red oceans represent all the industries in existence today—the known market space. In red oceans, industry boundaries are defined and accepted, and the competitive rules of the game are well understood. Here, companies try to outperform their rivals in order to grab a greater share of existing demand. As the space gets more and more crowded, prospects for profits and growth are reduced. Products turn into commodities, and increasing competition turns the water bloody—a red ocean.

Blue oceans denote all the industries not in existence today—the unknown market space, untainted by competition. In blue oceans, demand is created rather than fought over. There is ample opportunity for growth that is both profitable and rapid. There are two ways to create blue oceans. In a few cases, companies can give rise to completely new industries, as eBay did with the online auction industry. But in most cases, a blue ocean is created from within a red ocean when a company alters the boundaries of an existing industry. Cirque du Soleil is usually given as an example. In breaking through the boundary traditionally separating circus and theater, it created a new and profitable blue ocean from within the red ocean of the circus industry.

When I first read *Blue Ocean Strategy*, it had a profound impact on my thoughts on how to achieve a competitive advantage. It made so much sense. Business leaders shouldn't keep banging their heads against an extremely competitive environment. They should break free of the bloody red ocean and find a space untainted by competition—a blue ocean. In a now famous October 2004 article in the *Harvard Business Review* article also titled "Blue Ocean Strategy," Kim and Mauborgne indicate they have studied 150 blue ocean strategies in over 30 industries using data stretching back more than 100 years.

So although I really like the concept, the problem is it is very hard to develop a true blue ocean. So how does a management team develop a blue ocean strategy?

Let's look at a couple companies. The rise of Netflix is a textbook example of blue ocean strategy implementation. Starting out in a red ocean full of cutthroat competitors, Netflix disrupted the movie video market in a way that let them create a new blue ocean in which they initially played alone. In fact, their strategy was so successful that they put many video rental companies out of business. Remember Blockbuster?

Uber and Lyft are another example. These companies have experienced tremendous growth due to a lack of competition for the consumers who, until now, had no viable alternative to a traditional taxi. By making transportation easier, quicker, and more accessible, Uber and Lyft offered solutions to problems that public transportation official and taxi companies did not realize were previously unsolved. What are the common elements for most blue ocean strategies?

- Refuse to compete by all the factors other companies in the industry are competing by and identify one or two factors that really matter to the end users. For example, Uber identified that a moderate price and a clean car are more important to customers than a taxi with a city-approved taxi medallion.
- Reconstruct the market boundaries using blue ocean thinking and knowledge about alternative markets and all the participants in the customer value chain.
- Instead of adjusting to trends, use the trends to increase the value of your product.
- Go beyond existing demand by expanding your market by including various groups of current noncustomers that your management team believes could become a customer.
- Recognize pursuing a blue ocean strategy is a journey, not an event. Try, adjust, and try again is a part of developing a blue ocean strategy.

Recognizing it's very difficult to find and develop a blue ocean strategy, what's the alternative to a blue ocean strategy to gain a competitive advantage? Consider this concept: "the aggregation of marginal gains."

That phrase was coined by Sir David Brailsford, who turned the British cycling team into champions at the Beijing and London Olympics. This Olympic success stemmed not from one or two major innovations but a multitude of minor improvements, which when combined created a crushing advantage.

When Brailsford became head of British cycling in 2002, the team had almost no record of success: only a single gold medal in its seventy-six-year history. That quickly changed under Sir David's leadership. At the 2008 Beijing Olympics, his squad won seven out of ten gold medals available in track cycling, and they matched the achievement in London four years later. Sir David now leads Britain's first-ever professional cycling team, which has won three of the last four Tour de France events.

Sir David, a former professional cycler who holds an MBA, applied the theory of the aggregation of marginal gains to cycling. He and his team broke down everything they could think of that goes into competition on a bike, and then aimed to improve each element by 1 percent.

Eben Harrell chronicles Sir David's work in an October 30, 2015, article in the *Harvard Business Review* titled "How 1% Performance Improvements Led to Olympic Gold." Here is an excerpt of what Mr. Harrell wrote in this article:

> "By experimenting in a wind tunnel, we searched for small improvements to aerodynamics. By analyzing the mechanics area in the team truck, we discovered that dust was accumulating on the floor, undermining bike maintenance. So we painted the floor white, in order to spot any impurities. We hired a surgeon to teach our athletes about proper handwashing to avoid illnesses during competition (we also decided not to shake any hands during the Olympics). We were precise about food preparation. We brought our own mattresses and pillows so our athletes could sleep in the same posture every night. We searched for small improvements everywhere and found countless opportunities. Taken together, we felt they gave us a competitive advantage."

In William Green's book *Richer, Wiser, Happier,* Mr. Green discusses the concept of "the aggregation of marginal gains" and how Nicholas Sleep embraced the concept in his investment business. Mr. Sleep is a British fund manager and managed the Nomad Investment Partnership for over a decade and achieved above market results. Here is what Mr. Green wrote:

> "Sleep, who is an avid cyclist, says the best businesses share this obsession with securing even the most marginal gains. He recalls how Lord Harris, the founder of Carpetright, insisted on reusing old price tags, writing on both sides to save

a penny here, a penny there. "It's not one secret sauce," says Sleep, "You just have to care about all the little things and add them all together."

Years ago Charlie Munger coined the term the *lollapalooza effect*. You get the lollapalooza effect when two, three, or four forces are all operating in the same direction.

What causes the lollapalooza effect?

The combination of multiple factors that are all moving in the same direction is what creates the potential for a lollapalooza effect. According to Charlie Munger, lollapalooza effects occur when there are multiple forces or factors moving in the same direction. The key is that when forces combine, they don't just add up; each force builds off of and strengthens the other, creating an explosive effect with huge results. It is perfectly obvious. This is the way you win big in the world—by getting two or three forces working together in the same direction. The lollapalooza effect is an important form of the aggregational of marginal gains theory along with the theory of a virtuous cycle (see chapter 24).

Many times over the years an internal associate, board member, or distributor has asked me how Assurity can achieve a competitive advantage. They are typically looking for me to articulate one to three things—like our underwriting is going to be superior to our competitors, or we are going to have the most competitive products, and so on. My answer usually disappoints them. I'll say, "It's not one or two things, it's probably one hundred things we need to do better than our competitors, which when combined can give us a competitive advantage."

This is exactly what happened in Assurity's voluntary insurance business. Eastbridge, a consultancy, once benchmarked us to 156 different customer-facing (associate, employer, distributor) items. We then began the arduous work of becoming "best in class" on all 156. Albeit from a small base, our growth has been amazing since we embarked on this journey of improvement. Our success is a textbook example of "the aggregation of marginal gains."

A business leader should always be on the search for a blue ocean strategy. We just need to realize this is very rare. In the meantime, a focus on "the aggregation of marginal gains" can cause a business to achieve a competitive advantage.

CHAPTER 36
Expense Management

It is a rare business leader who enjoys his or her organizations annual budgeting process. Most business leaders look forward to budgeting season like they do to having a colonoscopy.

Corporate budgeting in its present form emerged in the 1950s as the numerical underpinning of corporate planning. Most corporate budgeting processes not only attempt to forecast and limit expenditures, but also predict revenue, profits, and capital expenditures.

Although a budgeting process is common in most major business, there are serious problems associated with many of them. Here are some of the major problems I've experienced with budgeting and expense management.

Time Required
It can be very time-consuming to create a budget. Usually it requires many iterations of the budget be developed before a final budget is approved. The time requirement can be unusually large if there is a participative budgeting process in place since this involves getting a large number of associates to come to a consensus.

Not Building in Flexibility
Uncertainty in economic conditions, the regulatory regime, geopolitical events, and the competitive environment have become so great to call into questions almost all projections.

Like I've stated in other chapters, a major blind spot for most management teams is the belief when they commit numbers to a projection or in a budget, they move expected results from inherent uncertainty to certainty. We need to remember that a budget is usually based on a set of assumptions that are generally not too far from the operating conditions under which the budget was formulated. If the business environment changes to any significant degree, the company's revenues or cost structure may change so radically that actual results will rapidly depart from the expectations delineated in the budget. This condition is a particular problem when there is a sudden economic downturn since the budget authorizes a certain level of spending that is no longer supportable under a reduced revenue level. Unless management acts quickly to override the budget, area managers will continue to spend under their original budgetary authorizations. As mentioned earlier, other conditions that can cause results to vary suddenly from budgeted expectations include changes in the competitive environment, new regulatory promulgations, or major geopolitical events.

When a company creates an annual budget, the senior management team will direct the focus of the organization to meeting the targets outlined in the budget. This can be a problem if the market shifts in a different direction sometime during the budget year. In this case, the company should shift along with the market, rather than slavishly adhering to the budget. Build in some wiggle room to allow responding to changing circumstances, to experiment, and to do things that might not work. Slack allows an organization to handle the inevitable shocks and surprises in the life of any enterprise. Here are some common budgeting problems I've encountered.

Not Exercising Good Judgment

As a business leader your primary responsibility is to exercise good judgment. You've heard me say this quite a few times in this book. Here are three scenarios around budgets that make me see "red." First, "I spent the money because it was in my budget." This statement makes no sense. Just because something is in a budget doesn't mean it should be spent. If business conditions have changed, we need to change. The second, if an area is allowed a certain amount of expenditures and it does not appear that the area will spend all of the funds during the budget period, the area manager may authorize excessive expenditures at the last minute on the concerns that his budget will be reduced in the next period unless he spends everything authorized in the current budget. Crazy, but I've heard area managers communicate this twisted logic. Finally, "We can't do X or Y because it isn't in our budget." If the expenditure makes sense and is important to achieving our long-term business objectives, we should expend the money even if the dollars haven't been budgeted. Many organization leaders become focused on a strict adherence to their budget. They should instead be obsessed with making sure they are doing the right thing.

Gamesmanship
Area managers may attempt to introduce budgetary slack, which involves deliberately reducing revenue estimates or increasing expense estimates so they can easily achieve favorable variances against the budget. This can be a serious problem and requires considerable oversight to spot and eliminate. We need to remember that anyone who "games" their budget is essentially being encouraged to engage in unethical behavior.

Several years ago I experienced one of the most hilarious moments ever in a budget review meeting. Our CFO and I were meeting with a new sales manager, and I started the meeting with what was supposed to be a humorous question. I said, "Tell me where the fat is in your budget?" The new young sales manager then began to offer up a number of areas where he indicated his budget was "fat" and suggested a number of expenses that could be reduced—much to the consternation of our senior VP of sales, his boss, who was also in the room. Don't "game the system."

Unrealistic Growth Expectations
In order to achieve some profitability objective some leaders will allow or even encourage unrealistic sales expectations in the budgetary assumptions. Growth can be a marvelous phenomenon—more jobs, greater scale, new products—all laudable aims for any business. But if increases in sales become an overwhelming objective, and

expenses are neglected, then normally grand plans run aground.

Too often more sales are seen as the antidote to everything. It allows business leaders to forget what they see as the drudgery of addressing bloated costs. Unfortunately, growth usually consumes cash and working capital—and if profits are anemic, then the cash runs out.

Other than for a startup every business leader needs to be mindful of achieving operating leverage. My simple definition for operating leverage is having sales growth exceed the growth in expenses. Too often this happens: expenses grow but there is not the accompanying growth in profitable sales, which results in negative operating leverage. A very pernicious development.

Thinking We Can Downsize Ourselves to Prosperity
Expense control is very important, but I've never known a business that was able to downsize itself to prosperity. A successful business needs to find a way to have profitable growth. Despite the importance of cost control to most businesses, cost reduction alone cannot guarantee success. For cost cutting to be effective, the sales and revenue end of the business must be healthy.

Avoiding Conflict and Not Making Difficult Decisions
I like "stop doing" lists. This is a list you develop to help you understand certain things you should stop doing, which are no longer moving you toward your goals. A corollary for budgeting and expense management is "zero-based budgeting." Stay with a clean slate and require all expenses be justified for each new period.

There are always a thousand excuses as to why costs cannot be cut. Managers are too embarrassed to ask for lower prices from suppliers; they are too squeamish to make surplus workers redundant; they lack the resolve to challenge how money is spent; they are comfortable with the status quo; they are too lazy to examine in detail where expenses arise and find intelligent ways to reduce them; and they are too scared of losing customers to re-engineer products to generate a fair return. More often than not, at the heart of the matter they avoid addressing expense issues because addressing them will involve conflict—with their peers, direct reports, suppliers, customers, and so on.

Costs come in every shape and size, from travel and office equipment to software and utility bills. An attitude should be developed that questions every line, every contract, and every quoted price. Small items can add up to big numbers. More can almost always be done with less if circumstances require it. Waste does not simply damage financial outcomes; it is a moral issue. Too often we don't challenge longstanding expenses. We just accept them as inevitable. Challenge each expense and don't assume they need to continue. Remember, saying no to an unnecessary expense provides funds for a bigger yes that will move the company forward.

One of my all-time favorite business books is titled *Memos from the Chairman*, written by the longstanding chairman of Bear Stearns, Alan C. Greenberg. This book is a collection of memos he authored to his staff over many years. Throughout this book he discusses the importance of expense control. But I especially like a memo dated July 10, 1990. In this memo, he discusses the ten things he thought Bear Stearns needed to focus on in the years ahead. What follows are numbers 3, 5 and 9.

3. Control expenses—even more so in good times
5. Reduce expenses
9. Cut expenses

So three of the ten involved expense control. These three are good advice for all of us.

Recently my wife and I and some friends visited Bentonville, Arkansas, to primarily see the amazing Crystal Bridges Museum and grounds. While in Bentonville we also toured the Walmart museum, which is housed in Sam Walton's original five-and-dime store. I highly recommend touring this interesting museum. In the museum they have an entire wall displaying the ten values Mr. Walton attempted to instill in the Walmart culture. I'm going to end this chapter with his value on expenses.

"Control your expenses better than your competition. This is where you can always find the competitive advantage. For twenty-five years running—long before Wal-Mart was known as the nation's largest retailer—we ranked number one in our industry for the lowest ratio of expenses to sales. You can make a lot of different mistakes and still recover if you run an efficient operation. Or you can be brilliant and still go out of business if you're too inefficient."

Wise words from an American business icon.

CHAPTER 37
Embrace Uncertainty

Many business leaders display a hubris about their ability to predict the future. They are very confident they know what the future holds for their company. They fail to acknowledge that fate provides an unending flow of unexpected events and circumstances. It is one thing to anticipate change, but it's quite another to have it foisted upon us when we least expect it. I've come to believe most business leaders would benefit from adopting an authentic humility about their ability to predict the future. We need to realize every company lives with a great deal of uncertainty and that failures to accurately predict the future often occur when the outcome is caused by events that never could have been credibly predicted—for example, a global pandemic.

We humans are enormously bad about predicting what will happen in the future. One way to realize how bad we are at foreseeing the future is to look back and read some old publications and see how often the world did something that wasn't even imagined. During my forty-plus-year business career, I've seen many predictions that turned out to be way off base. Here are a few of them:

1. In 1959, IBM said to Xerox, "The world wide potential market for copying machines is 5,000 at most."

2. In the 1980s, almost everyone in business believed the Japanese would soon rule the world as they were the acknowledged experts in manufacturing. Seminars abounded on how

to implement Japanese-style "Total Quality Management Programs," commonly known as "TQM." TQM programs were adopted by company after company. But the Japanese stock market peaked in the late 1980s, and by August 1990 the Nikkei stock index had plummeted to half its peak. The Japanese economy continued to decline for over two decades. Today, no one considers Japan to be our primary economic rival. "Japanification" is now a pejorative term.

3. Going into the 1990s, the prospect for economic growth wasn't good. Then Netscape and its browser went public in 1995. By 1999, the tech utopia was in full force. The Nasdaq composite index peaked on March 10, 2000, before crashing. I remember arguing with an investment analyst friend of mine in late 1999 about the value of Cisco. Cisco was, and still is, a great company, but my analyst friend argued Cisco was a bargain at a P/E of around 174. During the crash, Cisco lost more than 80 percent of its value.

4. Here is another prediction starting with a quote. "The concept is interesting and well-formed, but in order to earn better than a 'C,' the idea must be feasible." This was a Yale University management professor's grading of Fred Smith's paper proposing reliable overnight delivery service. (Smith went on to found Federal Express Corp.)

5. Two more bad predictions, just to hammer home the point:
The first in 2006, by David Pogue, Tech Correspondent for the *New York Times*: "Everyone's always asking me when Apple will come out with a cellphone. My answer is, probably never."
The second in 2007, by Steve Ballmer, former CEO of Microsoft: "There is no chance that the IPhone is going to get any significant market share."

All these predictions remind me of a famous quote by John Kenneth

Galbraith: "There are two kinds of forecasters: those who don't know, and those who don't know they don't know."

So given that predictions about the future are usually meaningless, what should leaders of companies do? Here are some thoughts.

1. **Be smart about probabilities.** It is helpful to think about alternative futures in a probabilistic way—avoid absolutism. Probabilistic thinking doesn't mean that we should bet everything on what we believe is the most likely outcome. Probabilistic thinking is more about considering the most realistic outcomes—it's rejecting futures with low probabilities and assigning the remainder a percentage probability. Always keep in mind a way to avoid the worst-case scenario and take any other actions within the organization's overall risk appetite.

   We should also all become "Bayesians." Thomas Bayes was an obscure country preacher who dabbled in math. He is remembered for "Bayes' Theorem," which shows how to use new evidence to adjust probabilities. Bayes realized probabilities are ever-changing. As we acquire new information, our probabilities need to change as well. Business leaders should not think in binary terms but in probabilities.

2. **Build in optionality.** This means having plenty of irons in the fire. Hindsight bias causes us to think that a successful firm's success was guaranteed. But this is not the case. Consider Amazon. It's had its share of flops (think the Fire Phone and expansion in China) even as it got the future right with its big bets on cloud computing and the Kindle. I acknowledge options are expensive to maintain since they often burn cash. But I believe building in optionality is almost always worth the effort. One of the most successful entrepreneurs I know often closes his management meeting by saying, "We need to get comfortable with having a number of lines in the water because we never know where we might get a bite."

Harry Singleton was one of the most brilliant engineers and businessmen of the twentieth century. He built Teledyne Corp into one of the most successful conglomerates ever. Singleton said, "I know a lot of people have very strong and definite plans they've worked out on all kinds of things, but we're subject to a tremendous number of outside influences and the vast majority of them cannot be predicted, so my idea is to stay flexible. My only plan is to keep coming to work every day."

Mr. Singleton's comment indicates he was practicing something I believe in called "strategic opportunism." I discussed the concept of strategic opportunism in chapter 32. But most management teams and boards of directors won't easily accept this concept. They want concrete, detailed plans. Here is a rhetorical question: when was the last time that your organization's detailed plan came about just as you envisioned it would during your planning sessions?

3. **Build knowledge and manage decisions adaptively.** We should learn as much as possible before making a decision. Knowledge makes the new seem more familiar. We also need to be adaptable when new information comes to light. We need to easily modify our path when conditions change. Build awareness around "consistency bias," which I discussed in chapter 21.

   Remember Ralph Waldo Emerson's famous quote: "A foolish consistency is the hobgoblin of little minds. A great person does not have to think consistently from one day to the next."

4. **Be careful about outsourcing uncertainty.** So often when management teams feel uncertain about something their first step is to bring in a consultant. Consciously or unconsciously, they believe this helps them avoid responsibility if something goes wrong.

5. **Focus on what won't change.** This approach was made famous by Amazon CEO Jeff Bezos. He was on stage at a press event when a reporter asked him, "Jeff, what do you think is going to change most in the next ten years?" Bezos replied, "Here is a better question: What's not going to change in the next ten years?"

    He went on to say that, from his perspective at Amazon, what won't change is people's desire for *lower prices* and *faster delivery*. Accordingly, Bezos built Amazon to focus on and invest billions into figuring out how to lower prices and increase the speed with which items are shipped to you. "When you have something that you know is true," he said, "even over the long term, you can afford to put a lot of energy into it."

    I think this is a very important exercise and something we've done at Assurity for a number of years as we start our annual planning process. It is really hard to know what will change. It's much easier to think about what won't change. I believe you can effectively build a strategic direction around what won't change.

6. **Be skeptical about all forecasts.** As I've stated several times in this book, many management teams tend to believe that a forecast coming out of their models is gospel. By having a sophisticated model that produces a forecast, they believe they can convert inherent uncertainty into certainty. They express surprise and sometimes dismay when actual results vary significantly from forecasted results. Even when actual results come close to forecasted results, it rarely unfolds exactly as planned. We need to remember our carefully developed strategic plan or budget is only one possibility in a sea of many potential outcomes. We need to remember all models are based on a certain set of assumptions. Small errors in assumptions can really alter model results.

    The very idea that a forecaster can spin a bunch of outcomes whose probabilities add up to 100 percent is a kind of hubris. Risk means that more things can happen than will happen, which in turn means that the scenarios we spin will never add up to 100 percent of future possibilities except as a matter of luck. Like it or not, the unimaginable outcomes are the ones that make the biggest spread between expected and actual results. Be wary of clinging to false precision in a complex world. Unfortunately, the future is never really knowable. Forecast is a polite synonym for "guess"; the best forecasts are informed guesses but sill inherently uncertain. I've long liked this quote from the author Peter Bernstein: "Forecasts create the mirage that the future is knowable."

In today's business world, uncertainty seems to be the only certainty. Uncertainty can be scary and lead to personal stress and anxiety. As humans, we tend to respond to uncertainty with denial or avoidance. If you can become more comfortable with uncertainty and ambiguity, many more possibilities open up in your life as a business leader. Fear will no longer be a dominant factor in what you do and no longer prevent you from taking action to initiate change. Remember that you can't predict the unpredictable. You can only control the things which are controllable.

The investment writer Morgan Housel in a recent newsletter said the following on forecasts and uncertainty. "The inability to forecast the past has no impact on our desire to forecast the future, certainty is so valuable that we'll never give up our quest for it, and most people couldn't get out of bed in the morning if they were honest about how uncertain the future is."

Annie Duke, author of *Thinking in Bets: Making Smarter Decisions When You Don't Have All the Facts*, said that "wrapping our arms around uncertainty and giving it a big hug will help us become better decision makers." I agree, embrace uncertainty. One of my favorite writers on personal finance is Jason Zweig who is a columnist with the *Wall Street Journal*. I'm going to conclude with this chapter with a quote from Mr. Zweig in an October 28, 2022 article in the *Wall Street Journal* with the title "What To Do When You Know What Stocks Will Do Next".

"And just think of the cocksure certainty with which gold bugs and bitcoin fans had been proclaiming for years that the precious metal and the digital currency were perfect ways to protect your purchasing power. So far in 2022, with inflation raging, gold is down 9%; bitcoin has lost more than 50%."

A wise observation from Mr. Zweig on the dangers of pursuing the illusion of certainty.

CHAPTER 38
Risk

I've had the privilege of chairing a number of risk committees for publicly traded companies. In addition, I helped design the enterprise risk management (ERM) process we utilize at Assurity. The 2008 economic crisis exposed the fragility of many organizations' bureaucratic approach to ERM. As a result of that painful experience, corporate America has become much better at risk identification and mitigation. Many companies are now very good at identifying and mitigating risk. What I don't think they are very good at is *taking* risks. In many firms, I believe we tend to think all risk is bad. In this chapter, I want to discuss the need to take risks, as well as the danger of not taking risks and trying new things.

In chapter 25, I introduced you to Charles Handy's book *21 Letters on Life and Its Challenges*. In this book, Mr. Handy also reminded me of something I learned about years ago, "the concept of an S curve." The S curve framework, displayed atop the next page, is used in business to represent the typical difficult beginning, then good growth and ultimate decline of any business. In the beginning most businesses usually experience a tough start but hopefully the business gains traction and begins to grow and do well. But inevitably the business products or services become mature, and the business begins to decline. It would be best if the company took a risk and started something new while things are going well at the top of the S curve, and before the inevitable decline begins.

Starting something new when the S curve is still going up is very hard to do. To quote Mr. Handy, "Psychologically it is very hard to leave a party while it is still at its height, and you are enjoying it." But it is at this time when you need to take a risk and start something new.

Before this curve starts to dip, you should try something new. You need to innovate and take a risk. But starting something new is scary. It's risky. Most business leaders want to avoid risk. In my thirty-plus years in the insurance industry, I would have a much larger bank balance if I had $100 for every time one of my colleagues or a board member said something like, "We should stick to our own knitting," "We should stay with what we know," or "Let's not get out of our lane," "We are a life insurance company and let's focus on being a life insurance company." Risk tolerance is a very scarce resource in most companies. The ironic thing is not taking a risk or making a change may be the riskiest of all.

As consumers' preferences and values have changed, many long-established industries are being disrupted. They are painfully discovering the consequences of not trying new things—taking a risk.

Let me give you my top reasons for taking risk:

1. Achieving big goals and playing it safe are incompatible. You can't achieve great things without taking risks. You have to get out of your comfort zone and try something new.

2. The world is not stagnant—almost every old, established industry is being disrupted. Think of all the old, well-established industries that have been disrupted due to changing consumer preferences and technological change. Here are a few off the top of my head:
   - Newspaper publishers and much of print media

- Telecommunication companies based on landlines
- Department stores
- Greeting card companies
- Brick-and-mortar bookstores and many other retailers
- Men's tie manufacturers
- Printing companies
- Directory and mailing list publishers
- Travel agencies
- Traditional radio
- Photo finishing
- Traditional depository financial institutions

I'm sure management at most of these companies felt they should stick to what they know. Bad idea. It's okay to stick to your knitting but not so if you have a bad basket of knitting.

3. Unforeseen opportunities often come from risk taking. While some risks don't pay out, it's important to remember that some do. Reframing risk as an opportunity to succeed rather than a path to failure is important in establishing the right attitude toward risk.

4. We learn from risks—and these lessons may lead us on an important new path. Yes, if we are smart, we will learn from the risks we take. We will be smarter and more formidable competitors.

5. Embracing risk—Taking risks helps you overcome a fear of failure. There are two inherent biases in the human mind that skew our perceptions of risk. The first is that we tend to exaggerate the possibility for failure. People tend to pessimistically predict failure more than real situations would warrant. The second is that we greatly exaggerate the consequences of those failures—we envision the worst-case scenario when the reality is far more manageable. Keep this in mind when imagining the negative possibilities associated with your

risks. Don't let fear overtake your own good judgment.

6. Risk is a differentiator—Some risks offer the promise of higher value. Some risks offer smaller potential consequences than others. Some risks could make or break a business. But there's one key element all risks have in common: their differentiators. Because most people are unwilling to take risks, the risk-takers of the world naturally stand out in the crowd, and as we all know, entrepreneurs and businesses that stand out are the only ones with a shot at breakout success.

In taking risks, here are some key things to remember:

1. There are different types of risks. I'm not just referring to "big risks" and "small risks" here—though those exist too. There are calculable risks, which involve a series of knowns that allow you to reasonably predict the odds of success. For example, you might be able to infer from historical data that there's a 30 percent chance a new product will achieve its production objectives.

   There are ambiguous risks, which involve some knowns and some unknowns. Ambiguous risks complicate the decision-making process. Most business risks fall into this category, because so many factors, like consumer behavior and economic shifts, are difficult to quantify or predict. Then there are completely unknown risks, which arrive when you bring something truly unique to the market. Knowing the differences between these risks can help you better understand how much risk you are actually assuming.

2. Some risks won't pay off. The optimistic risk-taker will always see things as half-full. These optimistic risk takers are fortified by the cultural ideal that risk taking is generally a rewarding strategy. However, don't be fooled into thinking that all risks work out. Remember the "overconfidence bias" from chapter 21. Many risks we take will fail.

Organizationally we need to get comfortable with failure. Failing is an opportunity to learn.

3. To take a risk, you can't be a persistent pessimist. But pessimism sounds smart—optimism naïve. Focusing only on established products and proven markets naturally leads to pessimism. For the organization to move forward you have to try new things. As a business leader you need to guard against the narrative that most new things won't work.

4. Understand the "J curve." It is somewhat akin to the S curve. The J curve represents the tendency of any new business or venture to post negative returns in the initial years and then post increasing returns in later years. The negative returns at the onset will cause detractors. Those who were against taking the risk will point out things aren't working. Organizationally we can't fall for that kind of naysaying.

5. "Everything looks like a failure in the middle." Harvard professor Rosabeth Moss Kanter popularized this phrase. It's been referred to as "Kanter's Law." Here is how she explained it in an August 12, 2009, *Harvard Business Review* article: "Welcome to the miserable middles of change. This is the time when Kanter's Law kicks in. Everything looks like a failure in the middle. Everyone loves inspiring beginnings and happy endings; it is just the middles that involve hard work."

6. Be aware of single-risk obsession. From my experience it is one of the costliest kinds of errors to which business leaders fall prey. Business leaders become so focused on one particular risk, say "rising interest rates," they fail to take notice of other risks but more importantly fail to see the opportunities this one risk could provide.

Taking a risk and starting something new is very hard. At some point in the process, usually the middle, even wide-eyed optimists will feel anxiety. They will start to question what they are doing and whether they will ever succeed. This is not the time to give up—this is the time to be persistent and double your efforts. Recognize the struggle of the "middle." Persist and preserve.

You can't be successful in business without taking risks. In our fast-moving current environment, risk taking is more important than ever. If an organization can become really good at taking risks and starting new things, it will surely have an inherent competitive advantage.

CHAPTER 39
Measurement and Metrics

In this chapter, I want to provide some thoughts on establishing metrics. I've long been an advocate of using appropriate metrics to ensure accountability. Tracking accountability involves measuring. A couple of my favorite aphorisms about measuring are:

- "Measurement improves performance."
- "What gets measured gets done."

I've also long believed in the maxim "you can't manage what you can't measure." As I matured as a business leader, I came to recognize the dark side of measuring. I now contend that addressing the right questions in the right way is more important than focusing on following certain metrics. Let me share a few problems with measurement and metrics. Have you heard of a concept called surrogation? Here is my definition of surrogation:

> Surrogation is a phenomenon in which a metric designed to measure progress toward the execution of a strategy instead becomes the goal itself.

I experienced this firsthand several years ago when I bought a new Lexus. After all, the paperwork was done, but before I left the dealership, the sales manager came up to me and said the following:

"You'll soon be getting a customer satisfaction survey from Lexus. We would appreciate you completing the survey. But in completing the survey you need to give us the highest rating on each question. Anything but the highest rating will impact our vehicle allocation from Lexus and our bonus payments from Lexus. Do you see any reason that you won't give us the highest rating on each question? If there is any reason you won't give us the highest rating, we need to fix this right now before you leave the dealership."

This sales manager wasn't primarily interested in a good experience for his customer; he was interested in getting a good score on the Lexus customer satisfaction survey. Later I thought to myself, "This is happening at Lexus dealerships across the country." I'm sure Lexus had good intentions when they initiated the survey, but it now was not accomplishing their original objective. The score had become what's important, not true customer satisfaction.

Another very common measurement problem is measuring the wrong thing. Most business leaders understand their principal objective is to create value—make their company more valuable than in the past. In the insurance industry, typically one of the measurements that ostensibly measures the creation of value is something around sales growth. Yet in my industry, if sales growth in and of itself is the principal measure, it will usually lead to some very poor outcomes. What usually happens is a company books unprofitable business just to achieve a certain sales growth metric. I once heard a seasoned insurance sales manager say, "Sales are for today, profits are somebody else's responsibility in the future." Unfortunately, a too-common practice is a sales growth metric without an accompanying sales quality metric. It is important to identify and understand the key issues involved in any sales environment rather than just monitoring a sales growth metric. Over the long term, quality of sales is more important than the quantity of sales.

Another common problem with measuring is not carefully considering cause and effect in choosing what to measure. What you're after are statistics that reliably reveal cause and effect. These have two defining characteristics. One, they are persistent, meaning that the outcome of a given action at one time will be similar to the outcome of the same action at another time; and two, they are predictive—there is a direct relationship between the actions the statistic measures and the desired outcome. Persistent statistics reflect performance that can be relied upon to produce a consistent result. If we do "A," we will see "B."

Many business leaders fail to distinguish between skill and luck. Think of persistence as occurring on a continuum. At one extreme, the outcome being measured is the product of pure skill. At the other, it is due to luck, so persistence is low. When you spin a roulette wheel, the outcomes are random; what happens on the first spin provides no clue about what will happen on the next.

All this seems like common sense, right? Yet companies often rely on statistics, which are neither very persistent nor predictive. Because these metrics do not reveal cause and effect, they will likely not measure progress toward achieving the company's broader goals.

Wise business leaders bring a healthy dose of skepticism in reviewing any set of statistics.

Another measurement problem is the misuse of lagging and leading metrics. Business leaders need to think carefully about leading and lagging metrics. If you measure your business solely on lagging indicators, you will start to manage your business based on history. These lagging metrics may not reflect the current reality. But picking the right leading metrics is very difficult. You need to find those leading metrics that are truly predictive. Some leading indicators give a false sense of causality. Metrics are by definition reductionist. They give an indication of something. They are the symptom, not the root cause. Choosing the wrong leading metrics can give a false sense of achievement. I love predictive leading indicators, but they need to be carefully chosen and with new information may need to be modified or abandoned.

Be wary of metrics that are easily gamed. Placing too much emphasis on metric performance can incentivize fraud and conflicts of interest. Incentive plans are usually based on a number of metrics. As a result, participants may attempt to "game" the system for their own advantage. Recognizing this will happen calls for us to carefully consider the metrics chosen and provide for an "out" if the metrics don't produce the intended result.

The proliferation of dashboards requires me to spend some time discussing this popular management tool. Dashboards can provide easily digested "snapshots" of key performance indicators (KPIs) for the whole organization or about any subset. If properly created dashboards can provide just-in-time views of what's working and what isn't.

Dashboards represent an improvement from complicated spreadsheets. Dashboards should provide business leaders essential information in a visually attractive way. Dashboards usually have an appealing design and a level of interactivity allowing a reduced cost of admission to data.

Although I like dashboards, they can bring their own set of problems. Some of the problems are identical to any metric-based scorecard, which I already discussed in this chapter. But there are some unique challenges with dashboards.

One of the most common problems with dashboard design is including too much information. It is generally believed that best-practice dashboards should be limited in size to a single page in order to provide the user with an at-a-glance summary of the key performance indicators. However, with such a limited amount of space, it is easy to fall into the trap of cramming in as much data as possible. This can lead to dashboards becoming cluttered, unclear, and difficult to interpret—something that ultimately defeats their purpose. Unfortunately, most "risk dashboards" reflect this problem. In order to fix this problem you should be extremely strict when it comes to editing the information that needs to be included. Members of the group who will use the dashboard will always want to cram in more—this needs to be resisted.

The proliferation of dashboards are also a problem. Dashboards seem to be everywhere. The VP of sales, operations, engineering, and so on all want a unique dashboard or dashboards for their area of responsibility. Fair enough, and this might be the right thing to do—but we also need to carefully consider whether it is worth the time and energy to populate all these dashboards.

Analytical types are especially vulnerable to the disease I call "not my dashboard." Managers who weren't involved in the creation of the dashboard begin to disparage the dashboard as "wrong," perhaps blatantly ignoring it. They may see the dashboard as a threat to their positions, and if they see numbers they didn't expect, they chalk it up to "bad data." This sort of event usually develops into a serious trust problem. And in most cases you can't send them the raw data to rebuild trust. In summary, dashboards can be very useful, but be careful.

We also need to remember how important intangible factors are to any organization's long-term success. Ethics, corporate culture, trust, and sustainability practices are all important and not easily measured. I'm reminded of an Albert Einstein quote: "Not everything that can be counted counts and not everything that counts can be counted."

Remember metrics can never replace judgment. In the complex environment in which most companies operate, it is difficult to assemble a group of metrics that perfectly captures progress toward the organization's broad objectives. Again, business leaders need to exercise judgment and base decisions on more than what comes from a possibly flawed set of metrics.

CHAPTER 40
Too Hard

Most business leaders would benefit their organization if they better understood some problems are not realistically solvable. At least they are not solvable within the resource and time constraints inherent for every business.

I'm friends with Steve Lacy, the now retired Chairman of Meredith Corp. We serve together on the board of First Interstate Bancorp and I've come to admire Steve's business acumen. On May 23, 2019, the *Wall Street Journal* published an article on Meredith, and how at Meredith the executive teams divides the issues they are facing into problems and situations. Under their definition problems can't be solved but situations can. In this *Wall Street Journal* article, they discuss Meredith's acquisition of *Time Inc*. They identified the problems; magazines like *Time, Money* and *Sports Illustrated*. Although these publications had historically been successful, they were being profoundly impacted by the travails facing all print publications. These publications couldn't be fixed with reasonable amounts of investment, management's attention, and time. On the other hand, they felt *People* magazine was a situation. *People* magazine was experiencing the difficulty endemic to all print publishing, but this publication had other advantages not present in the afore mentioned sister publications. The *Wall Street Journal* article includes this great advice.

"It's a practical approach: Invest in assets with the promise of profitable growth; don't waste money trying to fix hopelessly weak ones, no matter how strong the romantic attachment."

Many management teams believe their primary responsibility is to solve difficult problems. I maintain a management team's primary responsibility is to avoid difficult problems. I endorse Warren Buffett's comments in his 1989 annual report letter: "After 25 years of buying and supervising a great variety of businesses, Charlie and I have not learned how to solve difficult business problems. What we have learned is to avoid them. To the extent we have been successful, it is because we concentrated on identifying one-foot hurdles that we could step over rather than because we acquired any ability to clear seven footers."

In American business today, due to changing consumer preferences and values and disruptive competitors, there are so many formerly successful business models which are now facing an insurmountable hostile environment.

Let's consider men's ties, which I briefly mentioned in chapter 30. Tie sales peaked in the US in 1995 at $1.8 billion. By 2009, the figure had dwindled to $418 million, down by more than 75 percent. Don't you suppose executive leadership at the tie manufactures have discussed for years how to turn tie sales around? The discussion probably goes something like this: "If we only had better or more diverse fabrics or better designs; let's bypass retail stores and sell direct to the consumer." All kinds of futile ideas would be discussed and probably tried.

Unfortunately, there is a whole host of businesses similar to the men's tie business, and there is no credible way to turn around these businesses. They are "too hard."

Management teams that focus on trying to turnaround a fundamentally bad business are pursuing a futile effort. Here is another quote from Warren Buffett, which was also in his 1989 annual report letter: "I've said many times that when a management team with a reputation for brilliance tackles a business with a reputation for bad economics, it is the reputation of the business that remains intact."

Over the years, I've observed capital is more often consumed in poor businesses than propagated in good ones. Or, as Chris Bradley,

Martin Hirt, and Sven Smit wrote in their book *Strategy Beyond the Hockey Stick*,

> "Industry is a much bigger reason than most people understand or want to accept, both on the upside (when tailwinds help us sail along) and on the downside (when the writing on the wall tells tough times are coming and we don't like the news)."

Management teams usually favor incrementalism and continuing to deal with familiar but unsolvable problems. A mentor of mine in the banking business often said when we were discussing certain problem credits, "I don't care how smart you are or how hard you work, if you have too many things going against you the business won't be successful." A very true assertion.

Yet so many management teams resist facing reality. They spend time, effort, and money trying to solve a business condition that isn't salvageable. The many excuses for following this path usually include the following:

1. This is our basic business; how can we abandon the line of business that built this company?

2. Most of our people are involved in supporting this business line; what happens to them if we exit this business line?

3. The business isn't bad; we just have the wrong sales leadership or operations leadership, etc. If we make some personnel changes, we will get things turned around.

4. We just need to try harder and be smarter in what we do every day. We need better execution.

All of these reasons are fatuous. Why the company finds itself in this position is because years before the executive management didn't take appropriate risks. Remember the "S curve" from chapter 28.

Start something new before your basic business has started to decline. This is why I believe in diversification. Try new things, look for new opportunities. Get comfortable with trying new approaches and exploring new markets.

A course more business leaders should follow is to embark on a courageous and unremitting reallocation of resources from the too hard pile to new business models and show a willingness to get into new businesses with better growth and profitability dynamics.

CHAPTER 41
The Pygmalion Effect

The Pygmalion effect is a tendency named after a Greek mythological figure. Pygmalion worked as a sculptor. He carved a female statue out of ivory that was so beautiful and so perfect that he fell in love with it. Indeed, the statue was so perfect that no living being could possibly be its equal. Upon the festival day for Aphrodite, goddess of love, Pygmalion made offerings but was too afraid to say anything about his love for the sculpture. Instead, he wished for a bride that would be the likeness of his ivory sculpture. Returning back home, he gave a kiss to the statue, and it turned into a woman; the goddess of love made his wish come true. He called her Galatea. The two of them had a daughter, Paphos, whose name was later given to a coastal city in southwest Cyprus.

It's a beautiful story with a wonderful lesson. The Pygmalion effect explains why all of our relationships and attendant expectations are, in a very real sense, self-fulfilling prophecies. The Pygmalion effect in business is a psychological phenomenon where higher expectations lead to an increase in performance. The Pygmalion effect was popularly defined by psychologist Robert Rosenthal, who described it as "the phenomenon whereby one person's expectation for another person's behavior comes to serve as a self-fulfilling prophecy."

To study the effect, Rosenthal joined forces with a Californian elementary school principal named Lenore Jacobsen. During the study, each student completed an IQ test, but the results were not disclosed to teachers. However, they were told the names of students who were identified as having great potential.

One year later, the students took the test again. While all managed to achieve a higher score, the students identified as having greater potential made the most progress. In other words, students who had higher expectations placed on them by the teacher performed better.

Teachers were more likely to pay closer attention to these students by providing in-depth feedback and continuing to challenge them. The mood and attitude of each teacher toward the students with potential were also hypothesized to be a contributing factor to high performance.

The Pygmalion effect explains why people tend to perform up to the level that others expect of them. This effect explains why our relationships are usually self-fulfilling prophecies. Once you set expectations for somebody, that person will tend to live up to that expectation, whether it's good or bad.

In general, people tend to perform up to the level that others expect them to perform. If you don't expect much from the people you work with, it's likely you won't inspire them to perform to the limits of their capabilities. Let them know you expect great things from them, and more often than not, you'll find that they will perform up to or beyond our expectations.

The medical professions have long recognized that a physician's expectations can have a formidable influence on a patient's physical or mental health. If a physician is positive about a patient's illness and offers a positive prognosis from the prescribed treatment, it is more likely the patient will experience a good result. In the medical profession, sometimes this is referred to as the placebo effect.

But there are detractors to the Pygmalion theory. In fact, the original research may be flawed. For the last fifty years, no one has really been able to replicate Rosenthal's work. In fact, some researchers claim the impact of high expectations in the classroom is significantly exaggerated while others even claim that the Pygmalion effect is likely an illusion and the underlying research is "bad science."

I'll leave others to debate the science, but I've certainly seen this effect in the business world. When a leader thinks an associate is a high performer, the leader usually gives the associate more opportunities to develop, and the associate usually performs at a high level. The leader compliments and encourages the associate, thus creating a positive feedback loop. In parallel, if associates believe a leader is successful, the associates are more attentive and supportive, which likely improves the leader's performance.

I believe the reverse of the Pygmalion effect can also be an issue. If a leader's expectation of an associate is low, the leader will likely treat the associate (intentionally or unintentionally) in a way that will lead to poorer performance than the associate is capable of achieving. In psychology, this is called the Golem effect, the self-fulfilling prophecy that people live up (or, in this case, down) to expectations.

A young person's first manager is likely to be very influential in that person's career. In that regard I was very lucky. My first boss out of college, whom I introduced in chapter 20, was a high-energy, enthusiastic individual by the name of David Shindeldecker. Dave was an expert at setting realistic but high expectations. He was also adept at providing timely and personalized recognition for a job well done, thus creating a positive feedback loop. I would have done almost anything to not disappoint him. An associate's first manager will help build the foundation for future career success.

A truly great leader doesn't just motivate their highest-potential associates but also makes sure other associates aren't stigmatized with the badge of low expectations. The goal isn't to get someone to do something they aren't capable of but rather to ensure that everyone believes they have an opportunity to meet their own full potential.

As I've indicated repeatedly in this book, communication is so important. A business leader's communication skills come into play in getting the most out of the Pygmalion effect. The business leader needs to publicly recognize and highlight associates who are performing at a high level. One of my favorite self-help books of all time is Dale Carnegie's *How to Win Friends & Influence People*. In this book, Carnegie recommends "giving others a good reputation to live up to." I've used that concept in many business settings. Here is an example: If a distributor wants us to do something on the regulatory edge, I will usually say something like, "I know you always conduct your business affairs in a highly ethical way. I know you wouldn't want to do anything that would be considered unethical." I just gave this distributor a reputation to live up to.

I personally believe in the Pygmalion effect. Here are what I consider to be some best practices for using it in a business setting:

Manage Expectations.
It's important to note that the Pygmalion effect works both ways. While positive expectations contribute to high performance, negative expectations contribute to poor performance. Leaders should therefore seek to identify strengths in their team members and not dwell on weaknesses. By using this style of leadership, the manager will be primarily focusing on the associate's strengths. This will allow the associate to perform at his or her best.

Set challenges that are ambitious.
With the bar set high, overcoming these challenges increases a feeling of empowerment in associates. Leaders who set high standards are also likely to do everything they can to help someone else reach their goal. Ultimately, this enhances the culture of an organization.

Use positive language.
Perhaps an obvious point but one that bears repeating. Words are inherently potent, so leaders should use them to their advantage. Complimenting the positive attributes of an associate is vital. Give them a reputation to live up to.

As a business leader, the expectations you have of your associates and the expectations they have of their own work is very powerful. The Pygmalion effect can help to encourage associates to work to their full potential. I've long believed in the concept of a self-fulfilling prophecy. When an associate believes he can perform at a high level, they usually will do so. Therefore, a business leader should take every action possible to increase an associate's expectations of what they can accomplish.

A business leader can employ the Pygmalion effect on himself or herself by whom they associate with. Years ago one of my mentors said to me, "Carefully pick your business friends! You will end up being the average of the five people you spend the most time with." I've found this to be very true.

Fortunately for me, I joined a Young Presidents Organization (YPO) forum. Here was a group of business leaders who provided me positive role models on how to be a better business leader. Warren Buffet once said, "It's better to hang out with people better than you. Pick out associates whose behavior is better than yours and you'll drift in their direction."

Consciously consider who you allow in your life. Ask yourself about the people you meet and spend time with: Are they making you better? Do they help you set expectations to be a better version of yourself.

CHAPTER 42
Mentors

Occasionally, a new book comes out with a very clever title that I admire. Such is the case of a book by Tim Ferriss with the brilliant title *Tribe of Mentors*.

Tim Ferriss is the *New York Times* bestselling author who is probably best known for his book *The 4-Hour Workweek*. In *Tribe of Mentors*, Mr. Ferriss shares the ultimate compilation of tools, tactics, and habits from more than 130 of the world's top performers. This book contains practical and tactical advice from these mentors on how to achieve extraordinary results and transform your life. This book makes a strong case for the importance of mentors.

It has been my good fortune to have had many great mentors over the years. I attribute a good amount of whatever business success I have achieved to the knowledge and insights I gained from these mentors.

I've known some business leaders who make a point that they are self-made. They feel they don't need anyone's help—they are advocates of going it alone. Usually they believe they are already the smartest people in the room and don't believe they will learn much from others. I feel these narcissists are very misguided. Most thoughtful business leaders embrace and understand the value mentors have provided them over the years.

Many times well intended HR areas advocate for a formal structured mentoring program. For example, new associates would receive a "buddy" to learn the ropes. Associates with a few years of experience would be matched with a career mentor to help them grow in their position. And many firms have developed a formal mentoring program where they attempt to match up mentor and mentee. Although I think these programs can work, I'm not an advocate of this very structured approach to mentoring. These programs usually start with a lot of enthusiasm, but that enthusiasm usually wanes, and the mentoring program deteriorates into a bureaucratic check-the-box program—"Please provide HR with an acknowledgement that you and your mentor met this last quarter."

When I think back on all the mentors I've had over the years, never once did I anoint or announce at the time that they were my mentor. It just happened as our relationship developed.

So, how do you find good mentors? Here has been my approach:

1. You have to start with humility. You have to believe deep in your heart you can learn something from others. Talk less—listen more.

2. You need to be curious. You need to have curiosity about how to get better. Do you know you pay a prospective mentor a great compliment by asking for their opinion and truly listening to what they have to say? Many mentoring relationships I've had started with me paying the prospective mentor a sincere compliment: "I was really impressed how you handled X," or "Your success in the XYZ market is stunning—tell me more about how you made this happen."

3. Realize no one individual will have all the answers you need to achieve your professional objectives. This is where the tribe of mentors concept comes into play. Right now I probably have about a dozen mentors.

4. Be realistic about who can be a potential mentor. When I was president of NBC Bank, we started a formal mentoring program. Unfortunately, it ran out of steam in a couple of years. When the program first started, one junior loan

officer wrote to the then-CEO of Bank of America and asked the CEO to be his mentor. He was frustrated that he never received a response. Talk about an egomaniac! Why would he think that the CEO of one of the nation's biggest banks would agree to be a mentor to a junior loan officer in Lincoln, Nebraska? Strangers (especially people in the media and the public eye who've become "huge" successes) will virtually always have to say no to mentoring requests from strangers. Why? Because their time is already spoken for, and they're drowning in similar requests. Secondly, they don't have a relationship with you and therefore can't know how you operate or if it's a great investment of their time to help you. Be realistic.

5. Find great mentors through the inspiring people you're already interacting and working with now. They need to be people to whom you have already demonstrated your potential—who know how you think, act, communicate, and contribute. And they have to already like, trust, and believe in you. They also need to believe with absolute certainty that you'll put to great use their input and feedback.

6. Mentorship is typically a long game. I've had individuals who mentored me for thirty-plus years. Many were quite a bit older than me and have passed away. Even though in their later years we might not have had such frequent contact, I would light up when one of them would reach out and suggest we meet or just have a phone conversation. I still have a file with letters and notes of encouragement from these mentors.

7. Find your mentors among the people you know who are ten steps ahead of you in your field, role, or industry. When I was on the Board of the American Council of Life Insurers (ACLI), I developed a friendship with a couple of the CEOs of very large companies. At industry events I made a point

to connect with them and listen to their views on industry issues. We would also exchange emails from time to time. Although both are now retired from their companies, they are still doing interesting things in our industry, and I make it a point to connect with them a couple of times a year. Connect with people whom you can help and who will find it a mutually rewarding and beneficial experience to support you.

8. Put yourself in a potential mentor's shoes. If the tables were turned, what would you want to see from this individual asking for help? If you were inundated with requests for help every day, what type of person would you choose to assist and why? Go out and become that person who others would love to support and nurture.

9. Remember that most of mentoring is "caught not taught." We have all heard that roughly 90 percent of communication is nonverbal. Many mentors don't realize that their lasting imprint on a mentee is often how they conduct their life, whether at work, home, or in other settings. Over the years I've had mentors who I've spent little time with, but I've watched their success. I watched how they ran their business and how they lived their lives. They were a role model and an inspiration to me.

10. When thinking of mentors, we usually think of a "relationship between a young person (the mentee) and an older person (the mentor)." This view is way too limiting. Some of my most important mentors were peers. As I mentioned earlier, I was in the Young Presidents' Organization (YPO) and belonged to a YPO Forum. Most of these forum members ended up being important mentors to me. Many of our current and former board members were and continue to be mentors to me. Today some of my mentors are young people. I find their perspective and knowledge on current technology and contemporary culture to be invaluable.

You also need to give back. Be a mentor to others. At this point in my career I get a great deal of satisfaction when others seek my thoughts. As mentioned earlier, it is the highest compliment. I recently received a handwritten note from an individual with whom I've had a twenty-plus-year business relationship. He wrote how much my advice has meant to him over the years. His note meant a great deal to me. As I quoted earlier in this book, "Even an old dog likes to be petted once in a while."

Psychologist and Wharton professor Adam Grant, in his book *Give and Take,* describes three types of people in the world: givers, takers, and matchers. Takers might give, but only minimally and with the sole objective of getting what they want. Matchers, somewhat similarly, expect to receive in-kind for what they give. But givers share their knowledge and connections freely without any expectation of return. Which of these types do you think is most successful? While it might seem counterintuitive, Grant's data show that it's the givers. Despite not directly pursuing returns, those who freely give are consistently rewarded with promotions, profits, and more. Why? Because all those they've helped want to return the favor.

Mentoring is key to business success; get a tribe of mentors to help you, and in turn, give back by mentoring others.

CHAPTER 43
Being a Business Leader During a Crisis

I received my undergraduate degree from the University of Nebraska—Lincoln in May of 1975, and in early June of 1975, I started my working career at UMB—Bancshares in Kansas City. I've been in the workforce for over forty-six years, and during the past forty-six years I've witnessed many business crises. Here are the ones that are memorable to me:

- 1973–1975 recession, oil price shock, nifty-fifty stock crash.
- 1981–1982 recession, to break the back of inflation. The ten-year treasury rate peaked at 15.08 percent on September 21, 1981.
- 1982–1987 farm crisis. Farm real estate values in many areas declined by over 50 percent. Many multigeneration farm families were forced into bankruptcy.
- October 19, 1987. Black Monday. Stock market declined by 22.6 percent in one day.
- Late 1980s to the early 1990s, the savings and loan (S&L) crisis occurred. 1,043 out of 3,234 S& Ls failed or were forced to merge.
- 2000–2002 dotcom bubble burst. Nasdaq composite falls 78 percent.
- 9/11 attacks on the World Trade Center
- 2008–2010 Great Recession. Residential real estate value

collapsed in many parts of the country.
- 2020 COVID-19 Pandemic

Now these weren't all the major crises. I didn't mention the numerous wars or rumors of wars plus the many crises that impacted certain developing countries or a number of energy price shocks and various countries' currency and banking crises. Suffice it to say, I've lived through many crises over my working career. For many of these years—since 1982—I've been leading a financial institution through these crises. So what have I learned?

First, successfully navigating a crisis is mostly about leading and not managing. I was going to title this chapter "Managing Through a Crisis" but thought the better of it and feel leadership is much more important when a crisis occurs. So how does a great leader handle a crisis?

A leader needs to first identify the crisis they are facing. Crises can be bifurcated into two broad types: routine and novel. Routine crises occur from known risks for which an organization can plan and develop mitigation procedures. Examples include liquidity plans for financial institutions, disaster recovery, and IT security plans for all companies.

Novel crises are those crises that exhibit unusual frequency or impact. Organizations typically don't have plans for such events. A novel crisis may be a confluence of two or three events that strike at the same time period, or they may simply be too big or unusual to be imagined (like the COVID-19 pandemic). You need to decide which type of crisis you're facing so you can develop the appropriate response.

But whether routine or novel, here are some key things all leaders need to do:

1. Continuously frame the crisis: Rather than holding fast to first impressions in analysis of the crisis, be flexible to embrace new information and data as it comes along. Cast a wide net for information, and separate the noise from what is real. If new analysis suggests a remake of the original

plan, remake the plan. Harkening back to my chapter on narratives, the leaders need to control the narrative, clearly defining the crisis.

2. Actively communicate: You can't communicate enough through a crisis. The people you work with crave direction. Communication, however, needs to be authentic and honest. Most people want certainty and look to their leaders to provide it. But if you don't know, you need to say you don't know. Don't try to create certainty when it isn't available. What you can always say is that this crisis, like all others, will eventually end.

3. Build trust: Trust is always important but never more so than during difficult times. It is important that leadership establish a trusting environment. This is primarily accomplished through authentic and transparent communication.

4. Be ready for the unexpected: Under extreme pressure, the leader should understand that customers, vendors, distributors, and associates may act differently than they do normally. Remember the usual organization rules may not apply during a crisis.

5. You have to be resilient. You have to be persistent. Leading through a crisis is tough. It's a slog. The most important thing a leader can do is just go back to the battle each and every day. Look for the opportunities. In every crisis there is an opportunity. If nothing else, it is an opportunity for your key leaders to grow as they deal with the crisis. Remember, "smooth seas do not make skillful sailors." Through adversity we all grow and gain valuable experience.

6. Be measured. Resist the urge to do something immediately. Many times the best thing is to take no immediate action or, in some instances, to do nothing at all. In the white-hot

moment of dealing with a crisis, when so much of our time and attention is focused on instantaneous reaction, it seems almost inconceivable that doing nothing might be the best—but many times, inaction is the best move.

7. Conversely, be aware of "abdication bias." Don't adopt the attitude that there is nothing I can do. There is always something a leader can do. Don't eschew responsibility or blame others.

8. Stay calm. As a leader, you have to stay calm as others may become panicked. I learned a great lesson on this during the ag crisis in the mid-eighties. Although we were facing growing difficulties, including the realistic prospect of several of our banks failing, I never saw my boss lose his cool. He was unflappable and a calming influence on all of us. Remember that calm is contagious.

9. Stay rational—be aware of your biases. The great investment manager and author Howard Marks once wrote in his quarterly letter to his clients that we should all be aware of our own biases. He goes on to say, "I admit to mine. I'm more of a worrier than a dreamer." Like Mr. Marks, in my own case, I tend to focus more on what can go wrong. I attribute this to my early training as a credit analyst and a specialist in handling problem credits. In these roles, you are always thinking about what can go wrong. To combat this, I always try to remember my natural bias is to think about the worst outcomes. In fact, one of my early bosses at UMB, who ran our investment area, had a line he used when discussing a stock idea: "This company could be susceptible to good news." I try to remember those wise words.

It is important to be realistic with associates as to what we are facing. Unrealistic pessimism or optimism will come back to bite the leader. What people need is a straight, authentic analysis of the situation. As I've mentioned several times, I personally aim to be a realist with a hopeful nature. I don't always get there, but that's my aim.

10. Finally, you need to take care of yourself and not let worry overtake you. Be careful of awfulizing and catastrophizing. I always liked this quote by Mark Twain: "I've had a lot of worries in my life, most of which never happened." Be careful not to let your mind acclimate to a present circumstance and think the bad times will never end. Lift your gaze—think about the future and what you can do now to ensure a better one.

    I introduced you to Dr. Otis Young in chapter 29. In approximately 1992, Dr. Young penned his congregants the following advice on how to conquer worry:

- "Recognize that there is a big difference between nervous worry and healthy concern."
- "Get enough rest. Your problems look bigger when you are tired than when you are relaxed and refreshed."
- "Remember that problems have a way of diminishing in size as you get closer to them. Tomorrow's troubles look so much bigger today than they will look tomorrow."
- "Remember there is just as much a chance it will not happen as that it will."
- "Count on your hidden reserves. You have deep within you sleeping powers, which come forth in hours of crisis."
- "Learn to distinguish between those parts of life you can control and those parts you cannot."
- "Be wary of jealousy. Other people only look like they do not have a worry. Do not get the idea that worry has singled you out for its victim."
- "Check your goals. You may be worrying over false ambitions that are not worth the effort."
- "When you are anxious, check in with a family member, a shut-in, or a troubled friend. In extending yourself, you will lose your frustrations."

Although this advice is over thirty years old, it is still relevant today. A business leader cannot succumb to immobilizing worry.

CHAPTER 44
How to Guarantee You'll Be Miserable in Business

In 1986, Berkshire Hathaway vice chairman Charlie Munger delivered a commencement speech at a Los Angeles prep school that some of his children attended. It was an unusual talk in that he didn't follow the usual commencement speaker's playbook of discussing how to live a good life or the search for success or happiness in life. Instead, he titled the talk "Prescriptions for Guaranteed Misery in Life," borrowing a concept from a talk Johnny Carson gave several years earlier.

Carson had discussed three sure things he knew would lead to misery: (1) ingesting chemicals in an effort to alter mood or perception, (2) envy, and (3) resentment. If you focused on just those three things, you would have the most miserable life.

Munger liked Carson's speech so much he expanded Carson's list to include the following:

- Be unreliable.
- Avoid comprise.
- Harbor resentment.
- Seek revenge.
- Indulge in envy.
- Take drugs.
- Become addicted to alcohol.
- Neglect to learn from your good and bad experiences.

- Cling defiantly to your existing belief.
- Stay down when you are inevitably struck down by the challenges in life.

Mr. Munger's list, if followed, will guarantee a miserable personal life. Mr. Munger's list caused me to think about a similar list for business. So here is my list on how you can guarantee you'll be miserable in business. You'll see there is quite a bit of duplication from Mr. Munger's list.

1. Don't be trustworthy—Trust is the foundation of all business activity. If you become known as untrustworthy, your success as a business leader will be severely impaired. Your colleagues won't trust you, and neither will your associates, customers, suppliers, or other business leaders. You'll be an outcast.

2. Be unreliable—Don't follow through on your words or commitments. Be late or miss meetings altogether. Don't respond to legitimate emails in a timely manner. Never complete assigned projects on time. No one will take you seriously because no one can count on you. You will likely be the laughingstock.

3. Attempt to always negotiate an unfair advantage—We all know businesspeople who are known as tough negotiators. They usually take great pride in their negotiation prowess. They have a reputation as being someone you don't want to face in any negotiation. These individuals may gain a temporary advantage but their approach to negotiation will hurt them over the long run. The hard negotiator sees any negotiation as a contest of will in which the side that takes the more extreme position and holds out longer fares better. However, this type of negotiation usually produces an equally hard response from the other side. This approach to negotiation usually exhausts all involved and will hurt long-term relationships with the other side.

These types of negotiators don't understand the only thing that works long term is a "principled approach to negotiation" with a win-win attitude. This method was popularized by Roger Fisher and William Ury in their classic book *Getting to Yes*.

4. Cling defiantly to your existing beliefs—If you cling defiantly to your existing beliefs in the face of new or better information, you are setting yourself up to be miserable. Conditions are always changing. If you refuse to take in new information and adjust your views, you'll be known as someone who is backward and not a forward thinker. You'll be miserable.

5. Take all the credit or deflect the blame to others—We all know businesspeople who take credit for anything that has gone well but deflect the blame to others when things go wrong. These individuals will be despised by their coworkers and won't be trusted by their supervisors.

6. Go down and stay down when you are struck down—My final prescription for misery is to go down and stay down when you get your first, second, or third reversal in your business life. Because there is so much adversity out there—even for the lucky and wise—this will guarantee that, in due course, you will be permanently mired in misery. You'll be known as a quitter, not resilient—you'll be miserable.

All these things are commonsense things to avoid, but I've seen many succumb to what may be their initial allure. Remember that to be a successful business leader you need to play a long game. More on playing the long game in the next chapter.

CHAPTER 45
Marathon or Sprint?

Is achieving success in business more like running a marathon or a sprint? I think it is mostly a marathon with an occasional sprint. When do you sprint? If you are working on a special project, launching a new product, making an acquisition, merging in a new company, and so on, you are going to have to sprint. You'll need to work longer hours, expend more effort, and experience more stress to get the ball over the goal line.

Doing a sprint from time to time is essential for business success, but you can't sprint all the time. If you are always sprinting, you'll burn yourself out and everyone around you. One thing I've observed over the years is that many startup founders experience severe burnout, vowing never to do a startup again. Getting a startup up and running does require a sprint, but it's such a long sprint the founders end up becoming exhausted.

Anything worthwhile takes time, including business success. If success comes too quickly, there is usually something wrong. It may prove fleeting and transitory.

In chapter 36 I mentioned my wife and I had recently visited Bentonville, AR and toured the Walmart Museum. In the museum they have an electronic display showing the growth of Walmart stores over the years. Today Walmart is this bemouth with over 10,000 stores and employs over 2.3 million people. But this wasn't always the case. When Sam Walton started his Five and Dime business in 1950 in downtown Bentonville, he had one store. In fact, it was 7 years before he added a second store. It wasn't until the 1970s that Walmart started to experience fast growth. In the decade of the 1970s they added 258 Walmart stores.

It is important to remember that in business slow growth at first is the norm not the exception. The media loves to spotlight fast growing businesses giving the impression that hyper-growth is easily achieved. It is not, most new businesses, over many years, stumble and fail toward ultimate success.

So anything worthwhile takes time. It reminds me of a Beverly Sills quote when the press was calling her an overnight sensation for singing Cleopatra in Handel's Julius Caesar. She said, "My overnight sensation was twenty years in the making."

Another reality is that no business's result goes consistently up and to the right unless management is cooking the books. We need to remember the inherent nature of business is volatility in results. Hopefully, the trend line is positive, but consistent year over year increase in results does not occur without undo manipulation.

Stephen Covey, the famous motivational author and speaker, created the term "the Law of the Farm." What is the Law of the Farm, and how is such a term connected to business leadership? The Law of the Farm states that a farmer will have a good harvest only if he plans and works diligently over a period of time on the farm. He has to do many tasks at the right time in the right order if he wants to get a bumper crop. The farmer has to prepare the field; plant the seeds; nourish the soil and seeds; water the plants; provide protection to the plants from insects, diseases, and stray animals and birds; take care of weeds; and regularly watch over the crops. This will help get a good harvest. If the farmer just plants the seeds and expects them to grow to crops on their own, he is mistaken. He is going against the Law of the Farm and cannot expect to reap good results. In other words, a good farmer has to run a marathon to be successful.

We also need to be mindful of the "J Curve" effect. The J Curve represents the tendency of any new business or investment to post negative returns in the initial years and then post increasing returns in later years as the business or investment grows. So you need to be patient to experience long-term success. You need to effectively run a marathon.

What about fast-growing startups? Launching a startup and having initial success can happen very quickly. But making it a real business takes a lot of time. I've done a great deal of research on Angel investing, and I've observed at Assurity Ventures that for a startup it usually takes at least four years just to get pointed toward a real business—and I'd argue it takes seven to ten years for a surviving startup to be considered successful.

So if success in business is more like running a marathon, what should you do? Here are three things:

First and most importantly, take care of yourself. You have got to take care of yourself because you are playing a long game. You have to eat right, get regular exercise, control stress, and get adequate sleep. You need to find your own work-life balance. You need to have the discipline to exercise, control stress, eat right, and so on week after week.

Are you familiar with the concept of "sharpening the saw?" Covey popularized this concept in his book *The 7 Habits of Highly Effective People*. Here is what he wrote:

> "Sharpening the Saw means preserving and enhancing the greatest asset you have—you. It means having a balanced program for self-renewal in four areas of your life: physical, social/emotional, mental, and spiritual. Here are some examples of activities:
> - Beneficial eating, exercising, and resting
> - Making social and meaningful connections with others
> - Learning, reading, writing and teaching
> - Spending time in nature, expanding spiritual self through meditation, music, art, prayer, or service"

Take time to sharpen your saw.

Another repeating theme in this book is the importance of trust. Build long-term trust with the people who you interact with every day—superiors, peers, distributors, suppliers, and any person or organization essential for your business's long-term success. Building trust is like making a deposit in a savings account—you need to make deposits and then finally you can make a withdrawal. Be true to your word and follow through with your actions. Value the relationships that you have, and don't take them for granted. Always be honest. Help others whenever you can. Be careful about cutting people off. So often, whatever goes around comes around.

Here is an important third thing. We all know about the power of financial compounding when growing our money and investments, but are you aware of the power of knowledge compounding? I'm going to repeat a quote from Warren Buffet, which I used in chapter 11.

> "Read 500 pages every day. That's how knowledge works. It builds up, like compound interest. All of you can do it, but I guarantee not many of you will do it."

This is why we see a tremendous difference between people's success, happiness, and energy as they age. For most of the population, education ends when they finish schooling. But for the individuals who take it upon themselves to learn with greater vigor once formal learning is complete, the effect of their learning over time compounds. Put it simply, if Jeff Bezos or Bill Gates read an interesting book on human behavior right now, they'd get a lot more value out of it than you and I. That's because they have so many interesting mental models that allow them to test findings and incorporate learnings. It is these mental models that differentiate master/learning machines from everyone else.

Running a business is mostly a marathon. Take care of yourself, build long-term business relationships, and keep learning. A mentor of mine once said, "A lot of good advice in business simply boils down to thinking long term." Remember, you are running a marathon.

CHAPTER 46
Culture

A lot has been written over the years on the importance of a company's culture to its business success. In fact, one recurring feature in almost all CEO annual report letters is that they talk a great deal about their corporate culture, about norms in the company, about what behaviors are expected and rewarded. The CEO might use different language to discuss their company's culture. They might talk about guiding principles or the mission and values statement. But make no mistake, culture is very important to CEOs. Businesses are nothing more than collections of people trying to achieve common aims. Culture is the shared grooves of habit, character, and practice in the business. Peter Drucker once pronounced, "Culture eats strategy for breakfast." Drucker's point wasn't that strategy is unimportant, but rather that a powerful and empowering culture is a more sure route to organizational success.

I think it is fair to say that all successful business leaders recognize the value of a great company culture. In this chapter I want to discuss the common elements present in companies with a great culture, the benefits of a great corporate culture, and some of the unique challenges to fostering and maintaining a great company culture with a remote workforce.

It is true every company with a great culture has aspects unique to that company. But there are many commonalities. What follows are some elements I've observed present in any company with a great corporate culture:

Clear mission and values: An inspired company culture doesn't just manifest itself out of thin air. First, it has to be articulated and communicated through an emphasis on the company's mission and corporate values. The foundation of any great company's culture is its mission and values—they're something every associate should know and understand.

Provide purpose beyond just making money. The majority of associates crave meaning and purpose in their work. They want to know that their work has a higher calling. Building a great culture requires company leaders to continually stress the "why" of everyday work.

Communication. Great companies realize the importance of effective communication to a great corporate culture. Excellent communication can ensure that everyone in the company is on the same page. Company leaders recognize a big part of their job is communication. They also recognize good communication requires a lot of effort.

Transparency: Hand in hand with good communication is transparency. Secrets, and in general a lack of communication from the top down, create a culture of insecurity and uncertainty. Workplaces with positive cultures support a philosophy of transparency so that every team member feels they know where they stand, where the company is headed, and in general, they feel "in the loop." Transparency is bracingly positive.

Corporatewide, area and individual goals. No organization can have a positive corporate culture without clear goals. This is why I particularly like EOS developed by Gino Wickman. With EOS, everyone has goals and rocks. Associates also are communicated the area and corporate goals and rocks. They can see how what they do every day supports the company's near- and long-term goals. Ultimately, associates want to know where the company is going and how what they do every day contributes to the company's overall success.

Encourage positivity in order to build a positive culture. Winning begets winning. Companies with a positive culture get the flywheel going in a positive way. They are also careful to only bring on new associates who will help build on the positive culture. Business leaders need to be watchful for pockets of negativity in their company. These pockets of negativity are a workplace contagion few businesses can withstand.

Foster social connections. Workplace relationships are an essential element to a positive company culture. Leaders provide associates with opportunities for social interactions in the workplace. Like Gallup's Q12 suggests, most associates need to have a best friend at work. With a work friend, they have someone to call and lean on in times of stress, plus offering them day-to-day encouragement.

Recognition: Great companies have innovative and frequent programs in place for recognizing the achievements of their associates. This recognition happens in private and also in public ways.

Leaders are visible and accessible: Company leaders are transparent, accessible, honest, and authentic. They do not hide in their offices. They make it clear we are all in this together. They are in the trenches every day. It is also important for leaders to be empathetic and demonstrate emotional intelligence. Leaders need to "walk their talk." Fostering a great corporate culture is less about what a leader says and more about what they do.

Inspiring physical workspace: Having a physically inspiring place to work is very important. If people feel good about where they go to work every day, it will be reflected in how they treat the company's customers and each other.

No office politics: The company has largely eliminated company politics. Gossip, backbiting, meetings before meetings, and so on don't happen.

Ongoing professional development opportunities: Associates want to grow. They want an individualized, customized plan for their professional growth and development. Companies with great cultures are all about associate development.

Culture first: Company leaders are always thinking about how they build the company's culture. They are mindful of this when organizing company activities and policies.

Benefits of a Great Corporate Culture

Here are what I feel are some of the primary benefits of a great corporate culture:

- **Recruitment.** Many HR professionals agree that a strong company culture is one of the best ways to attract potential associates. Having a reputation as a great place to work gives an organization a competitive advantage in hiring the best and brightest. People want to work for companies with a good reputation from previous and current associates. Culture is a company's "talent brand." It is how associates think, feel, and share about the company as a place to work.

- **Associate loyalty.** Not only will a positive culture help recruitment efforts, it will also help retain top talent as well. A positive culture fosters a sense of associate loyalty. Associates are much more likely to stay with their current employer when they feel they are treated right and enjoy going to work every day.

- **Job satisfaction.** It's no surprise that job satisfaction is higher at companies with a positive corporate culture.

- **Collaboration.** Associates are much more likely to come together as a team at companies with a strong culture. A positive culture facilitates social interaction, teamwork, and open communication.

- **Being a high-performing business.** Strong company cultures have been linked to higher rates of productivity and financial success. This is because associates tend to be more motivated and dedicated to employers who invest in their well-being and happiness.

- **Associate morale.** Maintaining a positive company culture is a guaranteed way to boost associate morale. A company cannot be considered a great place to work without a positive corporate culture.

- **Less stress.** A positive company culture will help significantly reduce workplace stress. Companies with a strong corporate culture tend to seem less stressed.

Unique Challenges to Fostering and Maintaining a Great Company Culture with a Remote Workforce

It's now clear remote work will be a big part of corporate America's future. This is why progressive companies are designing a customized experience specifically for their remote workers. Here are some ideas on how to foster and maintain a great corporate culture with a remote workforce.

- **Onboarding.** Remote associates require an onboarding exercise unique to their circumstances. Ideally, new associates will spend some initial time physically in the company's headquarters, periodically revisiting from time to time. After that initial time in the home office, the supervisor needs to be sure they regularly engage with new remote associates in a meaningful way.

- **Celebrate with your remote workers.** Company cultures become stronger in times of celebration. Unfortunately, it can be tough to celebrate when everyone is remote. Companies need to be creative in ensuring remote workers are a part of company events. Send a celebratory gift to their home. Schedule a companywide Friday Afternoon Club (FAC). Send a pack of craft beer or bottle of wine to each associate. There are a lot of companies doing interesting things. Do some research and plagiarize the best ideas.

- **Communication.** Communication is key to maintaining a cohesive company culture. Your remote team culture will flourish or fail purely on communication. Set aside regular times every week for an all-hands video call if at all possible. Cover what the team is working on, give details on any decisions that may affect the team, and reiterate that you want feedback and open dialogue. During the early months of the pandemic, I did an almost weekly video update. Don't forget the power of an individual written communication sent to an individual via the USPS.

- **Find ways to constantly reinforce your core values.** You need to have programs and initiatives in place that regularly reinforce the company's core values to remote associates. Management needs to strive for these associates to live our values.

- **Capitalize on technological tools.** There are a growing number of technological tools that make scaling a company culture across a remote workforce more manageable. You need to become proficient at using all these tools, whether Cisco Jabber, Microsoft Teams, Zoom calls, or Cisco WebEx, not to mention a regular text, telephone call, or email. These tools are integral to staying connected with people who aren't physically in the office every day.

- **Be creative.** When using these technical tools, encourage associates to hook up for virtual coffee breaks, FACs, and other times. Randomly contact remote associates to seek their advice on an area or corporate issues.

- **Be considerate.** Whether all or part of your company is working remotely, colleagues need to be extra considerate. Be especially thoughtful when scheduling time on your colleague's calendar. This is particularly true if colleagues have children. Be mindful of any time zone changes, and make sure the meeting is necessary. Being considerate in these minor ways adds up to big differences in associate satisfaction, and your remote team will appreciate you all the more for it.

- **Build trust.** Supervisors with remote workers need to be more intentional and more organized and work harder to establish trust.

Having a great corporate culture requires constant attention. It can never be taken for granted. Corporate culture is not static; it needs to evolve. Great cultures incorporate change as new approaches come to light. Company culture is also not just about social events. It is more than free food in the cafeteria, doggy daycare centers, onsite barber shops, or any other over-the-top benefits provided by some Silicon Valley companies. Frontline supervisors play an oversized role in tending and promoting a great corporate culture. How an associate feels about their immediate supervisor is largely how they feel about the company.

For most companies, what they are attempting is at least partially aspirational. A company is always becoming something more, for better or worse. Aim for a good corporate culture and it's likely you'll get positive business results. Nurture a good corporate culture and achieving long-term corporate goals will become more assured.

CHAPTER 47
To Thine Own Self Be True

Shakespeare used the phrase "To Thine Own Self Be True" in Act 1, Scene III, Lines 78-82 of his play "Hamlet." Over the years, Shakespearean scholars have argued as to the exact meaning of the phrase. They've concluded this phrase implies a multiplicity of meanings. For purposes of this chapter, I'm going to interpret that this phrase means being true to your real self. Don't try to be someone else; aim to be the best version of yourself.

By reading this far, you know I believe in the importance of being a talent- and strengths-based organization. This means business leaders need to be sure what we ask someone to do every day fits with their natural strengths. Skills, knowledge, and experience can be acquired, but talent is innate. Many years ago at Assurity we added the "strengths or innate talents" required to every position description. At the time we did this, it was a novel practice. Every company lists the desired skills, knowledge, and experience on their position descriptions. Adding required strengths or innate talents was totally new, and I would argue they are the most important part of any position description.

I start with the premise that people do best when they work in their areas of strength. One cannot build high performance on weaknesses. Weaknesses can be coached to average, but strengths can be leveraged to the moon. This is such a commonsense idea, but so few firms seem to be devoted to being strengths based.

So how do we discover our strengths? Personal reflection, of course. Think about a time when you're doing work and are in "the flow." Time goes quickly and the work seems effortless. When this happens, you are likely working in your areas of strength. Another important way is to take advantage of the instruments available to help you know yourself better. This is why I've been a longtime fan of using instruments like the Myers-Briggs Type Indicator, Kolbe Index, and the Gallup Top 5 CliftonStrengths Assessment. In fact, at Assurity we have the Myers-Briggs Type Indicator and the Gallup Top 5 CliftonStrengths on the name plate of each associates' office. This information helps colleagues better understand each other, but it also helps us better understand ourselves.

Over my long business career, I know I've taken over twenty different individual assessments, some of them several times. They all present a little different information, and it has helped me build an understanding of myself. It has helped me create a mosaic of my strengths. I know what I do well and where I will struggle. A long-standing career objective of mine is to work more and more in my areas of strength and less and less in what I don't do well. I would encourage you to adopt this objective as well. I've consciously attempted to surround myself with people who shore up my weaknesses. I hire for my weaknesses, and I make sure I continually show my appreciation to these colleagues whose strengths are very different from mine but critical for the company's success.

We also need to remember our strengths all have "balcony" and "basement" qualities. It's important you understand this about yourself as well. Let me give you a personal example. One of my Gallup Top Strengths is "Activator." Here is what Gallup says about this strength.

Activator Strength

"You are impatient for action. You may concede that analysis has its uses or that debate, and discussion can occasionally yield some valuable insights, but deep down you know that only action is real. Only action can make things happen. Only action leads to performance

You make a decision, you take action, you look at the result, and you learn. This learning informs your next action and your next. The bottom line is this: You know you will be judged not by what you say, not by what you think, but by what you get done. This does not frighten you. It pleases you."

So the balcony quality of this strength is a strong bias to action – to get something worthwhile done, to move the ball across the goal line.

But there are basement qualities to this strength. I know I tend to act prematurely – to launch sooner than we should. I can move forward in a way that will ultimately cost more time and money. In contrast if I would have slowed down and been more thoughtful, I would have been more effective. One of my mentors once said to me, "Every now and again, you should look over your shoulder to see if your troops are still with you or are you on the battlefield or are you there by yourself." Wise words for me. Be mindful of the balcony and basement qualities of your strengths.

I offer one caveat of just working in your areas of strength and not on your weaknesses. As you further advance into the executive ranks, the more difficulty you'll encounter if you have any glaring weaknesses. In fact, Dr. Bradford Smart states in his excellent book "Topgrading" the following: "Executives make it to the big leagues when their strengths are solid, and they have no serious weaknesses."

As an example, over the years I've heard a number of sales management leaders say something like, "I'm just not good at math." Now, to be a top performing sales manager, you do not have to be a math wizard, but you better have a good working knowledge of probability and statistics. Conversely, an actuary who aspires to be in a top management position can't hide behind, "I'm just not good at working with people or making presentations." If you want to be in executive management, you better be good at working with people and effectively presenting to groups. If you aspire to be a top executive, it's hard to have any glaring weaknesses.

In chapter 10 I introduced Dan Sullivan, the founder of "The Strategic Coach" consulting firm. In chapter 10 I also discussed his concept of "unique ability". Mr. Sullivan defines "unique ability" as the characteristics and values entirely unique to you. In other words, your strengths. He is an advocate for people primarily working in their areas of strength and further, that everyone should work on developing their strengths.

Dan Sullivan counsels his clients to not work on their weaknesses. I love this line from Mr. Sullivan, "If you spend too much time working on your weaknesses, all you end up with is a lot of strong weaknesses." And I'll add – remember they will still be your weaknesses.

But what is most important is that you spend the time to know yourself and that you primarily work in your areas of strength and work on improving your strengths. This is where you'll do your best and contribute most to the success of the company. In the end, "To Thine Own Self Be True."

CHAPTER 48
Purpose in Business

What should be the goal of any business? For a long time, the prevailing view in corporate America was that advanced by the economist Milton Friedman in a September 1970 New York Times article where he said, "The social responsibility of business is to increase its profits." I once believed this true. I was wrong. Fortunately, for many business leaders our thinking has changed. It's been changed because society has changed.

In 1994, John Elkington—the famed British management consultant and sustainability guru—was ahead of his time when he coined the phrase the "triple bottom line." The triple bottom line in economics believes that companies should commit to focusing as much on social and environmental concerns as they do on profits. Triple bottom line theory posits that instead of one bottom line, there should be three: profit, people, and the planet. A triple bottom line seeks to gauge a corporation's level of commitment to corporate social responsibility and its impact on the environment over time. The idea was that a company can be managed in a way that not only makes money but that also improves people's lives and the planet.

Larry Fink, the CEO of investment giant BlackRock, created quite a stir with his 2018 missive titled "A Sense of Purpose." In this letter he advocated that for a company to prosper over time, every company must not only deliver financial performance but also demonstrate how it makes a positive contribution to society. Additionally, in an August 2019 statement, the Business Roundtable elevated "stakeholder" interests to the same level as shareholders

BOOST! | 267

interest. McKinsey & Company recently reported that only 7 percent of Fortune 500 CEOs believe their companies should mainly focus on making profits and not be distracted by social goals. Eighty-nine percent of executives surveyed in a 2015 E&Y survey said a strong sense of collective purpose drives associate satisfaction, 84 percent said it can affect an organization's ability to transform, and 80 percent said it helps increase customer loyalty. Across corporate America, the Environmental, Social and Governance movement—commonly known as ESG—has gained traction. Most large publicly traded companies now feel compelled to annually file a "Corporate Social Responsibility Report," commonly known as a CSR.

The CSR reports show how the company is contributing to the common good. In addition, there is a growing number of Certified B-Corps. B-Corps believe in using business as a force for good. In other words, operating the business for a purpose that is about more than just the bottom line.

Customers and associates are gravitating toward companies that are trying to have a positive impact on the world. Millennials especially want workplaces with social purpose. It is estimated by 2025, 75 percent of the workforce will be composed of millennials.

Millennials have high expectations for the actions of business when it comes to social purpose and accountability, and they want to work for companies that uphold these values. In other words, they want a company which is about more than just making money; they want a company with purpose.

Another unfortunate fact is most associates are not very engaged in their work. Many executives and frontline managers apply conventional economic logic in how they manage their associates. They view their associates as self-interested agents and design organizational procedures and culture around a contractional approach to managing their human resources. It is unfortunate, but many business leaders don't understand you can't build something special or unique in the marketplace unless you also build something special or unique in the workplace.

So what's the answer? Executives and managers need to engage associates in the company's purpose. By purpose, I mean more than just the company's mission and values statement. An inspiring mission statement is foundational, but purpose goes beyond the mission statement and the company's stated values.

Ernst & Young in its publication, "The Business Case for Purpose" defines purpose as an aspirational reason for being that is grounded in humanity and inspires a call to action. It is big picture and long term and it allows an organization to create value beyond financial metrics.

Purpose means the company is about more than just the bottom line. Personally, I believe the potential is extraordinary for business to serves as a force for good. Embracing an authentic purpose requires a higher level of maturity in a company's own awareness.

In the April 2020 issue of McKinsey Quarterly, they stated the following on purpose: "We suggest that the disconnects between public perceptions of business and its potential for good, or between associates' desire for meaning at work versus what they experience, reflect a purpose gap." I too believe we have a "purpose gap."

Some people think 'purpose' means diverting from profitability—but it doesn't. The purpose of a company is not just to produce profits, it is to produce solutions to problems of people and the planet, and in the process they will produce profits. I concede it's a difficult balance, but business leaders need to solve simultaneously for the interests of associates, communities, suppliers, the environment, customers, and the company's bottom line. All business leaders need to remember creating financial value within a business and addressing relevant societal challenges are not mutually exclusive ideas.

A book that had a powerful influence on my thoughts on the importance of purpose in business was Simon Sinek's book *Start with Why*. Mr. Sinek started a movement to help people become more inspired at work, and in turn inspire their colleagues and customers. Since then, millions have been touched by the power of his ideas, including more than 28 million who've watched his TED Talk based on *Start with Why*. Mr. Sinek recognized the reality that there are only two ways to influence behavior: you can manipulate it, or you can inspire it by stressing the company's why, or its purpose. Mr. Sinek said inspiring leaders start with why. People don't buy what you do, they buy why you do it—your purpose.

The desire to balance profit and purpose is arguably a return to the model that many American companies once followed. Henry Ford declared that, instead of boosting dividends, he'd rather use the money to build better cars and pay better wages. And Johnson & Johnson's credo, written in 1943, states that the company's "first responsibility" was not to investors but to doctors, nurses, and patients, to mothers and fathers and all others who use their products and services.

The idea that corporations should be only lean, mean, profit-maximizing machines isn't dictated by the inherent nature of capitalism, let alone by human nature. As individuals, we try to make our work not just profitable but also meaningful. So how does a business define its purpose?

A purpose doesn't describe the company's products, services or target market segment. It's not about the annual plan and accompanying metrics. The company's purpose is inspiring and makes associates feel proud of working for the company. Ideally the company's purpose is timeless. It is relevant now and for years to come.

So what does management need to do to make purpose come alive in their company? Here are six key things:

Communication
In a purpose-driven organization, the purpose needs to be continuously discussed. Leaders need to discuss the organization's impact on the lives of its customers, associates, and the greater community. Conversations should happen as part of sales meetings, business reviews, and other associate communications. By discussing the purpose frequently, the message will be constantly reinforced. Frequent and straightforward communication around a company's broader purpose is required, but it is not enough. Creative approaches to communicating a company's purpose makes the difference. Storytelling is particularly effective. Stories about how the company is living its purpose are especially powerful. Tell company legends about the company's core values and purpose.

Walk the Talk

Executives and managers need to walk the talk. Saying the environment is important but then not backing a comprehensive recycling program totally sends the wrong message. It is like during the height of the COVID-19 pandemic where some public officials were encouraging citizens to avoid big family holiday parties or holiday travel and it then came out that these same public officials were attending events with many people. Everyone recognizes hypocrisy, and associates will become more cynical. We need to remember everyone is watching what leaders do. By far the most important way to make core values and purpose come alive in an organization is to ensure that leadership lives them out every day.

Associates' Alignment with the Company's Purpose

We need to be sure and recruit people who align with the company's purpose. We need to be sure that each individual associate is able to clearly see how what they do every day contributes to the achievement of the company's purpose.

Be Consistent

The purpose of an organization should not change. The strategy and tactics will need to change but not the purpose. It is critical for leaders to be consistent in how they discuss the purpose of the organization internally and externally. The actions being taken by the organization should support the purpose and should be easy to understand. By being clear and consistent, every person in the organization should know how their actions impact the larger organization and the purpose. And if they don't, asking for clarification is not only acceptable, it is expected.

Recognition

We need to recognize and reward those individuals who are living out our purpose every day. I've long championed public recognition for associates who are exemplars of living the company's purpose. Others many prefer recognition that is less public. No matter the approach, we need to recognize those individuals who are aligned with and promoting the company's purpose.

Measure what you can, and learn from what you measure
We all know that what gets measured get done. But how do you measure progress on living a company's purpose? A place to start is to think what data and evidence are critical to understanding your organization's total social, environmental, and financial impact. And what metrics do your performance-management systems take into account? Seventh Generation, a maker of cleaning and personal-care products, recently built sustainability targets into the incentive system for its entire workforce in service of its goal of being a zero-waste company by 2025. Ultimately a shared purpose should create corporate clarity on what is really important.

Most forward-thinking business leaders would argue that an executive's most important role is to be a steward of the organization's purpose. Being a purpose-driven organization does not guarantee financial success, but I would argue it gives an organization a much better chance at reaching its financial goals. I believe business has an opportunity and an obligation to engage on the urgent needs of our planet and the greater society. Purpose is just not a lofty idea; it has practical implications.

Purpose puts a premium on leadership. Move too fast, and you will be criticized for swinging too far. Move too slowly, and you will be viewed as a corporate ostrich. But adopting a business-as-usual mentality is probably the most dangerous. Another danger is if you claim to be delivering on purpose but are ultimately viewed as inauthentic, you will lose credibility in front of your associates and society alike. For example, will you stick to your purpose during economic turbulence or only when times are good?

To be authentic, you must be unrelenting in elevating and stimulating debate about uncomfortable truths and tensions you may be tempted to sweep under the rug. You also need your own genuine way of talking about the symbiotic relationship between corporate purpose and corporate performance. At Assurity I felt we could not call ourselves successful unless we were also contributing to the greater good and helping society address some of its most difficult problems.

A company's purpose is bigger than its product, service, technology, charismatic leader, or team. It's the idea of who you are as a company and why you exist beyond bottom-line profitability. It's a great journey becoming a purpose-based organization—a journey that I believe more and more companies will embark on in the years ahead. This reflects the growing understanding among business leaders everywhere for the need to revise their social contract with society. "Corporate leaders today have the challenge of envisioning how to renew the corporate-society contract in the twenty-first century, such that firms contribute in distinct, relevant ways to societal well-being. To use business as a force for good!"

CHAPTER 49
Personal Purpose

Chapter 48 was about purpose in business. In this chapter I want to discuss personal purpose. A very fortunate thing for me early in my career was participation in a management training program, which included a course from the Success Motivation Institute (SMI), now known as Leadership Management International, Inc. (LMI). Paul J. Meyer of Waco, Texas, was the founder of SMI. The course was called "The Dynamics of Goal Setting."

Being exposed to this course's content at age twenty-three has proven to be very important to me. It was a great example of the oft-cited quote, "When the student is ready, the teacher will appear." I didn't know I was ready, but I was, and it made a huge difference in my life.

Here are some of the key things I learned in this course from SMI that I follow to this day:

1. Foundational to any effective goals program is the establishment of a personal mission statement and becoming clear about your own values. In this course, we spent a great deal of time becoming clear about our personal values, writing, rewriting, and reflecting on a personal mission statement. Although I had previously read Benjamin Franklin's autobiography, this course brought to life the process Franklin went through to establish his "thirteen virtues" or values. It made me a lifelong student of Franklin.

2. The ability to set goals and make plans for their accomplishment is critical to personal and professional success. Goal setting will help you achieve the things you want in life more than anything else.

3. To be effective, goals must be in writing. SMI postulated that few individuals have written goals.

4. To be effective, goals must be SMART: Specific, Measurable, Achievable, Relevant ,and Time bound. Almost all credible goal setting or planning systems are advocates of SMART goals.

5. Use a form of space repetition to internalize your goals. Daily review of your goals is key to internalizing the accomplishment of these goals.

6. Set goals in all key dimensions of your life: spiritual, family, physical, educational, career, financial, and social.

7. Goals should be of different durations: long-term goals, midterm goals, goals for the current year, and quarterly goals—all of which should drive the development of a daily task list.

8. Develop a plan for achieving your goals and a deadline for their attainment. Plan your progress carefully. Well-thought-through activity will help maintain enthusiasm for the accomplishment of your goals.

9. Develop a sincere desire for the things you want in life. A burning desire is the greatest motivator of every human action. The desire for success creates a vigorous and ever-increasing habit of success. Get your personal flywheel going in a positive direction.

10. Develop supreme confidence in yourself and your own abilities. Enter every activity without giving mental recognition to the possibility of defeat. Concentrate on your strengths instead of your weaknesses.

11. Develop a dogged determination to follow through on your plan, regardless of obstacles, criticism, or circumstances . . . or what other people say, think, or do.

12. Review your goals on a daily, weekly, and monthly basis for course correction. In order to achieve something significant, you will likely need to make changes along the way. When appropriate, you'll need to course correct as you gain additional information.

The SMI course had a positive impact on me. Forty-six years later, I still follow the precepts I learned in this course, and it has made a huge difference to me.

Stephen Covey's book *The 7 Habits of Highly Effective People* also had a big impact on my goal-setting process. Three concepts from that book have been especially impactful to me.

1. **Begin with the end in mind.**
   When setting goals, you have to know where you're headed. When writing down your goals, make sure that you understand the path to your final destination. After all, a goal without a clear roadmap is just a pipedream. Once you have your goal on paper, write out what you'll need to do to get there. These are your subgoals and the resources you will need to support you along the way.

2. **Law of the farm.**
   In chapter 45 I introduced Stephen Covey's concept, the law of the farm. Being a farmer myself, I've seen the law of the farm at work time and time again. I recently experienced this with the seeding of native grasses and pollinators at our

wildlife farm. Only in year three did this seeding come in to its own and now looks like what I imagined when I did the planting three years ago. It took time to have a great result.

Cramming doesn't work in a natural system like a farm. You can go for "quick fixes" but most won't produce a lasting result. Anything worthwhile takes time.

3. **Prioritizing Your Goals and Daily Activities**

   In *The 7 Habits of Highly Effective People,* Covey presents a technique for prioritizing that impressed me and soon became a central part of my personal planning process. This is sometimes referred to as the Eisenhower Decision Matrix. I understand this matrix guided President Eisenhower through his entire successful career as general and president. I briefly discussed this concept in chapter 15. In closing this chapter, I'll provide more information on this important productivity tool.

   The matrix consists of a square divided into four boxes, or quadrants, labeled as follows: (1) Urgent/Important; (2) Not Urgent/Important; (3) Urgent/Not Important, and (4) Not Urgent/Not Important.

EISENHOWER DECISION MATRIX

What is important is seldom urgent & what is urgent is seldom important.

	URGENT	NOT URGENT
IMPORTANT	**Quadrant 1** Important And Urgent Crises Deadlines Problems	**Quadrant 2** Important But Not Urgent Relationships Planning Recreation
NOT IMPORTANT	**Quadrant 3** Not Important But Urgent Interruptions Meetings Activities	**Quadrant 4** Not Important, Not Urgent Time Wasters Pleasant Activities Trivia

Quadrant 1: Urgent and Important Tasks

Quadrant 1 tasks are both urgent and important. They're tasks that require our immediate attention and also work toward fulfilling our long-term goals and mission in life. With a bit of planning and organization, many Quadrant 1 tasks can be made more efficient or even eliminated outright.

While we'll never be able to completely eliminate urgent and important tasks, we can significantly reduce them with a bit of proactivity and by spending more time in Quadrant 2. Quadrant 2 activities are where all substantial progress is made.

Quadrant 2: Not Urgent but Important Tasks

Quadrant 2 tasks are the activities that don't have a pressing deadline but nonetheless help you achieve your important goals. According to Covey, we should seek to spend most of our time in Quadrant 2 activities as they're the ones that provide us lasting happiness, fulfillment, and success. Unfortunately, there are a couple key challenges that keep us from investing enough time and energy into Quadrant 2 tasks:

- **You don't know what's truly important to you.** If you don't have any idea what values and goals matter most to you, you obviously won't know what things you should be spending your time on to reach those aims. Instead, you'll latch on to whatever stimuli and to-dos are most urgent.

- **Present bias.** We all have an inclination to focus on whatever is most pressing at the moment. Doing so is our default mode. It's hard to get motivated to do something when there isn't a deadline looming over our head.

Because Quadrant 2 activities aren't pressing for your attention, we typically keep them forever on the backburner of our lives and tell ourselves, "I'll get to those things someday after I've taken care of this." But "someday" will never come; if you're waiting to do the important stuff until your schedule clears up a little, trust me when I say that it won't. You'll always feel about as busy as you are now, and if anything, life just gets busier as you get older.

To overcome our inherent present-bias that prevents us from focusing on Quadrant 2 activities, we must live our lives intentionally and proactively. You can't run your life in default mode. You have to consciously decide "I'm going to make time for these things come hell or high water."

Quadrant 3: Urgent and Not Important Tasks

Quadrant 3 tasks are activities that require our attention now (urgent) but don't help us achieve our goals. Most Quadrant 3 tasks are interruptions from other people and often involve helping them meet their own goals and fulfill their priorities.

Quadrant 4: Not Urgent and Not Important Tasks
Quadrant 4 activities aren't urgent and aren't important. Quadrant 4 activities aren't pressing, nor do they help you achieve long-term goals. They're primarily distractions. I think if most of us did an audit on ourselves, we'd find that we spend an inordinate amount of time on Quadrant 4 activities like mindlessly watching TV. I'm sure most of us have those "I'm wasting my life" moments after we've spent hours surfing the web and realize we should have used that time to pursue our more ennobling life goals.

Developing a personal mission statement and understanding your values is foundational to personal success. With this in place, commit to developing goals in all key dimensions of your life: spiritual, family, physical, educational, professional, financial, and social. Your goals must be in writing to be optimally impactful and include long-term goals (five-plus years), midterm goals (two to five years), and current year and quarterly goals. The accomplishment of your quarterly goals should drive a daily to-do list.

If you follow these steps, you will be in rarefied company. You will have a huge competitive advantage. As Oliver Wendell Holmes said, "Most of us go to our graves with our music still inside us, unplayed." Don't let that happen to you—define in writing your personal purpose, mission, values, and goals in all dimensions of your life. Let your music out!

CHAPTER 50
Perspective

One of the ongoing challenges for every business leader is to maintain perspective. In the heat of any business problem, challenge, or opportunity, it is so easy to become overly emotional—to become so vested in a result you become immobilized. You must have passion to achieve success, but too much emotion and you will start to make mistakes.

Success or failure in business is often all about perspective. Short-term failures can be hidden long-term successes, while quick wins can sometime lead to future losses. It is impossible to know the future and how events will unfold.

Let's consider two of our country's most successful businesses, Amazon and Apple. Amazon has an impressive stock price history over the past two-plus decades. But you'd be hard-pressed to find anyone—outside of founder Jeff Bezos—who has been able to hold onto their shares for the entire ride. The stock has had its share of massive sell-offs. Since going public, there have been four times when the stock declined over 50 percent. In fact, during the dotcom bust, Amazon stock declined by 94 percent, and it experienced a particularly painful thirty-five-month period starting in 2003 when the price fell from $57.50 to $26.00 a share. Worries about the viability of online retailing, failed attempts at launching a smartphone, and missteps in attempting to sell in China caused investors to lose faith in the company's long-term success. Yet today no one can argue that Amazon isn't one of the most successful companies in human history.

Now consider Apple. Apple's stock hasn't been quite as volatile as Amazon, but over the past forty-one years there have been five times when the stock declined over 30 percent—during the dotcom bust, the stock declined by 71 percent. Concerns about the lack of new products—would the iPhone work, would anyone want an iPad?—caused the stock to decline. But today Apple is one of the most valuable companies in the world.

The point is it's impossible to tell whether things that happen will ultimately turn out for good or for ill. You never know what the consequences of misfortune or good fortune will be, as only time will tell the whole story. Things may look great at the start, but over time it may not become what you had imagined it to be. Similarly, you feel bad about something, but someday it could be one of the best things that happened to you.

At his seventieth birthday party, one of my favorite mentors said, "There are very few advantages to getting old other than experience and perspective." He went on to say, "When I was younger, I suffered through so many imagined worries. Now with the perspective of age, I do not."

So how do we maintain perspective?

One tool we can use was invented by Suzy Welch, wife of former GE CEO Jack Welch and a business writer for publications such as *Bloomberg, Businessweek,* and *O* magazine. It's called 10-10-10, which Welch describes in a book of the same name. I briefly introduced this tool in chapter 14. To use 10-10-10, we should think about our decisions on three different timeframes:

- How will we feel about it 10 minutes from now?
- How about 10 months from now?
- How about 10 years from now?

The three timeframes provide an elegant way of forcing us to get some distance on our decisions. 10-10-10 helps to level the emotional playing field. What we're feeling now is intense and sharp, while the future feels fuzzier. That discrepancy gives the present too much power because our present emotions are always in the spotlight. 10-10-10 forces us to shift our spotlight, asking us to imagine a moment

10 months into the future.

This shift can help us to keep our short-term emotions in perspective. It's not that we should ignore our short-term emotions; often, they are telling us something useful about what we want in a situation. But we should not let them dictate how we react.

For example, if you've been avoiding a difficult conversation with a coworker, then you're letting short-term emotions rule you. If you commit to having the conversation, then ten minutes from now you'll probably be anxious—but ten months from now, you will be glad you didn't avoid short-term conflict.

Another way to maintain perspective is to embrace certain stoic principles. Stoic philosophers have a valuable practice they call "negative visualization." When bad things happen to you, before you get engulfed by sadness and self-pity, realize that it could have been a lot worse. For those of us who were only indirectly impacted by the virus, 2020 was just a mediocre year, especially if you compare it to what a generation or two before us suffered in Europe in the late 1930s through the mid-1940s. Stoicism helped me put 2020 in a broader historical context and helped me compare what happened, which was bad, to what could have happened and how much worse it could have been for my company and me personally.

At its heart, stoicism is about accepting things that are in your power to control and ditching the rest. Stoicism also helps us all understand the impermanence of everything.

To further keep perspective, remember that "one day, most people still living will not remember you." This is not meant to be a morbid sentiment; it is just the truth. There is no getting away from the fact that one day we will all die. The further time advances past this point, the more we will all be forgotten. Life goes on. It waits for nobody. No matter how famous you are or how many followers you currently have on Instagram or Twitter, you will start to be forgotten once you die. Some may think this is a depressing perspective. It may appear that way, but it isn't. It's a dose of reality and also liberating. Don't take yourself too seriously.

I think of all the local, regional, and national business leaders I've known over the years who have built incredible businesses or run big organizations. Five years after they are gone—for sure ten years—other than their family and a few close colleagues, nobody remembers what they did or who they were. The stress and sleepless nights they experienced in building their businesses or running their organizations will be remembered by no one. One of my predecessors stopped to see me about ten years after he retired and remarked in coming to my office he saw few people he recognized. He went on to say he supposed not many people at the company now knew who he was. I didn't have the heart to tell him that virtually no one at the company now knows who he is.

The BBC wrote an interesting article in December 2017 titled "Who Will Be Remembered in 1,000 Years?" The article's conclusion is virtually no one.

It is a sobering thought, but the reality is after you die you will most likely be totally forgotten after three generations. Here is my own experience. I'm a fourth generation Nebraskan. My great grandparents on both sides were German immigrants and they homesteaded in Nebraska in the middle 1860s. My father's side of the family established their homestead in 1866 in southwest Lancaster County Nebraska; one year before Nebraska became a state. They had to be courageous people to leave their native Germany and move out to the wind-swept prairie and initially live in a dugout. I know a few family stories about the pioneer hardships they faced but no personal details. I do remember my great grandfather Henning's first name but for my other great grandparents I would have to consult research a cousin completed several years ago to be reminded of their names.

The steady march of time will cause us all to be eventually forgotten. Even people who have risen to dizzying heights of fame during their lives will most likely be forgotten in three generations. An important truism: we are all mortal, and all glory is fleeting.

On a reporting trip to Bhutan, Michael Easter, author of *The Comfort Crisis*, learned to reimagine his fear of dying. In Bhutan, people think of the Buddhist concept of mitakpa, or impermanence, every day. The lama Damcho Gyeltshen explained to Easter that nothing lasts, and therefore, nothing can be held onto. All things change. All things die. The lama told Easter to think of mitakpa three times a day—in the morning, afternoon, and evening. Pondering mitakpa can be terrifying at first, but it adds clarity and urgency to every moment. There's no procrastinating or saying, "I'll do X when Y happens." Easter concluded this story with the following comment: "The practice has helped me reprioritize my life and made me calmer and more grateful and happy."

We all should realize our place in the cosmos. When I've gotten a little too puffed up with my successes or a little too dejected with my failures, I remember what it means in the scheme of everything—which is nothing. This reality check gives me some much-needed perspective.

Stoics have another piece of advice for us. Epictetus said, "People are not disturbed by things, but by the views they take of them." It is amazing how much impact "the view we take" has on our well-being. Though you cannot change reality, you can do plenty with how you interpret it and thus how you feel. Remember: work on what you can control and forget the rest. This attitude is essential to keeping a healthy perspective.

Finally, to keep perspective, remember that nothing is permanent. In life, there'll always be good and bad times. However, nothing lasts forever. All the tough things you may be experiencing today will come to an end. A few years from now, you'll not remember them.

Good things come to an end as well. That's why you need to avoid getting too puffed up in fleeting success. Just cherish the good times. Don't be afraid if you are in the middle of a crisis. It will come to an end. Embrace the good experiences in life. And always keep in mind that everything is temporary. And remember lasting happiness in life does not come from outcomes; it comes from the journey.

I'll end with a quote from the English writer and theologian G. K. Chesterton: "Angels can fly because they take themselves lightly." I encourage you all to take yourselves lightly.

Acknowledgments

My deepest gratitude to my colleagues at Assurity Life, past and present, who encouraged me to share in writing what wisdom I've gleaned over the years on how to be a better business leader.

Special thanks to Susan Becker, vice president of human resources at Assurity, who edited each blog, the foundation for these chapters. I'm also indebted to the marketing area at Assurity for their helpful edits to my initial blogs.

Finally, special thanks to my assistant of thirty-two years, Tammy Halvorsen, for patiently assisting me in the many iterations of writing each chapter.

Tom's Favorite Business Leadership and Management Books

Author	Book Title
David Allen	"Getting Things Done: The Art of Stress-Free Productivity"
Dan Ariely	"Payoff"
Peter Bevelin	"Seeking Wisdom: From Darwin to Munger"
Ken Blanchard & Spencer Johnson, M.D.	"The One Minute Manager"
Marcus Buckingham	"Now Discover Your Strengths"
Marcus Buckingham & Curt Coffman	"First, Break All The Rules"
Warren Buffett & Lawrence A. Cunningham	"The Essays of Warren Buffett"
Jan Carlzon	"Moments of Truth"
Dale Carnegie	"How to Win Friends and Influence People"
Rob Chapman	"Everybody Matters"
Clayton M. Christensen	"The Innovator's Dilemma"
Robert B. Cialdini	"Influence The Psychology of Persuasion"
Jim Collins	"Good To Great"
Jim Collins	"Good to Great: Why Some Companies Make the Leap… and Others Don't"
Stephen Covey	"First Things First"
Stephen R. Covey	"The 7 Habits of Highly Effective People"
Stephen R. Covey	"The 8th Habit"

Stephen M.R. Covey	"The Speed of Trust"
Ray Dalio	"Principles"
Max De Pree	"Leadership is an Art"
Dr. Peter H. Diamandis	"Abundance: The Future is Better Than You Think"
Rolf Dobelli	"The Art of the Good Life"
Rolf Dobelli	"The Art of Thinking Clearly"
David Dotlich, Peter Cairo & Cade Cowan	"The Unfinished Leader"
Peter F. Drucker	"The Effective Executive"
Annie Duke	"Thinking in Bets: Making Smarter Decisions When You Don't Have All the Facts"
Harold Evans	"Do I Make Myself Clear?"
Tim Ferriss	"Tribe of Mentors"
Robert Frank	"Success and Luck: Good Fortune and the Myth of Meritocracy"
Benjamin Franklin	"The Autobiography of Benjamin Franklin"
Jason Fried & David Heinemeier Hansson	"It Doesn't Have to Be Crazy at Work"
Gallup	"Driving Employee Engagement Workbook"
Adam Grant	"Think Again" & "Give and Take"
Alan C. Greenberg	"Memos From The Chairman"
Robert K. Greenleaf	"Servant Leadership"
Charles Handy	"21 Letters on Life and its Challenges"
Chip & Dan Heath	"Decisive"
Ryan Holiday	"The Obstacle is the Way: The Timeless Art of Turning Trials into Triumph"
Walter Isaacson	"Steve Jobs"
Ralph Jacobson	"Getting Unstuck: Using Leadership Paradox to Execute with Confidence"
Spencer Johnson	"Who Moved My Cheese?"
Daniel Kahneman	"Thinking, Fast and Slow"
Robert S. Kaplan & David P. Norton	"Alignment"
Robert S. Kaplan & David P. Norton	"Strategy Maps"
Robert S. Kaplan & David P. Norton	"The Balanced Scorecard: Training Strategy into Action"

Robert S. Kaplan & David P. Norton	"The Execution Premium"
Dacher Keltner	"The Power Paradox"
W. Chan Kim & Renée Mauborgne	"Blue Ocean Strategy"
Nancy Koehn	"Forged in Crisis: The Power of Courageous Leadership in Turbulent Times"
A.G. Lafley & Roger L. Martin	"Playing To Win: How Strategy Really Works"
Alan Lakein	"How to Get Control of Your Time and Your Life"
Daniel Levitin	"The Organized Mind: Thinking Straight in the Age of Information Overload"
William Manchester	Volumes 1, 2, & 3 Biographies on Winston Churchill
Leonard Mlodinow	"The Drunkard's Walk"
Edmund Morris	Volumes 1, 2, & 3 Biographies on Theodore Roosevelt
Satya Nadella	"Hit Refresh: The Quest to Rediscover Microsoft's Soul and Imagine a Better Future for Everyone"
Bob Nelson	"1001 Ways To Reward Employees"
Cal Newport	"Deep Work: Rules for Focused Success in a Distracted World"
Paul R. Niven	"The Balanced Scorecard Step-by-Step"
Daniel H. Pink	"When: The Scientific Secrets of Perfect Timing"
William Putsis	"Compete Smarter, Not Harder"
Tom Rath & Dr. Don Clifton	"How Full is Your Bucket"
Phil Rosenzweig	"The Halo Effect"
Richard P. Rumelt	"Good Strategy Bad Strategy"
Ricardo Semler	"Maverick: This Success Story Behind the World's Most Unusual Workplace"
Howard Schultz	"Onward: How Starbucks Fought for Its Life Without Losing Its Soul"
Kim Scott	"Radical Candor"
Susan Scott	"Fierce Conversations"
Simon Sinek	"Start with Why"
Bradford D. Smart, Ph.D.	"Topgrading"
Hyrum W. Smith	"The 10 Natural Laws of Successful Time and Life Management"
Dan Sullivan	"The Laws of Lifetime Growth"
Nassim Nicholas Taleb	"Fooled by Randomness: The Hidden Role of Chance in Life and in the Markets"

Richard Thaler & Cass Sunstein	"Nudge: Improving Decisions about Health, Wealth, and Happiness"
Gino Wickman	"Traction: Get a Grip on Your Business"
Dr. Otis Young	"Reach Out and Live"
William Zinsser	"On Writing Well"

About the Author

Tom Henning has been the CEO of a commercial bank or an insurance company for over thirty-eight years. The companies Tom has led have been known as progressive organizations that were also great places to work. For nearly twenty-seven years Tom served as CEO of Assurity Group Inc. or predecessor companies. Tom has also served on several publicly traded company boards, including current service on Nelnet Inc., First Interstate Bancorp and the Federal Home Loan Bank of Topeka's board. Tom has been inducted into the Nebraska Business Hall of Fame and received the Distinguished Service Award from the American Council of Life Insurers. Tom and his wife, Candy, also operate Henning Farms, which is committed to regenerative agriculture.

Bibliography

Collins, Jim. *Good to Great: Why Some Companies Make the Leap ... and Others Don't.* New York: HarperBusiness, 2001.

Greenleaf, Robert K. *Servant Leadership: A Journey into the Nature of Legitimate Power and Greatness.* Paulist Press, 1991.

Hesse, Hermann. *Journey to the East.* Mansfield Centre, Connecticut: Martino Publishing, 2011.

White, Sarah K. "What Is Servant Leadership? A Philosophy for People-First Leadership." Society of Human Resource Management, February 28, 2021. https://www.shrm.org/.

Spiro, Josh. "How to Become a Servant Leader." Inc. Magazine, August 31, 2010. https://www.inc.com/guides/2010/08/how-to-become-a-servant-leader.html.

Scott, Susan. *Fierce Conversations: Achieving Success at Work & In Life, One Conversation at a Time.* New York: New American Library, 2017.

Rath, Tom, and Donald Clifton. "How Full Is Your Bucket?" Gallup, 2004. https://store.gallup.com/p/en-us/10314how-full-is-your-bucket%3F-expanded-anniversary-edition.

Covey, Stephen R. *The Speed of Trust: The One Thing That Changes Everything.* New York: Simon & Schuster, 2006.

Kingswell. "The Berkshire Handshake, Munger Down Under, Costco Hot Dogs, and Dividend Snowballs. Kingswell, July 14, 2022. https://kingswell.substack.com/p/the-berkshire-handshake-munger-down.

Green, William. *Richer, Wiser, Happier: How the World's Greatest Investors Win in Markets and Life*. New York: Scribner, 2021.

William, *Richer, Wiser, Happier*, 28.

William, *Richer, Wiser, Happier*, 40.

William, *Richer, Wiser, Happier*, 131.

Chapman, Bob, and Rajendra Sisodia. *Everybody Matters: The Extraordinary Power of Caring for Your People like Family*. London: Penguin Random House, 2015.

Robbins, Mike. "Why Employees Need Both Recognition and Appreciation." Harvard Business Review, August 31, 2021. https://hbr.org/2019/11/why-employees-need-both-recognition-and-appreciation.

Spier, Guy. "Aquamarine Annual Reports." Aquamarine Funds, 2015. https://www.aquamarinefund.com/aqua-ar/.

Green, William. "RWH010 : HIGH-PERFORMANCE HABITS W/ GUY SPIER." Investor's Podcast Network, n.d. https://www.theinvestorspodcast.com/richer-wiser-happier/high-performance-habits-w-guy-spier/.

Schumpeter Column. "Getting a Handle on a Scandal." The Economist. The Economist Newspaper, March 30, 2018. https://www.economist.com/business/2018/03/28/getting-a-handle-on-a-scandal.

Holiday, Ryan. *Courage Is Calling*. London: Penguin Publishing Group, 2021.

Johnson, Spencer. *Who Moved My Cheese?* New York: G.P. Putnam's Sons, 2018.

Steinberg, Scott. *Make Change Work for You: 10 Ways to Future-Proof Yourself, Innovate Fearlessly, and Succeed despite Uncertainty*. London: Piatkus, 2015.

Smet, Aaron De, Gregor Jost, and Leigh Weiss. "Three Keys to Faster, Better Decisions." McKinsey & Company. McKinsey & Company, May 1, 2019. https://www.mckinsey.com/capabilities/people-and-organizational-performance/our-insights/three-keys-to-faster-better-decisions.

Heath, Chip, and Dan Heath. *Decisive: How to Make Better Choices in Life and Work*. New York: Crown Business, 2013.

Derman, Emanuel. *Models. Behaving. Badly: Why Confusing Illusion with Reality Can Lead to Disaster, on Wall Street and in Life*. Chichester: John Wiley, 2011.

Amazon Staff, and Jeff Bezos. "2016 Letter to Shareholders." US About Amazon, April 17, 2017. https://www.aboutamazon.com/news/company-news/2016-letter-to-shareholders.

Merle, Andrew. "The Reading Habits of Ultra-Successful People." HuffPost. HuffPost, April 14, 2016. https://www.huffpost.com/entry/the-reading-habits-of-ult_b_9688130.

Strunk, William, and E. B. White. *The Elements of Style*. London: Collier Macmillan, 1979.

The Economist. *The Economist Style Guide*. New York: PublicAffairs, 2015.

Dreyer, Benjamin. *Dreyer's English: An Utterly Correct Guide to Clarity and Style*. New York: Random House, 2020.

Evans, Harold. *Do I Make Myself Clear? Why Writing Well Matters*. New York: Little, Brown US, 2017.

Levitin, Daniel J. *The Organized Mind: Thinking Straight in the Age of Information Overload*. Toronto: Penguin Random House, 2015.

Hemp, Paul. "Death by Information Overload." Harvard Business Review, September 2009. https://hbr.org/2009/09/death-by-information-overload.

Linenberger, Michael. *Total Workday Control Using Microsoft Outlook*. San Ramon, CA: New Academy Publishing, 2010.

Schwartz, Tony. "'No' Is the New 'Yes': Four Practices to Reprioritize Your Life." Harvard Business Review, January 12, 2012. https://hbr.org/2012/01/no-is-the-new-yes-four-practic.

Welch, Suzy. *10-10-10: 10 Minutes, 10 Months, 10 Years: A Life-Transforming Idea*. New York: Thorndike Press, 2009.

Welch, *10-10-10*, 61.

Welch, *10-10-10*, 176.

Ury, William. *The Power of a Positive: No How to Say No and Still Get to Yes*. London: Hodder Mobius, 2008.

Parrish, Shane. "The Focus to Say No." Farnam Stree (blog), 2022. https://fs.blog/steve-jobs-saying-no/.

Burkeman, Oliver. *Four Thousand Weeks: Time Management for Mortals*. New York: Farrar, Straus and Giroux, 2021.

Burkeman, *Four Thousand Weeks*, 65.

Oncken, William, and Donald L. Wass. "Management Time: Who's Got the Monkey?" Harvard Business Review, September 22, 2022. https://hbr.org/1999/11/management-time-whos-got-the-monkey.

Lakein, Alan. *How to Get Control of Your Time and Your Life*. New York: New American Library, 1974.

Lakein, *How to Get Control*, 69.

Covey, Stephen R. *7 Habits of Highly Effective People*. New York: Simon & Schuster, 1992. "Leadership and Governance." Wells Fargo. Accessed 2022. https://www.wellsfargo.com/about/corporate/governance/.

Covey, *Highly Effective People*, 65.

Covey, *Highly Effective People*, 159.

Covey, *Highly Effective People*, 173.

Aurelius, Marcus, and George Long. *Thoughts of the Emperor Marcus Aurelius Antoninus*. Oxford, England: Benediction Classics, 2012.

Grant, Adam. "Tapping into the Power of Humble Narcissism." ideas.ted.com, March 14, 2018. https://ideas.ted.com/tapping-into-the-power-of-humble-narcissism/.

Isaacson, Walter. *Steve Jobs: Passion, Perfection, and Contradiction*. New York: Simon & Schuster, 2011.

Rodriguez, Diego. "Hiring: It's About Cultural Contribution, Not Cultural Fit." LinkedIn, September 10, 2015. https://www.linkedin.com/pulse/how-i-hire-its-all-cultural-contribution-fit-diego-rodriguez.

Duke, Annie. "Decision-Making: Morgan Housel in Conversation with Annie Duke." Interview by Morgan Housel. United States of America, n.d. https://podcasts.apple.com/us/podcast/decision-making-morgan-housel-in-conversation-with/id268942353?i=1000475296631.

Thompson, Erica. *Escape from Model Land: How Mathematical Models Can Lead Us Astray and What We Can Do About It*. New York: Basic Books, 2022.

Spier, Guy. "RWH010 : HIGH-PERFORMANCE HABITS W/ GUY SPIER." Interview by William Green. The Investor's Podcast, July 9, 2022. Accessed 2022. https://www.theinvestorspodcast.com/richer-wiser-happier/high-performance-habits-w-guy-spier/.

Duke, Annie. *Quit: The Power of Knowing When to Walk Away.* New York: Penguin Random House, 2022.

Dobelli, Rolf. *The Art of Thinking Clearly.* New York: Harper, 2013.

Kahneman, Daniel. *Thinking, Fast and Slow.* London: Penguin Publishing Group, 2011.

Kahneman, *Thinking, Fast and Slow*, 84.

Kahneman, *Thinking, Fast and Slow*, 117.

Kahneman, *Thinking, Fast and Slow*, 124.

Dobelli, Rolf. *The Art of the Good Life.* London: Hodder & Stoughton, 2017.

Lewis, Michael. *The Undoing Project: A Friendship That Changed Our Minds.* New York: W.W. Norton & Company, 2017.

Grant, Adam. *Think Again: The Power of Knowing What You Don't Know.* New York: Viking, 2021.

Kay, John, and Mervyn A. King. *Radical Uncertainty: Decision-Making Beyond the Numbers.* New York: W.W. Norton & Company, 2021.

Shiller, Robert J. *Narrative Economics: How Stories Go Viral and Drive Major Economic Events.* Princeton: Princeton University Press, 2019.

Taleb, Nassim Nicholas. *Fooled by Randomness: The Hidden Role of Chance in Life and in the Markets.* London: Penguin Publishing Group, 2007.

Rosenzweig, Phil. *The Halo Effect . . . and the Eight Other Business Delusions That Deceive Managers.* New York: Free Press, 2007.

Mlodinow, Leonard. *The Drunkard's Walk: How Randomness Rules Our Lives.* New York: Pantheon Books, 2008.

McCaffrey, Paul. "Daniel Kahneman: Four Keys to Better Decision Making." CFA Institute Enterprising Investor, August 12, 2021. https://blogs.cfainstitute.org/investor/2018/06/08/daniel-kahneman-four-keys-to-better-decision-making/.

Merriam-Webster. "Virtuous Circle." Merriam-Webster. Accessed 2022. https://www.merriam-webster.com/dictionary/virtuous%20circle.

Bird, Jon. "Feeding the Flywheel: Why Amazon Prime Day Is So Much More Than a Sale." Forbes. Forbes Magazine, July 24, 2018. https://www.forbes.com/sites/jonbird1/2018/07/22/feeding-the-flywheel-why-amazon-prime-day-is-so-much-more-than-a-sale/?sh=71abc42542db.

Diamond, Michael. "The Bezos Behemoth." Michael Diamond, February 3, 2021. https://www.michaeldiamond.com/bezos/.

Handy, Charles B. 21 *Letters on Life and Its Challenges*. London: Windmill Books, 2020.

Handy, *Life and Its Challenges*, 100.

Handy, *Life and Its Challenges*, 139.

Fried, Jason, and David Heinemeier. *It Doesn't Have to Be Crazy at Work*. New York: HarperCcollins Publishers, 2018.

Peck, M. Scott. *The Road Less Traveled: A New Psychology of Love, Traditional Values, and Spiritual Growth*. New York: Simon and Schuster, 1979.

Merriam-Webster. "Innovation Definition & Meaning." Merriam-Webster. Accessed 2022. https://www.merriam-webster.com/dictionary/innovation.

Dalio, Ray. *Principles: Life and Work*. New York: Simon and Schuster, 2017.

Wickman, Gino. *Traction: Get a Grip on Your Business*. Livonia, MI: EOS, 2007.

Schwartz, Harry. "Forrester's Law." The New York Times, June 14, 1971. https://www.nytimes.com/1971/06/14/archives/forresters-law.html.

Young, Otis. *Reach Out and Live: Reflections on Leadership in Ministry and Sermons*. Lincoln, NE: Lee Booksellers, 2008.

Bradley, Chris, Sven Smit, and Martin Hirt. *Strategy Beyond the Hockey Stick: People, Probabilities, and Big Moves to Beat the Odds*. Hoboken, NJ: Wiley, 2018.

Bradley, *Beyond the Hockey Stick*, 119.

Bradley, *Beyond the Hockey Stick*, 146.

Tasler, Nick. "3 Myths That Kill Strategic Planning." Harvard Business Review, November 2, 2014. https://hbr.org/2014/05/3-myths-that-kill-strategic-planning.

Maxfield, By: John J. "The Dinsdales and Chandlers." Bank Director, October 13, 2021. https://www.bankdirector.com/magazine/archives/4th-quarter-2021/the-dinsdales-and-chandlers/.

Lafley, A. G., and Roger L. Martin. *Playing to Win: How Strategy Really Works*. Boston: Harvard Business Review Press, 2013.

McCullough, David G. *John Adams*. New York: Simon & Schuster, 2004.

Collins, Jim, and Morten T. Hansen. *Great by Choice: Uncertainty, Chaos, and Luck: Why Some Thrive Despite Them All*. New York: HarperCollins Publishers, 2011.

Merriam-Webster. "Paradox Definition & Meaning." Merriam-Webster. Accessed 2022. https://www.merriam-webster.com/dictionary/paradox.

Kim, W. Chan, and Mauborgne Renée. *Blue Ocean Strategy: How to Create Uncontested Market Space and Make the Competition Irrelevant*. Boston: Harvard Business Review Press, 2004.

London, Simon. "Book Review: A Rheory That Swims Against the Tide." Financial Times, February 20, 2005. https://www.ft.com/content/e4e8824e-8362-11d9-bee3-00000e2511c8.

Kim, W. Chan, and Renée Mauborgne. "Blue Ocean Strategy." Harvard Business Review, January 12, 2023. https://hbr.org/2004/10/blue-ocean-strategy.

Harrell, Eben. "How 1% Performance Improvements Led to Olympic Gold." Harvard Business Review, October 30, 2015. https://hbr.org/2015/10/how-1-performance-improvements-led-to-olympic-gold.

Greenberg, Alan C. *Memos from the Chairman*. New York: John Wiley, 1997.

Walton, Sam. "Sam's Rules for Building a Business." Walmart Museum. Accessed 2022. https://www.walmartmuseum.com/content/walmartmuseum/en_us/timeline/decades/1990/artifact/2636.html.

Duke, Annie. *Thinking in Bets: Making Smarter Decisions When You Don't Have All the Facts*. Alberta: Portfolio, 2018.

Zweig, Jason. "What to Do When You Know What Stocks Will Do Next." The Wall Street Journal. Dow Jones & Company, October 28, 2022. https://www.wsj.com/articles/what-to-do-when-you-know-what-stocks-will-do-next-11666968602.

Kanter, Rosabeth Moss. "Change Is Hardest in the Middle." Harvard Business Review, July 23, 2014. https://hbr.org/2009/08/change-is-hardest-in-the-middl.

Trachtenberg, Jeffrey A. "Why a Magazine Giant Wanted Nothing to Do With Time and Fortune." The Wall Street Journal. Dow Jones & Company, May 24, 2019. https://www.wsj.com/articles/how-to-navigate-a-collapsing-business-magazine-giant-meredith-axes-nostalgia-11558624030.

Buffet, Warren. "Chairman's Letter - 1989." Berkshire Hathaway, March 2, 1990. https://www.berkshirehathaway.com/letters/1989.html.

Carnegie, Dale. *How to Win Friends and Influence People*. London: Vermilion, 2006.

Ferriss, Timothy. *Tribe of Mentors: Short Life Advice from the Best in the World*. Boston: Houghton Mifflin Harcourt, 2017.

Ferriss, Timothy. *The 4-Hour Workweek: Escape 9-5, Live Anywhere, and Join the New Rich*. New York: Crown, 2009.

Grant, Adam. *Give and Take: Why Helping Others Drives Our Sucess*. New York: Penguin Random House, 2014.

Munger, Charlie. "Prescriptions for Guaranteed Misery in Life." Commencement Speech. Speech presented at the Commencement Speech, 1986.

Fisher, Robert, and William Ury. *Getting to Yes: Negotiating Agreement Without Giving In*. Boston: Houghton Mifflin, 1981.

Gallup, Inc. "Activator." Gallup, May 26, 2022. https://www.gallup.com/cliftonstrengths/en/252140/activator-theme.aspx.

Smart, Bradford D. *Topgrading: The Proven Hiring and Promoting Method That Turbocharges Company Performance*. 3rd ed. New York: Penguin Random House, 2012.

Friedman, Milton. "A Friedman Doctrine-- The Social Responsibility of Business Is to Increase Its Profits." The New York Times. The New York Times Archives, September 13, 1970. https://www.nytimes.com/1970/09/13/archives/a-friedman-doctrine-the-social-responsibility-of-business-is-to.html.

Fink, Larry. "Larry Fink's 2018 Letter to CEOS." BlackRock, 2018. https://www.blackrock.com/corporate/investor-relations/2018-larry-fink-ceo-letter.

Ernst & Young Global Limited. Rep. *The Business Case for Purpose*. Boston: Harvard Business Review, 2015.

Gast, Arne, Pablo Illanes, Nina Probst, Bill Schaninger, and Bruce Simpson. "Purpose: Shifting from Why to How." McKinsey & Company, March 1, 2021. https://www.mckinsey.com/capabilities/people-and-organizational-performance/ our-insights/purpose-shifting-from-why-to-how.

Sinek, Simon. *Start With Why: How Great Leaders Inspire Everyone to Take Action*. London: Penguin Publishing Group, 2011.

Gorvett, Zaria. "Who Will Be Remembered in 1,000 Years?" BBC Future. BBC, December 21, 2017. https://www.bbc.com/future/article/20171220-how-to-be-remembered-in-1000-years.

Easter, Michael. *The Comfort Crisis: Embrace Discomfort to Reclaim Your Wild, Happy, Healthy Self*. Emmaus, PN: Rodale Books, 2021.